Mastering Computer Craft

1st Series

50 computer skills to learn for a lucrative career

Copy right page

Mastering Computer Craft 1st Series: 50 Computer Skills to learn for a lucrative career

For permission requests, please contact:

Micheal Ayandele

ayandelemayowa@gmail.com +2348130922826

Disclaimer: The information provided in this book is intended for educational and informational purposes only. The author and publisher are not responsible for any actions taken based on the information contained in this book.

Cover design by Micheal Ayandele

Author Page on Amazon

Author's Page

https://www.amazon.com/kindle-dbs/author?ref=dbs_G_A_C&asin=B0B9KD7G1D

Author's Website

Content

Introduction   1

Overview of the Transformative Role of Computers in Creativity and Productivity   2

The Importance of Computer Skills in Modern Life   3

How This Book Can Help Readers Explore Diverse Applications of Computer Technology   7

Introduction to Section 1: Creativity and Design   12

Part 1: Graphic Design Projects for Beginners   14

Part 2: Creating Custom Digital Art and Illustrations   20

26

Part 3: Designing Personalized Greeting Cards   27

33

Part 4: Making Logos for Small Businesses   34

41

Part 5: Exploring 3D Modeling and Printing   42

Part 6: Designing a Website from Scratch   49

58

Part 7: Digital Scrapbooking   59

72

Part 8. Print and Market Your Custom T-Shirts   73

Part 9: Designing Book Covers for Self-Publishing   74

Part 10: Making Interactive Presentations   83

Section 2: Multimedia Projects   91

92

Part 11: Basic Video Editing Projects   93

   101

Part 12: Crafting Photo Slideshows with Effects   102

   110

Part 13: Audio Editing and Podcast Creation   111

Part 14: Making Animations Using Free Software   120

   129

Part 15: Digital Storytelling Techniques   130

Part 16: Composing Music with Computer Software   137

Part 17: Designing E-Cards with Sound and Motion   145

   153

Part 18: Enhancing Photographs with Editing Tools   153

Part 19: Creating a Virtual Portfolio   162

Part 20: Producing Educational Videos   170

Part 21: Building a Personal Website Using HTML/CSS   179

Part 22: Writing Your First Python Script   189

Part 23: Developing a Basic Mobile App   198

Part 24: Automating Tasks with Macros in Excel   207

Part 25: Creating Custom Keyboard Shortcuts   215

Part 26: Building a Chatbot for Customer Service   222

Part 27: Designing a Simple Game   231

Part 28: Learning to Work with Raspberry Pi   239

Part 29: Coding Interactive Quizzes   246

Part 30: Creating an AI-Driven Tool   257

Part 31: Creating a Business Plan Template   267

Part 32: Designing Marketing Materials   273

Part 33: Making a Financial Budget Tracker 280

Part 34: Planning Projects Using Software 287

Part 35: Automating Email Campaigns 295

Part 36: Crafting PowerPoint Presentation 303

Part 37: Managing Tasks with Computer Tools 310

Part 38: Creating an Online Store 317

Part 39: Analyzing Data for Business Decisions 324

Part 40: Managing Customer Relations Digitally 332

Part 41: Designing Flashcards for Study 341

Part 42: Creating Online Quizzes 347

355

Part 43: Building Interactive eBooks 356

Part 44: Developing eLearning Modules 363

Part 45: Making Educational Infographics 371

Part 46: Recording and Editing Tutorials 379

Part 47: Building Simple Simulations for Teaching 387

Part 48: Developing Classroom Games 395

Part 49: Creating an Academic Portfolio 403

410

Part 50: Producing School Newsletters Digitally 411

Summary of Possibilities with Computer Craft 419

Encouragement to Explore and Innovate Further 423

Introduction

In the modern world, computers have become more than mere tools; they are the backbone of creativity, innovation, and productivity. From simple tasks like drafting documents to advanced endeavors such as designing virtual realities, the versatility of computers has transformed how we live, work, and create. This transformation has opened up endless possibilities for individuals to explore their potential and achieve their goals through the power of technology.

Creativity and Productivity in the Digital Age
The fusion of creativity and computing has given rise to new art forms, innovative solutions, and streamlined workflows. Whether you're a designer crafting stunning visual, a programmer developing groundbreaking applications, or a hobbyist exploring digital hobbies, the computer is a gateway to bringing your ideas to life. Its capacity to amplify productivity allows us to achieve more in less time, making once-daunting tasks manageable and accessible to everyone.

The Importance of Computer Skills
In today's technology-driven era, computer literacy is no longer optional—it's essential. From professional environments to personal projects, understanding and utilizing computer technology has become a critical skill. Mastering these skills not only opens doors to new opportunities but also empowers individuals to stay relevant and competitive in an ever-changing world.

What This Book Offers
This book, *100 Computer Crafts*, is a guide to unlocking the vast potential of computers in your daily life. Whether you're a beginner eager to explore simple projects or an expert seeking advanced challenges, this book provides insights and step-by-

1

step instructions for 100 unique ideas. From creative design to practical applications, each craft is carefully curated to inspire innovation and encourage exploration.

As you journey through this book, you'll discover how to harness the power of computers to create, solve problems, and express your unique ideas. Let this be your roadmap to a more imaginative, productive, and tech-savvy future.

Welcome to the exciting world of computer crafts!

Overview of the Transformative Role of Computers in Creativity and Productivity

Computers have revolutionized the way we think, work, and create. They have transformed almost every aspect of our lives, from how we communicate to how we solve complex problems. Their ability to process vast amounts of data, automate repetitive tasks, and provide limitless platforms for innovation makes them indispensable tools in modern life.

Creativity   Unleashed

The advent of computers has expanded the horizons of human creativity. Artists now use graphic design software to craft intricate digital artworks, musicians compose melodies with virtual instruments, and writers bring their visions to life with advanced text-editing tools. Beyond traditional art forms, computers enable new dimensions of creativity, such as 3D modeling, animation, and game development. These tools allow individuals to push the boundaries of what was once possible, turning imagination into reality with precision and efficiency.

Boosting   Productivity

Computers have equally transformed productivity, allowing

tasks to be completed faster and more accurately than ever before. Automation tools help streamline workflows, while sophisticated software simplifies data analysis, project management, and communication. In professional settings, computers enhance collaboration through cloud-based platforms, enabling teams across the globe to work together seamlessly. For individuals, they provide tools to manage personal goals, organize schedules, and even optimize daily routines.

A   Catalyst   for   Innovation
Perhaps most importantly, computers serve as a catalyst for innovation. They provide a space for experimentation, prototyping, and problem-solving. Whether it's developing groundbreaking applications or creating life-saving technologies, computers empower people to innovate in ways that were unimaginable just a few decades ago.

By bridging the gap between creativity and efficiency, computers have become more than machines—they are powerful allies in achieving human potential. Their role in transforming creativity and productivity continues to evolve, opening new doors for those willing to explore their full potential.

The Importance of Computer Skills in Modern Life

In the 21st century, computer skills are no longer a luxury—they are a necessity. As technology continues to shape the modern world, having a solid grasp of computer literacy is essential for navigating both personal and professional landscapes. Whether it's for education, communication, employment, or daily tasks, computer skills empower individuals to thrive in a digitally connected society.

1. Enhancing Education and Learning

Computers have revolutionized education by making knowledge accessible to anyone with an internet connection. E-learning platforms, digital libraries, and online courses provide opportunities for lifelong learning. Understanding how to navigate these resources enables individuals to acquire new skills, pursue certifications, and even earn degrees from the comfort of their homes.

- Students can use word processors for assignments, spreadsheets for data analysis, and presentation software to enhance their projects.

- Research tools like academic databases and search engines are indispensable for gathering information efficiently.

- Specialized tools like coding platforms or graphic design software expand learning into creative and technical domains.

2. Facilitating Communication and Connectivity

In today's interconnected world, computer skills are essential for communication. Social media platforms, email, and video conferencing have transformed how people interact, both personally and professionally.

- Individuals can connect with friends and family across the globe through messaging apps and video calls.

- Businesses rely on collaboration tools like Slack, Microsoft Teams, and Zoom to maintain seamless communication among employees.

- Networking opportunities are abundant through professional platforms like LinkedIn, which require basic knowledge of creating and managing online profiles.

3. Driving Career Opportunities and Professional Growth

Proficiency in computer skills is often a prerequisite for many jobs, as most workplaces rely on technology to some extent.

- Basic skills like using word processing, spreadsheets, and email are expected in almost every profession.

- Advanced skills, such as data analysis, programming, and cybersecurity, open doors to high-demand careers in tech.

- Creative fields, such as graphic design, video editing, and web development, rely heavily on computer expertise.

- Understanding productivity tools like project management software (e.g., Asana, Trello) enhances an employee's efficiency and value to an organization.

4. Empowering Daily Life and Personal Management

Computers simplify day-to-day activities, making them faster and more efficient. From online shopping to personal budgeting, computer skills provide tools for managing everyday tasks with ease.

- Online banking and payment platforms ensure secure and convenient financial management.

- Digital calendars and task managers help organize schedules and set reminders for important events.

- Social media and blogging platforms allow individuals to express their creativity and connect with like-minded communities.

5. Supporting Innovation and Problem-Solving

Computer skills foster innovation by giving individuals the tools to explore new ideas and solve complex problems.

- Entrepreneurs can use computers to start and manage online businesses, develop marketing strategies, and analyze consumer behavior.

- Engineers and scientists rely on simulations, modeling software, and data analysis tools to develop groundbreaking solutions.

- Innovators can prototype designs using 3D modeling or explore artificial intelligence to create smart solutions.

6. Bridging the Digital Divide

As the world becomes increasingly digital, the gap between those with and without computer skills grows wider.

- People who lack these skills face challenges in accessing job opportunities, education, and even basic services.

- Acquiring computer literacy levels the playing field, enabling individuals to participate fully in a technology-driven society.

7. Preparing for the Future

The future is being shaped by emerging technologies such as artificial intelligence, virtual reality, and the Internet of Things (IoT).

- Proficiency in computer skills prepares individuals to adapt to these advancements.

- Knowledge of coding, machine learning, and cloud computing positions individuals to stay relevant in a rapidly evolving job market.

- Awareness of cybersecurity ensures individuals can protect their digital assets in an increasingly connected world.

Conclusion

In modern life, computer skills are not just about convenience—they are a cornerstone of success, creativity, and adaptability. From enhancing education to advancing careers and managing daily life, these skills empower individuals to make the most of the digital age. By investing in computer literacy, people can unlock opportunities, overcome challenges, and contribute meaningfully to an interconnected and technology-driven society.

How This Book Can Help Readers Explore Diverse Applications of Computer Technology

The digital era has unlocked countless possibilities for applying computer technology in creative, productive, and innovative ways. This book, *100 Computer Crafts*, serves as a comprehensive guide to help readers discover and implement these applications. Whether you're a beginner eager to explore the basics or a seasoned user seeking advanced projects, this book is designed to broaden your understanding and inspire your creativity.

1. Inspiring Creativity Through Practical Projects

One of the keys focuses of this book is to show how computers can be used as tools for artistic and creative expression. With step-by-step guides to various crafts, readers can learn to:

- Design stunning graphics and digital art.

- Create engaging animations or short videos.

- Build immersive virtual environments using 3D modeling software.

- Develop personalized digital scrapbooks, photo collages, or custom greeting cards.

These projects allow readers to unleash their creativity while m astering essential software and tools.

2. Enhancing Productivity with Advanced Techniques

Beyond creativity, this book introduces readers to practical ways computers can simplify tasks, boost efficiency, and improve productivity. Through clear examples and tutorials, you'll learn how to:

- Organize your life using task management and scheduling tools.

- Use spreadsheet software to manage budgets or analyze data.

- Automate repetitive tasks with macros and scripts.

- Streamline work processes with project management platforms.

These skills will enable readers to work smarter and achieve more in less time.

3. Developing Technical and Problem-Solving Skills

For those interested in technical applications, this book delves into areas that help readers build valuable problem-solving abilities. With hands-on examples, readers can explore:

- Basics of programming and creating simple applications.

- Troubleshooting common computer issues.

- Understanding and managing computer networks.

- Developing websites or blogs from scratch.

These skills not only empower readers to handle technical challenges but also provide a foundation for pursuing advanced tech careers.

4. Discovering Career and Business Opportunities

Computers open doors to numerous career paths and business opportunities. This book highlights how readers can leverage technology to enhance their professional lives, including:

- Starting an online business or e-commerce store.

- Using graphic design tools to offer freelance services.

- Creating and selling digital products like eBooks, online courses, or stock photos.

- Learning video editing for content creation or marketing purposes.

By exploring these applications, readers can turn their hobbies into income-generating ventures.

5. Exploring Emerging Technologies

The book also provides a glimpse into cutting-edge applications of computer technology, such as:

- Experimenting with artificial intelligence tools for creative and analytical projects.

- Exploring augmented and virtual reality for gaming or professional purposes.

- Understanding blockchain and its potential applications beyond cryptocurrencies.

- Using IoT (Internet of Things) devices to automate homes or workplaces.

These insights prepare readers to adapt to and thrive in the rapidly changing technological landscape.

6. Making Technology Accessible and Enjoyable

This book is designed to demystify computers, making them accessible and enjoyable for readers of all skill levels. Whether you're a student, a professional, or a hobbyist, the projects and ideas in this book are tailored to provide value and inspire confidence.

- Each craft is explained in simple, actionable steps.

- Visual aids and practical examples ensure concepts are easy to grasp.

- A variety of applications cater to diverse interests, ensuring there's something for everyone.

7. Encouraging Lifelong Learning

Lastly, this book emphasizes the importance of continuous growth and learning in a technology-driven world. By engaging with these projects, readers will develop a mindset of curiosity and exploration, empowering them to:

- Stay updated with new tools and trends.

- Experiment with ideas beyond the book's scope.

- Cultivate a habit of innovation and problem-solving.

Conclusion

100 Computer Crafts is more than a guide—it's a gateway to discovering the incredible potential of computer technology. By providing a wide range of projects and applications, this book helps readers unlock new skills, expand their horizons, and harness the power of computers to transform their personal and professional lives. Whether you aim to create, innovate, or simply explore, this book is your trusted companion on the journey to mastering the digital world.

Introduction to Section 1: Creativity and Design

Creativity and design lie at the heart of human expression, and computers have become indispensable tools for unleashing imagination in ways once thought impossible. Whether you're sketching digital art, crafting a visually striking presentation, or designing an interactive website, the power of computer technology allows your ideas to take shape with precision and flair.

In this section, we explore how computers have revolutionized the creative process, offering tools and platforms that make design more accessible and impactful than ever before. From graphic design and animation to 3D modeling and multimedia creation, you'll discover a world of possibilities where innovation meets artistry.

Through practical projects and step-by-step guidance, this section aims to inspire readers to tap into their creative potential. Whether you're a beginner looking to create your first design or an experienced user seeking new techniques, the tools and insights provided here will help you push the boundaries of what you can achieve.

Join us as we dive into the exciting intersection of creativity and technology, where your imagination is the only limit!

Figure 1: Creativity and Design

Part 1: Graphic Design Projects for Beginners

Graphic design is a cornerstone of modern creativity, enabling individuals to communicate ideas visually through captivating designs. Whether you're designing a poster, logo, flyer, or social media post, mastering the basics of graphic design can elevate your creative potential. In this section, we introduce beginners to essential graphic design tools and provide step-by-step guidance on using them effectively.

Introduction to Graphic Design Tools

Graphic design tools are the foundation of any design project, offering a range of features to create and edit visuals. While some tools cater to professionals with advanced features, others provide user-friendly platforms for beginners. Here's an overview of popular tools:

1. **CorelDRAW**

   o **What It Is**: A professional vector graphics editor known for its precision and versatility.

   o **Best For**: Logo creation, detailed illustrations, and print design.

   o **Why Use It**: CorelDRAW offers powerful tools for creating scalable designs, making it ideal for projects like business cards, posters, and product packaging.

   o **Example Project**: Create a simple, professional logo for a fictional company using CorelDRAW's shape and text tools.

2. **Adobe Creative Suite (Illustrator, Photoshop)**

o **What It Is**: Industry-standard software for graphic design, photo editing, and digital illustration.

o **Best For**: Advanced projects requiring high customization, such as branding, photo manipulation, and custom artwork.

o **Why Use It**: Adobe tools provide unparalleled flexibility and precision, though they may have a steeper learning curve for beginners.

o **Example Project**: Design a creative poster using Adobe Illustrator's vector tools or a photo collage in Photoshop.

3. **Canva**

o **What It Is**: An easy-to-use online design platform with a vast library of templates and drag-and-drop functionality.

o **Best For**: Beginners and quick projects like social media posts, presentations, and infographics.

o **Why Use It**: Canva is accessible, intuitive, and offers pre-designed templates, making it ideal for those with no prior experience.

o **Example Project**: Create an eye-catching Instagram post using Canva's templates and customizable elements.

4. **Other Beginner-Friendly Tools**

o **Visme**: Great for infographics and presentations.

- o **Snappa**: Perfect for creating online graphics quickly.

- o **Figma**: A versatile design tool for both UI/UX and graphic design projects.

- o **Piktochart**: Excellent for visual storytelling through charts and reports.

Step-by-Step Beginner's Graphic Design Project

Project Title: Design a Social Media Post

Objective: Learn how to use Canva to create an engaging and visually appealing post for Instagram or Facebook.

Tools Required: Canva (free or premium account)

Steps:

1. **Sign Up and Login**

   - o Visit Canva's website or app and create an account.

   - o Choose a template size suitable for social media (e.g., 1080x1080 px for Instagram).

2. **Choose a Template**

   - o Browse Canva's library and select a template that matches your project's theme.

   - o For beginners, start with a pre-designed template to understand layout structure.

3. **Customize Text and Colors**

   - o Edit the text to include your desired message.

o Experiment with fonts and adjust colors to align with your theme or brand.

4. **Add Visual Elements**

o Insert images or graphics from Canva's library or upload your own.

o Use drag-and-drop features to position elements as needed.

5. **Finalize and Download**

o Review your design for alignment and spacing.

o Download the final design in your preferred format (JPEG, PNG, or PDF).

Illustration of Graphic Design Progression

Imagine starting with a blank canvas and transforming it into a visually stunning design:

1. **CorelDRAW Logo Design**: A simple yet professional logo using geometric shapes and text.

2. **Adobe Poster Creation**: A vibrant event poster combining custom illustrations and typography.

3. **Canva Social Media Post**: A polished Instagram post with bold fonts, bright colors, and appealing visuals.

Why Beginners Should Start with Canva

While professional tools like CorelDRAW and Adobe Creative Suite are powerful, they can be overwhelming for beginners. Canva and similar platforms provide:

- **Ease of Use**: Drag-and-drop features simplify the design process.

- **Templates**: Pre-made layouts eliminate the need for starting from scratch.

- **Accessibility**: Web-based tools are available on any device without installation.

Conclusion

Part 1 equips readers with the foundational skills and confidence needed to begin their graphic design journey. By exploring both professional and beginner-friendly tools, you'll understand the possibilities of graphic design and how to create compelling visuals for personal or professional use. Whether you're crafting a business logo, designing a poster, or creating a social media post, this section empowers you to turn your ideas into stunning designs.

STEP BY STEP
TUTORIAL

Figure 2: Digital Art and Illustration

Part 2: Creating Custom Digital Art and Illustrations

Digital art and illustrations have revolutionized the world of creativity, offering artists and enthusiasts an unlimited canvas to bring their imaginations to life. With the aid of computers and specialized tools, anyone can create stunning, custom artwork—whether you're sketching, painting, or designing intricate illustrations. This section explores the fundamentals of creating digital art, introduces essential tools, and provides step-by-step guidance for beginners and intermediate artists.

Understanding Digital Art and Illustrations

What is Digital Art?
Digital art refers to artwork created or enhanced using digital tools such as tablets, computers, and software. Unlike traditional mediums like paper and canvas, digital art offers flexibility, allowing creators to experiment with various styles, colors, and effects without physical limitations.

Why Create Custom Illustrations?
Custom illustrations can be tailored for specific purposes, such as:

- Designing personalized artwork for branding or marketing.

- Crafting characters, scenes, or environments for games or animations.

- Creating digital portraits or unique gifts.

- Enhancing storytelling with vivid visuals.

Essential Tools for Digital Art

1. **Graphics Tablets**

   o **Purpose**: Mimics the experience of traditional drawing while offering precision and control.

   o **Popular Options**: Wacom, Huion, XP-Pen.

2. **Art Software**

   o **Adobe Photoshop**: Versatile for creating detailed illustrations and digital paintings.

   o **Corel Painter**: Designed for replicating traditional painting techniques.

   o **Procreate** (iPad): User-friendly and perfect for beginners and professionals.

   o **Krita**: Free, open-source software for digital painting.

   o **Clip Studio Paint**: Excellent for comics, illustrations, and animation.

3. **Touchscreen Devices**

   o Devices like iPads or touchscreen laptops with a stylus offer portable solutions for creating digital art.

Step-by-Step Guide: Creating Custom Digital Art

Project Title: Design a Simple Digital Portrait

Objective: Create a stylized digital portrait using a drawing tablet or touchscreen device and software like Procreate or Photoshop.

Steps:

1. **Set Up Your Canvas**

    o Open your chosen art software and create a new canvas.

    o Recommended size: 3000 x 3000 pixels, 300 dpi for print-quality resolution.

2. **Sketch the Outline**

    o Use the pencil tool to create a rough sketch of your portrait.

    o Keep your strokes light and focus on the basic shapes (e.g., circles for the head, lines for proportions).

3. **Add Layers**

    o Separate your sketch, base colors, and details into different layers.

    o Lock layers as needed to avoid accidental changes.

4. **Apply Base Colors**

    o Use the fill or brush tool to add flat colors to your portrait.

    o Choose a color palette that complements your style or theme.

5. **Add Shadows and Highlights**

    o Use a soft brush to apply shadows and highlights, adding depth and dimension to your artwork.

o Experiment with blending modes for realistic effects.

6. **Refine Details**

o Focus on small details like facial features, hair, and textures.

o Use finer brushes for intricate areas and zoom in for precision.

7. **Final Touches**

o Adjust contrast, brightness, or saturation to enhance the overall look.

o Add a background or decorative elements if desired.

8. **Save and Export**

o Save your work in editable format (e.g., PSD or Procreate file).

o Export as JPEG or PNG for sharing or printing.

Exploring Different Styles and Techniques

1. **Vector Art**

o Tools: Adobe Illustrator, CorelDRAW.

o Applications: Logos, icons, and scalable graphics.

2. **Digital Painting**

o Tools: Photoshop, Procreate, Corel Painter.

o   Applications: Realistic or stylized artwork, concept art, and landscapes.

3. **Pixel Art**

   o   Tools: Aseprite, Piskel.

   o   Applications: Retro game designs and animations.

4. **3D Art and Sculpting**

   o   Tools: Blender, ZBrush.

   o   Applications: 3D models for games, animations, and visual effects.

5. **Anime/Manga Illustration**

   o   Tools: Clip Studio Paint, MediBang Paint.

   o   Applications: Character design, comic creation, and fan art.

Beginner-Friendly Digital Art Project Ideas

- **Abstract Art**: Use brushes and shapes to create colorful, abstract pieces.

- **Fantasy Landscapes**: Experiment with layers to build depth in scenic illustrations.

- **Custom Stickers**: Create simple, fun designs for digital or physical use.

- **Cartoon Characters**: Start with basic shapes and develop expressive, cartoon-style characters.

Benefits of Creating Custom Digital Art

- **Unlimited Revisions**: Edit, undo, and refine your work without the constraints of traditional media.

- **Cost-Effective**: No need for physical supplies like paints, canvases, or brushes.

- **Creative Freedom**: Explore endless styles, effects, and techniques with a single tool.

- **Shareability**: Easily share or sell your artwork online through platforms like Etsy, ArtStation, or Instagram.

Conclusion

Part 2 provides readers with the knowledge and tools to begin their journey into digital art and illustration. By exploring different tools, techniques, and project ideas, you'll learn to create stunning custom artwork that reflects your unique style and vision. Whether you're designing for personal enjoyment, professional projects, or commercial purposes, the skills gained here will empower you to turn your creative ideas into vibrant digital masterpieces.

Figure 3: Greeting Cards

Part 3: Designing Personalized Greeting Cards

Greeting cards are a timeless way to convey emotions, celebrate milestones, and connect with loved ones. In today's digital era, designing personalized greeting cards has become both easy and exciting, thanks to computer tools and templates. This part of the book guides you through the process of creating unique, custom greeting cards using simple yet powerful design tools.

Why Design Personalized Greeting Cards?

Personalized greeting cards offer:

- **A Unique Touch**: Unlike store-bought cards, custom designs reflect your personality and the recipient's preferences.

- **Creative Freedom**: Customize every element, from colors to text and graphics.

- **Cost-Effectiveness**: Save money by designing and printing cards yourself or sending them digitally.

- **Eco-Friendliness**: Choose digital formats to reduce waste and environmental impact.

Essential Tools for Greeting Card Design

1. **Beginner-Friendly Tools**

   o **Canva**: Offers a wide range of templates, drag-and-drop features, and ready-to-use design elements.

- o **Adobe Express**: Simple yet powerful for quick card creation with professional-quality results.

- o **Fotor**: A photo editing and design tool perfect for personalized designs.

2. **Advanced Tools**

- o **Adobe Photoshop**: For highly detailed and professional-grade designs.

- o **CorelDRAW**: Ideal for vector-based, scalable greeting card designs.

- o **Affinity Designer**: A cost-effective alternative to Adobe for precise designs.

3. **Optional Resources**

- o **Graphics Libraries**: Download icons, illustrations, and photos from resources like Freepik, Pexels, and Pixabay.

- o **Fonts**: Use platforms like Google Fonts or DaFont to access creative typography.

Types of Greeting Cards You Can Design

1. **Occasion-Based Cards**

- o Birthdays, anniversaries, weddings, graduations, and holidays like Christmas or Valentine's Day.

2. **Emotion-Based Cards**

- o Thank-you cards, sympathy cards, congratulations, and apologies.

3. **Custom Themes**

- o   Personalized cards for hobbies, favorite colors, or inside jokes between you and the recipient.

Step-by-Step Guide: Designing a Greeting Card

Project Title: Create a Personalized Birthday Greeting Card

Objective: Design a birthday card with a custom message, theme, and illustrations.

Steps:

1. **Set Your Canvas Size**

   - o   Open your chosen design tool (e.g., Canva or Photoshop).

   - o   Recommended size: 7 x 5 inches (standard card size).

2. **Choose a Theme or Template**

   - o   Start with a blank canvas or select a pre-made template.

   - o   Common themes: Balloons, cakes, flowers, or geometric patterns.

3. **Add a Background**

   - o   Use solid colors, gradients, or patterns for the background.

   - o   For digital cards, animated or textured backgrounds can add a dynamic touch.

4. **Insert Graphics or Illustrations**

   - o   Add icons like balloons, candles, or party hats from the tool's library.

- o Use royalty-free images or custom illustrations for a more personal feel.

5. **Write Your Message**

- o Use creative fonts to write a heartfelt message like:
  "Happy Birthday! Wishing you a day filled with laughter, love, and joy."

- o Highlight important words with bold colors or larger font sizes.

6. **Customize the Layout**

- o Align text and graphics for a clean, balanced look.

- o Use grids or guides if your tool supports them.

7. **Finalize with Decorative Elements**

- o Add borders, frames, or small accents like sparkles or stars.

- o Keep designs minimal for elegance or add more elements for a vibrant card.

8. **Save and Export**

- o Save in high-resolution formats like PDF for printing or PNG for digital sharing.

Tips for Designing Outstanding Greeting Cards

1. **Focus on the Recipient**

- o Incorporate their favorite colors, quotes, or hobbies.

2. **Use High-Quality Graphics**

   o   Avoid pixelated or low-resolution images to ensure a polished look.

3. **Experiment with Fonts**

   o   Combine decorative fonts with simple ones for a balanced design.

4. **Keep It Simple**

   o   Avoid overcrowding the card with too many elements.

5. **Test Your Design**

   o   Print a sample to check alignment, colors, and clarity before finalizing.

Project Ideas for Beginners

1. **Holiday Cards**

   o   Design themed cards for Christmas, Easter, or Halloween using seasonal colors and symbols.

2. **Thank-You Cards**

   o   Simple designs with floral or geometric patterns and a heartfelt message.

3. **Wedding Invitations**

   o   Elegant designs with script fonts and soft pastel colors.

4. **Digital Invitations**

   o   Create animated e-cards for birthdays, weddings, or parties.

5. **Photo Cards**

    o   Incorporate personal photos for a warm and memorable touch.

Benefits of Designing Greeting Cards

1. **Creative Expression**: Showcase your artistic side by crafting cards that stand out.

2. **Personalized Impact**: Show recipients that you've put thought and effort into their card.

3. **Skill Development**: Improve your design skills, which can be applied to other creative projects.

4. **Entrepreneurial Opportunities**: Turn your designs into a business by selling digital or physical greeting cards online.

Conclusion

Designing personalized greeting cards is a fulfilling and versatile skill that combines creativity with practical application. By using readily available tools and templates, you can create unique cards for every occasion and person. This chapter equips you with the knowledge and techniques to design cards that leave a lasting impression, whether for personal use or as a step toward starting your creative business.

Figure 4: Logo Design

Part 4: Making Logos for Small Businesses

Logos are the visual cornerstone of a brand's identity, encapsulating its mission, values, and personality in a simple, memorable design. For small businesses, a professionally crafted logo can set them apart in a competitive marketplace, create brand recognition, and build trust with customers. This section focuses on empowering readers to design impactful logos for small businesses, even with minimal experience in graphic design.

The Importance of a Well-Designed Logo

1. **Brand Identity**: A logo serves as the face of a business, representing its values and offerings at a glance.

2. **Memorability**: A unique logo helps customers remember a brand.

3. **Professionalism**: A high-quality logo communicates credibility and reliability.

4. **Marketing Tool**: Logos appear on all promotional materials, from business cards to websites and social media.

Essential Elements of a Great Logo

1. **Simplicity**

   o Avoid cluttered designs. A simple logo is easier to recognize and remember.

2. **Relevance**

o Reflect the business's industry, values, and target audience. For example, a logo for an eco-friendly brand might feature green tones and natural symbols.

3. **Scalability**

o Ensure the logo looks good at all sizes, from a website favicon to a billboard.

4. **Color Psychology**

o Colors evoke emotions and associations. For instance:

- Blue: Trust, professionalism (common for banks and tech companies).

- Green: Growth, nature (suitable for eco-friendly or wellness brands).

- Red: Energy, passion (ideal for food or entertainment businesses).

5. **Typography**

o Choose fonts that match the business's tone—modern, classic, playful, or formal.

o g professional logos based on business information.

o **Hatchful by Shopify**: A free tool for quick logo creation with ready-made templates.

2. **Advanced Tools**

o **Adobe Illustrator**: Industry-standard software for vector-based logo design.

- o **CorelDRAW**: Ideal for creating detailed and scalable logos.

- o **Affinity Designer**: A cost-effective alternative with powerful features for professional designs.

3. **Optional Resources**

   - o **Font Libraries**: Google Fonts, DaFont, or Font Squirrel for unique typography.

   - o **Icon and Vector Libraries**: Freepik, Flaticon, and Noun Project for symbols and illustrations.

Step-by-Step Guide: Designing a Logo for a Small Business

Project Title: Crafting a Logo for an Organic Juice Bar

Objective: Design a clean, nature-inspired logo that reflects the business's eco-friendly and health-conscious values.

Steps:

1. **Understand the Business**

   - o Name: "Green Sip Juice Bar."

   - o Mission: Promoting health and sustainability with fresh, organic juices.

   - o Target Audience: Health-conscious individuals and families.

2. **Sketch Initial Ideas**

   - o Use pen and paper to brainstorm concepts.

o Consider elements like a leaf, fruit, or juice drop integrated with the business name.

3. **Choose a Design Tool**

   o Open Canva for simplicity or Adobe Illustrator for more advanced options.

4. **Set Canvas Size and Resolution**

   o Standard size: 500x500 pixels for digital use or scalable vector art for print.

5. **Select a Color Palette**

   o Primary Colors: Green (nature, health), Orange (energy, vitality).

   o Accent Colors: White (purity, cleanliness).

6. **Add Shapes and Symbols**

   o Use geometric or organic shapes (e.g., a circular logo symbolizing inclusivity and balance).

   o Insert icons like a leaf or a juice glass.

7. **Incorporate Text**

   o Business Name: Use a clean, modern sans-serif font like "Montserrat."

   o Optional Tagline: "Fresh, Organic, Energizing."

8. **Refine the Design**

   o Adjust alignment, spacing, and proportions.

   o Test the logo in black-and-white to ensure clarity.

9. **Save and Export**

- o Save as a vector file (SVG or EPS) for scalability.

- o Export as PNG or JPEG for web and social media use.

Logo Design Tips

1. **Start with Black and White**

- o Focus on the design's form before adding colors.

2. **Keep it Timeless**

- o Avoid overly trendy designs that may become outdated.

3. **Use Negative Space Creatively**

- o Incorporate hidden symbols or messages within the logo.

4. **Get Feedback**

- o Share drafts with peers or clients for constructive criticism.

5. **Test in Various Contexts**

- o Check how the logo appears on different backgrounds, sizes, and mediums.

Common Mistakes to Avoid

1. **Overcomplicating the Design**

o Too many elements can make the logo confusing and hard to remember.

2. **Using Low-Quality Graphics**

   o Avoid pixelated images; always work with vectors.

3. **Relying Solely on Templates**

   o Customize templates to ensure originality and uniqueness.

4. **Ignoring Scalability**

   o Test how the logo looks when resized, especially for smaller applications.

Why Logo Design Skills Are Valuable

1. **For Entrepreneurs**: Create logos for your own businesses without hiring designers.

2. **Freelance Opportunities**: Offer logo design services to small businesses and startups.

3. **Portfolio Building**: Showcase your creativity and versatility in design.

4. **Branding Expertise**: Gain insights into creating cohesive brand identities.

Conclusion

Designing logos for small businesses is a rewarding skill that combines creativity with strategic thinking. With the right tools, techniques, and an understanding of the business's identity, you can craft logos that leave a lasting impression.

Whether you're designing for your own ventures or helping others establish their brand, this chapter equips you with the knowledge and inspiration to create professional, impactful logos.

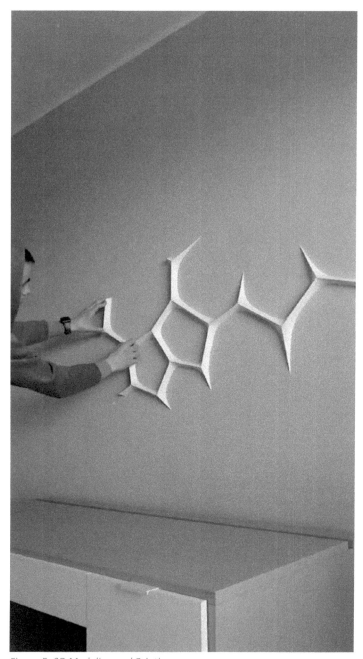

Figure 5: 3D Modeling and Printing

Part 5: Exploring 3D Modeling and Printing

3D modeling and printing represent a cutting-edge fusion of technology and creativity, enabling individuals to bring digital designs to life. From prototyping inventions to crafting art pieces, this field offers endless possibilities for innovation. This section provides a detailed guide to help readers understand the basics of 3D modeling, explore popular tools, and begin their journey into 3D printing.

What is 3D Modeling and Printing?

1. **3D Modeling**

   o The process of creating a three-dimensional representation of an object using specialized software.

   o Models can be viewed, edited, and manipulated from any angle.

2. **3D Printing**

   o A manufacturing process that transforms digital models into physical objects by building them layer by layer using materials like plastic, metal, or resin.

   o Often referred to as additive manufacturing.

Applications of 3D Modeling and Printing

1. **Prototyping**: Rapidly create prototypes for inventions, engineering projects, or industrial design.

2. **Art and Design**: Craft sculptures, jewelry, or decorative items.

3. **Medical**: Design prosthetics, dental implants, and surgical models.

4. **Education**: Teach concepts in geometry, architecture, and engineering.

5. **Manufacturing**: Produce custom parts or small-scale products.

6. **Gaming and Animation**: Develop characters, objects, and environments.

Popular 3D Modeling Tools

1. **Beginner-Friendly Software**

    o **Tinkercad**: A web-based, user-friendly tool ideal for beginners.

    o **SketchUp Free**: Intuitive software for designing simple 3D objects.

2. **Intermediate Tools**

    o **Fusion 360**: Versatile CAD software with advanced modeling and simulation features.

    o **Blender**: Open-source software for 3D modeling, animation, and rendering.

3. **Professional Tools**

    o **AutoCAD**: Industry-standard software for precise 3D modeling.

    o **Maya**: A favorite among professionals for complex 3D designs and animation.

o **SolidWorks**: Ideal for engineers and designers working on detailed projects.

Getting Started with 3D Modeling

1. **Choose a Project**

   o Decide on a simple object to model, such as a keychain, a cup, or a geometric figure.

2. **Understand the Workflow**

   o **Sketching**: Create 2D outlines of the object.

   o **Extruding**: Turn 2D sketches into 3D shapes.

   o **Refining**: Add details like textures, curves, or cutouts.

3. **Use Basic Tools and Techniques**

   o Learn essential operations like scaling, rotating, and mirroring.

   o Experiment with primitive shapes (cubes, spheres, cylinders) to build complex objects.

4. **Save in the Right Format**

   o Export your design as an STL or OBJ file for 3D printing.

Introduction to 3D Printing

1. **Types of 3D Printers**

   o **FDM (Fused Deposition Modeling)**: Uses thermoplastic filaments; ideal for beginners.

   o **SLA (Stereolithography)**: Offers high-resolution prints using resin.

- o **SLS (Selective Laser Sintering)**: Utilizes powder materials for detailed and durable objects.

2. **Materials for 3D Printing**

   - o **PLA**: Eco-friendly and easy to use; great for general projects.

   - o **ABS**: Durable and heat-resistant; suitable for functional parts.

   - o **Resin**: Provides smooth finishes; perfect for detailed designs.

   - o **Metal and Nylon**: Advanced materials for industrial applications.

3. **Preparing for Printing**

   - o **Slicing Software**: Use programs like Cura or PrusaSlicer to convert 3D models into printer instructions (G-code).

   - o **Printer Calibration**: Ensure the printer is correctly calibrated for accurate results.

   - o **Build Plate Preparation**: Apply adhesive to prevent the model from detaching during printing.

4. **Printing Process**

   - o Load the file into the printer.

   - o Monitor the progress to ensure no errors occur.

5. **Post-Processing**

o Remove supports, sand rough edges, and paint or polish the object for a professional finish.

Beginner Project: Design and Print a Custom Phone Stand

1. **Design**

   o Use Tinkercad to create a simple stand with slots to hold a smartphone.

   o Add personal touches like initials or patterns.

2. **Print**

   o Export the model as an STL file and slice it using Cura.

   o Choose PLA filament for ease of printing.

3. **Finish**

   o Sand and paint the stand to make it visually appealing.

Tips for Success in 3D Modeling and Printing

1. **Start Small**

   o Begin with simple projects to build confidence.

2. **Learn Through Practice**

   o Explore tutorials and practice replicating designs.

3. **Experiment with Tools**

   o Try different software and materials to expand your skills.

4. **Optimize for Efficiency**

o Design with print time and material usage in mind.

5. **Join a Community**

   o Engage with online forums and groups like Thingiverse or GrabCAD to share ideas and troubleshoot challenges.

Challenges and How to Overcome Them

1. **Failed Prints**: Analyze errors in slicing or calibration and adjust settings accordingly.

2. **Complex Designs**: Break down intricate models into smaller components.

3. **Material Limitations**: Experiment with different materials to find the best fit for your project.

Conclusion

Exploring 3D modeling and printing opens the door to a world of creativity and innovation. Whether you're crafting art, building prototypes, or designing functional items, these skills have applications in countless industries. By starting with the basics and gradually tackling more complex projects, you can turn your ideas into tangible creations, making 3D modeling and printing an exciting and rewarding pursuit.

Figure 6: Website Design

Part 6: Designing a Website from Scratch

Creating a website from scratch is a valuable skill that allows you to present ideas, products, or services in the digital world. Whether you're a beginner or looking to refine your skills, learning the fundamentals of web design will help you build functional, aesthetically pleasing websites that serve a specific purpose. This section will walk you through the process of designing a website from start to finish, from planning to execution, and introduce essential tools and coding techniques to make your website stand out.

What Is Website Design?

Website design is the process of planning, conceptualizing, and organizing content and structure for a website. It involves both the aesthetics (visual appeal) and the functionality (how it works). A well-designed website is user-friendly, intuitive, and serves its intended purpose, whether it's a portfolio, e-commerce site, blog, or informational platform.

The Basics of Website Design

1. **Purpose and Goal Setting**

   o Before diving into the design process, it's crucial to define the purpose of the website. What do you want to achieve with your site? This could range from providing information to selling products. Understanding the goal of the website will guide your design choices, from layout to content.

49

2. **User Experience (UX) and User Interface (UI) Design**

- o **UX Design**: Refers to creating a seamless and enjoyable experience for the user. It includes navigation, accessibility, and overall satisfaction while using the website.

- o **UI Design**: Focuses on the look and feel of the website, such as typography, color schemes, buttons, and interactive elements.

Step-by-Step Guide to Designing a Website from Scratch

1. Plan Your Website's Structure

Before you even open your code editor or design tool, you need to plan out your website's structure. A clear blueprint will ensure your design is organized and user-friendly.

- **Sitemap Creation:**
  - o Create a sitemap, which is essentially a visual representation of the site's structure. It includes all the main pages (Home, About, Services, Contact, etc.) and their subpages (Blog, FAQs, Product Categories).
  - o Tools like **MindNode** and **XMind** can help create simple and clear sitemaps.

- **Wireframes:**
  - o Wireframes are blueprints of your website's layout. They show where content, images, buttons, and navigation menus will be positioned.

o   Tools like **Balsamiq** and **Figma** are great for wireframing.

2. Choose the Right Tools

Selecting the right tools is key to building your website efficiently. There are two main options for website creation: using a website builder or coding from scratch.

- **Website   Builders**: If you want to avoid coding and need a quick solution, website builders like **Wix**, **Squarespace**, and **WordPress** are excellent choices. These platforms provide drag-and-drop interfaces and templates to speed up the design process.

- **Coding   from   Scratch**: If you want full control over your website's design and functionality, you can write the code yourself. The basic technologies you'll need are:

  o   **HTML (HyperText Markup Language)**: The foundation of web pages; HTML is used to structure your content (headings, paragraphs, links, etc.).

  o   **CSS (Cascading Style Sheets)**: Used for styling and laying out your content (colors, fonts, spacing, etc.).

  o   **JavaScript**: Adds interactivity and dynamic features like form validation, image sliders, etc.

3. Design and Style the Website

- **Color   Scheme**: Choose a color palette that reflects your brand or the mood you want to convey. You can use tools like

51

Coolors or **Adobe Color** to generate harmonious color schemes.

- **Typography**:
  Typography is essential in setting the tone for your website. Choose a legible font and ensure it complements the overall design. **Google Fonts** offers a wide variety of free fonts you can easily integrate into your website.

- **Imagery**:
  High-quality images and graphics are essential for a visually appealing website. Use free image resources like **Unsplash** and **Pexels**, or create custom graphics using design tools like **Canva** or **Adobe Photoshop**.

4. Write the Code

If you choose to code your website, you'll start writing the foundational code. Here's how you can structure it:

- **HTML**:
  The first step is to write the structure of your site in HTML. A basic HTML template includes essential tags like <html>, <head>, <body>, <header>, <footer>, <nav>, and <section>. You can use a code editor like **Visual Studio Code**, **Sublime Text**, or **Atom** for writing your HTML code.

Example of a basic HTML structure:

<!DOCTYPE html>

<html lang="en">

<head>

  <meta charset="UTF-8">

```
<meta name="viewport" content="width=device-width, initial-scale=1.0">

<title>My Website</title>

<link rel="stylesheet" href="styles.css">
</head>
<body>
  <header>
    <h1>Welcome to My Website</h1>
    <nav>
      <ul>
        <li><a href="#home">Home</a></li>
        <li><a href="#about">About</a></li>
        <li><a href="#contact">Contact</a></li>
      </ul>
    </nav>
  </header>
  <main>
    <section id="home">
      <h2>Home Section</h2>
      <p>This is the home section of the website.</p>
    </section>
    <section id="about">
      <h2>About Section</h2>
```

```
    <p>This is the about section.</p>

  </section>

</main>

<footer>

  <p>© 2025 My Website</p>

</footer>

</body>

</html>
```

- **CSS**:
  After HTML, apply styles using CSS. The CSS file controls the colors, layout, typography, and overall aesthetic. Link your CSS file in the <head> section of your HTML.

Example of basic CSS:

```
body {

  font-family: Arial, sans-serif;

  background-color: #f4f4f4;

}

header {

  background-color: #333;

  color: white;

  padding: 10px 0;

  text-align: center;

}
```

```css
nav ul {
   list-style-type: none;
   padding: 0;
}


nav ul li {
   display: inline;
   margin-right: 10px;
}


nav ul li a {
   color: white;
   text-decoration: none;
}


section {
   padding: 20px;
}
```

- **JavaScript**:
  To add interactivity, such as a form validation or dynamic content, you can use JavaScript.

Example of a simple script for form validation:

```javascript
function validateForm() {
```

```
let name = document.getElementById("name").value;

if (name == "") {

    alert("Name must be filled out");

    return false;

  }

}
```

5. Test and Debug

After coding your website, it's important to test it across different devices (desktop, tablet, mobile) and browsers (Chrome, Firefox, Safari, Edge) to ensure it looks and functions as expected.

- **Responsive   Design**: Use media queries in CSS to ensure your website adjusts to various screen sizes. Example of a responsive CSS rule:

- @media (max-width: 600px) {

- body {

- background-color: lightblue;

- }

- }

- **Debugging**: Tools like **Google Chrome Developer Tools** help identify layout issues, errors in code, and performance bottlenecks.

6. Launch Your Website

Once your website is designed, tested, and debugged, it's time to go live!

- **Choose a Domain Name**: Select a memorable domain name that reflects your website's purpose. You can register a domain through platforms like **GoDaddy**, **Namecheap**, or **Google Domains**.

- **Web Hosting**: You'll need a web hosting service to store your website's files. Popular options include **Bluehost**, **HostGator**, or **SiteGround**.

- **Deploy the Website**: After securing your domain and hosting, upload your website files to the server using **FileZilla** or the hosting provider's file manager.

Conclusion

Designing a website from scratch requires a combination of planning, creativity, and technical skills. By understanding the process and using the right tools, you can create a functional, aesthetically pleasing website that meets your goals. Whether you choose to code from scratch or use a website builder, the fundamental principles of design and user experience will always guide you in creating a successful online presence.

Figure 7: Digital Scrapbooking

Part 7: Digital Scrapbooking

Digital scrapbooking is a creative and modern way to preserve memories and create beautiful, personalized designs. Unlike traditional scrapbooking, which involves physical materials like paper, glue, and embellishments, digital scrapbooking uses computer software and tools to create scrapbook pages that can be printed or shared online. This method allows for limitless creativity without the mess of physical supplies, and it can be done from the comfort of your own home.

In this section, we will explore what digital scrapbooking is, the tools you'll need, and how to get started with creating stunning digital scrapbook pages. Whether you're looking to create a family photo album, a travel journal, or a special occasion memory book, digital scrapbooking can help you achieve professional-looking results with ease.

What is Digital Scrapbooking?

Digital scrapbooking is the art of creating scrapbook pages using digital tools and resources. Instead of manually cutting, pasting, and decorating photos and papers, you use graphic design software to arrange and manipulate digital elements. These elements can include:

- **Photos**: Your personal images, such as family photos, vacation snapshots, or event pictures.

- **Backgrounds**: Digital papers, textures, and patterns that serve as the base for your scrapbook page.

- **Embellishments**: Decorative elements such as buttons, ribbons, flowers, and shapes to add flair and personality to your page.

- **Fonts and Text**: Digital typography allows you to add meaningful captions, quotes, and titles to your pages.

- **Masks and Frames**: These tools help you creatively position and shape your photos, giving them unique effects.

Digital scrapbooking provides endless flexibility to mix and match these elements, giving you the ability to experiment with different layouts, themes, and styles until you're happy with the result.

Tools for Digital Scrapbooking

To create a digital scrapbook, you'll need a few essential tools. Fortunately, many of these tools are available for free or at an affordable price, making digital scrapbooking accessible to anyone.

1. **Software for Designing Scrapbook Pages**
   The first step in digital scrapbooking is selecting a software tool to design your pages. Some of the most popular options include:

   o **Adobe Photoshop**: The industry standard for graphic design and digital art. Photoshop provides powerful tools for photo editing, layout creation, and design. It's a great choice for experienced scrapbookers or those looking for advanced design features.

   o **Adobe Illustrator**: Ideal for creating vector-based elements such as illustrations, icons, and logos, Illustrator is a great choice for creating your own embellishments.

   o **Canva**: A beginner-friendly, web-based design tool with easy-to-use drag-and-drop functionality. Canva has templates and pre-made digital scrapbooking elements that you can quickly use to create scrapbook pages.

o **PicMonkey**: Similar to Canva, PicMonkey is a user-friendly tool that offers templates, photo editing features, and graphic design elements tailored to scrapbooking.

o **GIMP (GNU Image Manipulation Program)**: A free, open-source alternative to Photoshop. GIMP offers powerful editing tools but may have a steeper learning curve than Canva or PicMonkey.

o **Scrapbook Studio**: Specialized software for scrapbooking, designed specifically for creating digital scrapbooks with built-in templates and embellishments.

2. **Digital Scrapbook Kits**
These kits are pre-made collections of photos, backgrounds, fonts, and embellishments designed specifically for scrapbooking. You can find these kits on websites like **Etsy**, **Pixel Scrapper**, or **Design Bundles**. Digital kits can save you time and effort, especially when you're starting, as they offer themed sets of design elements that you can use in your pages.

3. **Fonts and Text**
Fonts are a critical component of digital scrapbooking, as they help convey the mood and style of your pages. Websites like **DaFont** and **Google Fonts** offer a wide range of free fonts you can use in your projects. Pay attention to font pairing to ensure readability and aesthetic appeal.

Getting Started with Digital Scrapbooking

1. **Select   a   Theme**
   Before beginning your digital scrapbook page, decide on the theme. The theme can be based on an event (wedding, birthday, vacation), a specific color scheme, or a mood (vintage, modern, minimalist). Selecting a theme helps guide your choices in backgrounds, fonts, and embellishments.

2. **Choose   Your   Photos**
   Collect and select the photos you want to include in your scrapbook. Digital scrapbooking allows you to use high-resolution images, so choose photos that are clear and well-composed. If you need to edit or enhance your images, you can do so using the photo editing tools in your design software.

3. **Create   the   Layout**
   The layout refers to the arrangement of your photos, text, and embellishments on the page. You can start with a blank canvas or use a template to guide your design.

   o **Grid Layout**: A common and clean approach where photos are arranged in rows and columns.

   o **Collage Style**: A more flexible, organic layout where photos are scattered or layered on the page.

   o **Journal Style**: A more structured layout that mimics traditional scrapbooking with a focus on captions, text, and journaling alongside images.

4. **Add Backgrounds and Embellishments**
Select a background that complements your photos and theme. Digital scrapbooking allows you to experiment with textured backgrounds, gradients, and patterns. Once you've chosen a background, start layering your photos and adding embellishments like ribbons, buttons, flowers, and frames.

You can adjust the size, angle, and opacity of each element to create depth and visual interest.

5. **Incorporate Text and Journaling**
Adding text is a great way to tell the story behind your photos. Whether it's a caption, quote, date, or short narrative, text helps personalize your scrapbook pages. Choose fonts that match your theme and make sure they're easy to read.

You can also add journaling to your pages to describe the memories, emotions, or significance behind the photos. This adds a personal touch to the scrapbook and allows you to capture stories that will be cherished for years to come.

Tips for Creating Stunning Digital Scrapbook Pages

1. **Use Layers**
One of the key advantages of digital scrapbooking is the ability to work with layers. This allows you to move, resize, and edit each element without affecting others. Take full advantage of this feature to adjust the placement of photos, text, and embellishments until everything fits perfectly.

2. **Experiment with Filters and Effects**
Digital scrapbooking offers an endless range of creative possibilities. You can apply filters to photos for unique effects, such as sepia tones, black and white,

or vintage looks. You can also experiment with shadow effects on text and embellishments to add depth to your pages.

3. **Incorporate Gradients and Textures**
   Adding subtle gradients or textures to your backgrounds can give your scrapbook pages a more dynamic, layered look. Use soft gradients to create a smooth transition between colors or add texture to give your background a tactile feel.

4. **Stay Consistent with Style**
   While experimenting with different design elements is fun, it's important to keep the overall design cohesive. Stick to a limited color palette, font choices, and embellishments to create a harmonious and visually pleasing scrapbook page.

Sharing and Printing Your Digital Scrapbook

Once you've created your digital scrapbook pages, there are many ways to preserve and share them.

1. **Create a Digital Photo Book**
   Websites like **Shutterfly**, **Mixbook**, and **Snapfish** allow you to upload your digital scrapbook pages and turn them into physical photo books. This is an excellent way to preserve your digital scrapbook as a keepsake.

2. **Print Pages for Traditional Scrapbooks**
   You can print individual scrapbook pages on high-quality paper and place them in traditional scrapbooking albums.

3. **Share Online**
   Share your digital scrapbooks online via social media

platforms or personal blogs. Websites like **Pinterest** or **Instagram** are great places to showcase your creative work and inspire others.

Conclusion

Digital scrapbooking is an enjoyable and creative way to preserve memories while showcasing your design skills. With the right tools and techniques, you can create beautiful scrapbook pages that are both personal and professional. Whether you're documenting family milestones or commemorating special events, digital scrapbooking allows you to express your creativity and share meaningful stories in a modern, digital format.

Part 8: Creating Custom T-Shirts with Graphic Software

Creating custom t-shirts has become a popular and accessible way to express personal style, advertise a brand, or commemorate special events. With the rise of on-demand printing services, anyone with basic graphic design skills can create unique designs and bring them to life on a t-shirt. In this section, we will explore the process of designing custom t-shirts using graphic software, tools, and techniques that will help you turn your ideas into wearable art.

What You'll Need to Create Custom T-Shirts

Before diving into the design process, it's important to understand the tools and resources you'll need to create custom t-shirt designs. These are the essential components:

1. **Graphic Design Software**
   The right software will enable you to create high-quality, print-ready designs. Some popular graphic design programs for t-shirt creation include:

- o **Adobe Illustrator**: A vector-based design tool that is perfect for creating clean, scalable designs. Illustrator is ideal for logos, typography, and designs that need to be resized without losing quality.

- o **Adobe Photoshop**: A raster-based tool that is best for photo editing and creating more complex, detailed designs. Photoshop allows you to work with images, textures, and effects, which can be used in t-shirt designs.

- o **CorelDRAW**: Another vector design tool similar to Illustrator. CorelDRAW is known for its user-friendly interface and is a great choice for beginners and professionals alike.

- o **Canva**: A beginner-friendly online design tool that offers pre-made templates, fonts, and graphics to help you create t-shirt designs quickly and easily. It's perfect for those who want a simple approach without advanced graphic design skills.

- o **Inkscape**: A free, open-source vector design software. While it may not have all the advanced features of Illustrator, it's a great choice for beginners on a budget who want to create vector-based t-shirt designs.

2. **Design   Resources**

In addition to software, you will need design elements to help you create your t-shirt design. These include:

- o **Fonts**: Typography plays a key role in t-shirt design. Choose fonts that are legible and match

66

the style you're going for, whether it's bold and modern or playful and quirky.

- o **Graphics and Illustrations**: You can use free or paid graphic elements such as illustrations, icons, patterns, or textures to enhance your design. Websites like **Freepik**, **Shutterstock**, or **Vecteezy** offer a wide range of graphics for download.

- o **Images**: You can incorporate photos into your t-shirt designs, either by using stock images or your own personal photos. Just ensure the images are of high quality and resolution for the best print results.

3. **Printing Platform or Equipment**
Once your design is complete, you'll need to choose how to bring it to life. If you don't have access to a professional printing machine, online printing services like **Printful**, **TeeSpring**, or **Redbubble** allow you to upload your design and have it printed on demand. Alternatively, if you want to create t-shirts yourself, you'll need:

- o **A Heat Press Machine**: A machine that transfers your design onto fabric using heat and pressure.

- o **Vinyl Cutter**: If you're creating designs using vinyl, you'll need a vinyl cutter to cut out shapes and letters.

- o **Inkjet Printer**: If you're using transfer paper to print your designs, an inkjet printer can help you print high-resolution images onto the transfer paper.

Step-by-Step Process for Creating Custom T-Shirt Designs

Creating a custom t-shirt design involves several steps, from initial brainstorming to finalizing the design and preparing it for printing. Here's a comprehensive breakdown of the process:

1. Define Your Design Concept

Before opening your design software, take some time to think about the concept of your t-shirt design. What message or theme do you want to convey? Some things to consider:

- **Purpose**: Is the design for a personal project, business branding, a special event, or just for fun? This will guide your design choices.

- **Target Audience**: Who will wear this t-shirt? Consider the preferences, interests, and style of your intended audience when choosing colors, typography, and graphics.

- **Theme**: Decide on the general theme of the design. For example, is it sports-themed, retro, minimalist, inspirational, or artistic? Themes will influence the choice of colors, fonts, and imagery.

2. Choose Your Design Software

Once you've established your concept, choose the graphic design software that suits your needs and skill level. If you're a beginner, **Canva** or **Inkscape** are great starting points. For more advanced designs, you may want to use **Adobe Illustrator** or **Photoshop**.

3. Start with the T-Shirt Template

In most design software, you can either create your design from scratch or use a pre-made template. Many platforms, such as **Canva** and **Placeit**, provide t-shirt templates with mockups so you can see how your design will look on a shirt. Working with a template ensures that your design fits within the printable area and helps you visualize the final product.

- **T-Shirt Templates**: You can find blank t-shirt mockups in your design software or download them from websites that offer free or paid resources. These templates serve as a reference for the size and placement of your design.

- **Printable Area**: Be sure to work within the printable area, which typically includes the front of the shirt (and optionally the back or sleeves, depending on the design). This will vary based on the printing service or equipment you're using.

4. Create Your Design Elements

Now it's time to create or import the elements that will make up your t-shirt design. Some design options include:

- **Text**: Choose a bold, readable font that suits the theme of your design. For t-shirt designs, consider fonts that are simple, large, and eye-catching. Use text to convey messages, quotes, or branding.

- **Graphics**: Add images, icons, or illustrations that complement your text. If you're going for a more complex design, consider combining multiple graphics to create a layered effect.

- **Colors**: Choose a color palette that reflects your style and resonates with your audience. Keep in mind that bright, bold colors tend to stand out, while muted

69

tones can create a more minimalist or vintage feel. If you're designing for a specific shirt color, make sure the colors contrast well with the fabric.

- **Effects**: Utilize design effects like shadows, gradients, textures, and outlines to enhance your design. These effects can give your design a more dynamic look.

5. Organize the Layout

Arrange your design elements (text, images, and graphics) in a visually appealing way. Ensure that there is enough space between elements, and keep the design balanced. Make sure the text is legible, and avoid overcrowding the design with too many elements. If you're working with a t-shirt template, be sure to center your design in the printable area.

6. Review and Finalize the Design

Before moving on to the printing process, review your design and make any necessary adjustments. Double-check that:

- The design is clear, balanced, and visually appealing.

- The text is easy to read from a distance.

- All design elements are properly aligned and placed.

- The colors work well on the chosen t-shirt color.

It's also a good idea to view your design in different sizes to ensure it looks good both in large and small formats.

7. Save and Export Your Design

Once your design is complete, save your file in the appropriate format for printing. Typically, for t-shirt printing, you'll need to save your design as:

- **PNG**: This format is best for designs with transparent backgrounds. It's widely accepted by printing services and ensures high-quality, crisp images.

- **SVG**: If you're using vector-based elements (created in Illustrator or Inkscape), saving your design as an SVG file ensures that it's scalable and will maintain its quality when resized.

- **PDF**: A good option if you're printing your design yourself or working with a print shop.

Be sure to save your file in high resolution (at least 300 dpi) to ensure the print quality is sharp and clear.

Figure 8: Customize T-Shirt Desing

Part 8. Print and Market Your Custom T-Shirts

Once you have your custom t-shirt design ready, it's time to print it! If you're using a printing service like **Printful**, **TeeSpring**, or **Redbubble**, you can simply upload your design, choose your shirt style and color, and they will handle the printing and shipping. Alternatively, if you're printing your t-shirts at home or through a local print shop, you'll need to use your heat press machine, vinyl cutter, or inkjet printer.

If you're designing t-shirts for a business or to sell, consider using **social media marketing** to showcase your designs. Platforms like **Instagram**, **Facebook**, and **Etsy** provide excellent opportunities to reach potential customers and promote your custom t-shirts.

Conclusion

Creating custom t-shirts using graphic software is an enjoyable and rewarding process that allows you to express your creativity and showcase your design skills. With the right tools, resources, and techniques, you can create eye-catching and unique t-shirt designs that stand out. Whether you're designing for fun, for a business, or as a personal project, the possibilities are endless. So, unleash your creativity, start designing, and see how your custom t-shirts come to life!

Part 9: Designing Book Covers for Self-Publishing

A book cover is often the first thing potential readers see, and it plays a significant role in attracting attention and sparking interest in your book. For self-published authors, designing a compelling book cover is a crucial step in presenting a professional and marketable product. In this section, we will explore the process of designing a book cover, from conceptualization to execution, using graphic design tools and techniques.

The Importance of a Book Cover

Before diving into the design process, it's essential to understand why the book cover is so important:

1. **First Impressions Matter**: A book cover is often the first visual impression readers have of your work. It must grab attention and convey the essence of the book's theme and genre. A well-designed cover can persuade a reader to pick up your book or click on it in an online store.

2. **Reflecting the Genre and Tone**: Your cover must reflect the genre and tone of the book. Whether it's a romance novel, thriller, fantasy, or non-fiction, the cover should communicate the feel of the book to potential readers. For example, bright, colorful covers may work well for a children's book, while darker, more subdued tones are appropriate for a mystery novel.

3. **Professionalism**: A professional-looking cover suggests that the book inside is also of high quality.

Self-published books must compete with traditionally published books, so creating a polished cover is essential for gaining credibility and standing out in the marketplace.

4. **Brand Identity**: For authors who plan to release multiple books, creating a consistent and recognizable cover style across their works helps build a personal brand. This consistency establishes a visual identity that readers will recognize and trust.

What You'll Need to Design a Book Cover

1. **Graphic   Design   Software**
   The right tools will allow you to create a professional-quality book cover. Here are some of the most popular graphic design software for book cover design:

   - **Adobe Photoshop**: A powerful raster-based software ideal for photo manipulation, detailed artwork, and complex cover designs. It's perfect if your cover requires photographs or intricate image effects.

   - **Adobe Illustrator**: A vector-based design tool that's ideal for creating clean, scalable designs such as typography, logos, and illustrations. Illustrator is often used for simple, graphic-driven covers.

   - **Canva**: An easy-to-use online design tool that offers pre-made templates, fonts, and images for those who don't have professional graphic design skills. It's an excellent tool for beginners and non-designers.

- o **GIMP**: A free, open-source alternative to Photoshop, offering powerful image manipulation tools for creating detailed designs without the cost.

- o **Affinity Designer**: A one-time purchase software that combines both vector and raster design capabilities, making it an affordable option for those who need a versatile tool for cover design.

- o **Book Cover Templates**: Whether you're using Photoshop or Canva, many design platforms offer pre-made templates specifically sized for book covers. These templates can help guide the design process and ensure your cover looks professional.

2. **Stock Photos and Illustrations**
   Stock imagery can be a useful resource for book cover design, especially if you don't have access to professional photos or illustrations. Websites like **Shutterstock, Adobe Stock**, and **Unsplash** offer high-quality images that you can license for use in your book cover designs. For illustrations or custom artwork, consider platforms like **IllustrationX** or working with freelance artists who can bring a unique, custom touch to your cover.

3. **Fonts**
   Typography is a crucial part of book cover design. The font should reflect the genre and tone of your book. Free font resources like **Google Fonts, DaFont**, and **FontSquirrel** offer a wide variety of typefaces that can suit different styles and themes.

4. **Color** Palette

Colors play a vital role in setting the mood and tone of your book cover. You should choose colors that align with the emotions or themes of your book. For example, dark blues and grays might suit a thriller or mystery novel, while bright pastels could work for a lighthearted romance or children's book.

Step-by-Step Process for Designing a Book Cover

Here's a step-by-step breakdown of how to design an effective book cover for self-publishing:

1. Define the Book's Theme, Genre, and Target Audience

Before opening any design software, it's crucial to understand the key elements of your book. Consider the following:

- **Theme**: What is the book's central message or storyline? Whether it's a love story, a historical drama, or a guide to success, the cover should reflect the theme visually.

- **Genre**: Different genres have different visual codes. For instance, a romance novel might feature soft colors and elegant fonts, while a thriller may use bold typography and dark, moody imagery.

- **Target Audience**: Who is the book for? A cover designed for young adult readers might look different from a cover aimed at a business or self-help audience. Make sure the design appeals to the specific demographic you are targeting.

2. Research Book Covers in Your Genre

Take a look at other books in your genre to see what works and what doesn't. Notice the common design elements such as

77

color schemes, typography, and imagery. This research will help you understand industry standards and trends, giving you a starting point for your own design.

- Pay attention to what stands out on the shelves (or in online stores) and analyze the success of bestselling book covers. Look for patterns in composition, style, and how titles are presented.

- Study the cover art of books by successful authors in your genre to determine what elements might resonate with your readers.

3. Start with a Blank Canvas or Template

Using your design software, start with the correct dimensions for your book cover. The typical size for an eBook cover is 1600x2560 pixels, while print covers may require different dimensions based on the trim size of the book. Many self-publishing platforms, such as **Amazon Kindle Direct Publishing (KDP)**, provide specific cover size guidelines, including bleed and margin areas for print books.

- **Bleed**: If your design extends to the edges of the cover, make sure to include bleed in your design, which is extra space around the edges that gets trimmed off during the printing process.

- **Margins**: Ensure important elements like the title, author name, and central graphics are placed within the safe zone to avoid being cut off.

4. Choose the Right Images and Graphics

Images should visually convey the book's essence. Depending on your book's theme, you might choose:

- **Photographs**: Realistic and detailed images can give your cover a polished, professional feel. If your book is a memoir or biography, consider using a photo of the subject.

- **Illustrations**: Custom illustrations or artwork can make your book stand out and offer a unique, artistic touch. If your book is fictional or fantasy, you may opt for illustrated covers.

- **Abstract Graphics**: For self-help, business, or non-fiction books, abstract designs or simple patterns can work well to create a clean, modern look.

5. Typography and Layout

Typography is one of the most critical design elements of a book cover. The title should be legible and easy to read, even at small sizes (especially for eBooks). Consider these typography tips:

- **Font Style**: Choose a font that reflects your genre. Serif fonts may be more appropriate for classic novels or historical fiction, while sans-serif fonts are often used for modern or minimalist designs.

- **Font Size**: Ensure the title is large enough to be readable at thumbnail size. The author's name should be smaller but still visible.

- **Alignment**: Place the title and author's name in an aligned and aesthetically pleasing way. Typically, the title goes at the top or center, with the author's name placed beneath it.

Use contrast to make your text stand out against the background. If the background is dark, use light text, and if the background is light, use darker text.

6. Play with Colors and Contrast

Your color scheme should align with the book's mood and genre. Use complementary or contrasting colors to create visual interest, but avoid overcrowding the design with too many colors.

- **Warm Colors (Red, Yellow, Orange)**: Often used for books with action or drama. Great for romance or thrillers.

- **Cool Colors (Blue, Green, Purple)**: Ideal for calm, serene designs. Used for self-help books, spirituality, or books about nature.

- **Monochromatic Schemes**: Works well for minimalist designs or when you want to create a clean, sleek aesthetic.

7. Add the Back Cover (For Print Books)

If you are designing a print book cover, don't forget the back cover and spine. The back cover typically contains a brief description or blurb, ISBN, bar code, and any other relevant information.

- **Back Cover Blurb**: Keep the text concise but enticing. Write a short summary of the book that sparks curiosity and compels readers to purchase the book.

- **Spine**: The spine should include the title, author name, and possibly a small logo or graphic, especially for books with multiple titles in a series.

8. Save, Export, and Upload

Once the design is complete, save your file in the correct format:

- **For eBooks**: Save your cover as a high-resolution PNG or JPEG file (usually 72 dpi for eBooks).

- **For Print Books**: Save your cover as a PDF or TIFF with 300 dpi resolution for crisp, high-quality prints.

Ensure your design meets the self-publishing platform's specifications before uploading. Platforms like **Amazon KDP** offer detailed guidelines for uploading cover art, including size, file format, and resolution.

Conclusion

Designing a book cover for self-publishing can be an exciting and rewarding process. By understanding the importance of visual appeal, reflecting the book's genre and tone, and using the right design tools and techniques, you can create a cover that will attract readers and make your book stand out in a crowded market. Whether you're designing the cover yourself or working with a professional designer, taking the time to craft a stunning book cover will set the foundation for your book's success.

Figure 9: Interactive Presentation

Part 10: Making Interactive Presentations

In today's digital world, the art of making engaging and interactive presentations is crucial in various fields, from business and education to marketing and personal projects. Interactive presentations are more than just a collection of slides filled with text and images—they involve creating dynamic, engaging content that captivates your audience and enhances their experience. In this part, we will explore how to create interactive presentations that leave a lasting impression using different tools and techniques.

What Makes a Presentation Interactive?

An interactive presentation goes beyond the traditional slide format. It allows the audience to engage with the content in a way that keeps them focused, enhances retention, and provides a more personalized experience. Here are some key features of an interactive presentation:

- **User Input**: Incorporating elements like quizzes, polls, and surveys where the audience can provide feedback or answer questions in real-time.

- **Multimedia**: Using videos, sound effects, and animations to make the content more lively and engaging.

- **Hyperlinks and Navigation**: Allowing the audience to navigate through content at their own pace, jumping between slides or topics based on their interests.

- **Interactive Tools**: Tools such as live Q&A sessions, clickable elements, and interactive graphics help involve the audience directly in the presentation.

Why Create Interactive Presentations?

1. **Engagement**: Interactive elements keep the audience involved, making them more likely to remember and understand the information being presented.

2. **Improved Retention**: When the audience is actively participating, they are more likely to retain key information, especially through quizzes, polls, and decision-based interactions.

3. **Customizability**: Interactive presentations can be customized to fit the needs and interests of different audiences, making them more relevant and personal.

4. **Feedback Opportunities**: Incorporating feedback tools gives the presenter immediate insights into how well the audience is understanding the material.

5. **Flexibility and Innovation**: Interactive presentations allow for creative freedom. Whether it's adding animations, voiceovers, or using unconventional formats, these presentations can break free from traditional, static slides.

Tools for Creating Interactive Presentations

There are several software tools available that allow you to create interactive presentations, ranging from user-friendly programs to professional-grade software for complex designs. Here are some of the most popular options:

1. Microsoft PowerPoint

PowerPoint remains one of the most widely used tools for creating presentations. With the right techniques, it can be transformed into a powerful interactive platform. Features like hyperlinks, embedded videos, animations, and triggers can turn a standard presentation into an interactive one.

- **Hyperlinks and Navigation**: You can add clickable links to different parts of your presentation, allowing users to navigate through different sections.

- **Triggers and Animations**: Set specific actions, such as a button press, to trigger animations, transitions, or reveal content, creating a more dynamic user experience.

- **Embedded Polls and Quizzes**: You can use add-ons like Mentimeter or Slido to incorporate live polls and quizzes, or even embed YouTube videos to make the presentation more interactive.

2. Prezi

Prezi is a popular tool that uses a non-linear format to create more visually dynamic and engaging presentations. Unlike traditional slide-based presentations, Prezi allows you to zoom in and out of different parts of the canvas to showcase various sections and points.

- **Zooming User Interface (ZUI)**: Prezi's unique zooming effect allows the presenter to zoom in on key points, providing a dynamic feel to the presentation.

- o **Interactive Navigation**: The audience can interact with the Prezi presentation by clicking on different points to navigate the content. This allows them to explore specific topics or areas of interest.

- o **Collaborative Features**: Multiple users can work on the same presentation simultaneously, making it an ideal tool for group projects or collaborative presentations.

3. **Canva**

Canva is a highly intuitive and user-friendly design platform, perfect for creating interactive presentations with a more visually appealing design. While primarily known for static designs, Canva offers several interactive features that can be used in presentations.

- o **Drag-and-Drop Interface**: Canva's simple interface makes it easy to create beautiful slides with various interactive elements.

- o **Embedded Videos and Animations**: You can enhance your presentations with embedded videos, animated text, and elements that move to grab attention.

- o **Interactive PDFs**: Canva allows you to export presentations as interactive PDFs that include hyperlinks, enabling the audience to click and navigate through different sections.

4. **Google Slides**

Google Slides offers a free and collaborative platform that can be used to create interactive presentations. Like PowerPoint,

Google Slides has a variety of features that can help increase engagement.

- o **Collaboration**: Multiple team members can work on the presentation at the same time, and changes are immediately reflected across all devices.

- o **Add-ons for Interaction**: Use third-party add-ons such as Pear Deck, which turns Google Slides into a fully interactive presentation tool. Pear Deck allows you to add interactive questions, polls, and activities to keep your audience engaged.

- o **Linking and Navigation**: You can easily add clickable links to slides or external websites, making the presentation more flexible and interactive.

5. **Mentimeter**

Mentimeter is a tool designed specifically to make presentations interactive. It allows you to incorporate real-time polls, surveys, quizzes, and audience feedback. Mentimeter is ideal for situations where you need to engage a large audience and collect data during the presentation.

- o **Live Polling and Q&A**: Use live polls and Q&A sessions to get instant feedback from your audience and address their questions in real-time.

- o **Quizzes and Surveys**: You can use quizzes and surveys to test your audience's knowledge and adjust the content based on their understanding.

- o **Word Clouds**: Mentimeter also allows you to create word clouds, which visually display the most common responses to questions.

Techniques for Making Your Presentation Interactive

1. Interactive Quizzes and Polls

Adding quizzes and polls is one of the best ways to increase interaction and gauge your audience's understanding of the material. Tools like PowerPoint (with add-ons), Mentimeter, and Kahoot allow you to create fun and engaging quizzes where your audience can respond in real time. By incorporating interactive questions, you create a two-way communication channel between you and your audience.

2. Click-to-Reveal Content

With features like triggers and animations, you can hide and reveal content with a simple click. This is useful for step-by-step explanations, building suspense, or allowing the audience to navigate through specific details at their own pace. For instance, you can hide answers to questions and reveal them when the audience is ready to see them.

3. Gamify the Experience

Transform your presentation into a game by adding elements like points, scores, and challenges. For example, you can create a quiz with a leaderboard, making the audience feel like they're participating in a fun competition. This approach works well for corporate presentations, classroom learning, and educational workshops.

4. Interactive Timelines and Flowcharts

Using interactive visuals like timelines and flowcharts, where users can click through different stages or steps, helps present complex information in a clear, understandable way. Tools like Prezi, Canva, and Google Slides allow you to create clickable elements that navigate between different stages or branches in a process.

5. Embed Videos and Multimedia

Adding videos, audio clips, and other multimedia elements can make your presentation more engaging and dynamic. By embedding relevant videos, you can provide additional context or explain complex concepts visually. Interactive video platforms like YouTube or Vimeo allow you to link or embed videos directly into your presentation.

6. Live Q&A and Audience Feedback

Encourage audience interaction by incorporating live Q&A sessions during your presentation. Platforms like Google Slides, Mentimeter, and Zoom allow you to field questions from the audience in real-time, making the presentation feel more personal and responsive to their needs.

Tips for Creating Engaging Interactive Presentations

1. **Keep It Simple**: Avoid overwhelming your audience with too many interactive elements. Focus on one or two key interactive features that enhance understanding without cluttering the presentation.

2. **Use Consistent Design**: Keep the design consistent and clean across all slides to maintain a professional appearance. Use a cohesive color scheme and font style to ensure the presentation is visually appealing.

3. **Know Your Audience**: Tailor the level of interactivity based on your audience. For example, corporate audiences may appreciate quick polls or surveys, while

a classroom setting may benefit from more extensive quizzes or discussions.

4. **Practice**: Interactive presentations require smooth transitions and timing. Be sure to practice the presentation beforehand to ensure everything works as planned and to familiarize yourself with any interactive features.

5. **Be Ready for Technical Issues**: Ensure you have backups for any technical issues that may arise during your presentation. Always have a static version of your slides ready in case there are problems with the interactive elements.

Conclusion

Creating an interactive presentation can significantly boost engagement, enhance learning, and provide a more enjoyable experience for your audience. By utilizing the right tools, incorporating interactive features like quizzes, polls, and multimedia, and maintaining a clear, focused design, you can deliver a dynamic presentation that leaves a lasting impression. Whether you're presenting in a classroom, business meeting, or online webinar, interactive presentations help keep your audience involved and invested in the content.

Section 2: Multimedia Projects

Introduction

In today's digital landscape, the ability to work with multimedia is an essential skill for individuals and businesses alike. Multimedia projects, which integrate a combination of text, audio, images, video, and interactive elements, are a powerful tool for storytelling, education, marketing, entertainment, and more. The merging of different media formats allows creators to communicate ideas in ways that engage multiple senses, making information more compelling, memorable, and accessible.

This section, *Multimedia Projects*, will guide you through the process of creating dynamic multimedia content using a range of tools and techniques. Whether you're aiming to produce captivating videos, compelling audio presentations, or interactive websites, this section will offer practical insights into how to combine various forms of media into cohesive, high-quality projects.

Throughout this section, we will delve into key multimedia projects, focusing on the necessary skills and the software tools required to bring your creative ideas to life. From understanding the foundational principles of multimedia design to mastering the use of industry-standard programs, we'll explore the ways in which multimedia projects can elevate your content and enhance your creative expression. By the end of this section, you'll have a solid understanding of how to effectively create multimedia content that not only captures attention but also communicates your message in powerful and engaging ways.

We will begin by introducing fundamental multimedia concepts, followed by a deep dive into practical projects such

91

as video production, audio editing, animation, and interactive media design. These projects will not only improve your technical proficiency but will also provide a platform for you to express your creativity, produce professional-quality work, and explore the endless possibilities that multimedia has to offer.

In short, this section is dedicated to giving you the tools, techniques, and knowledge you need to successfully create multimedia projects that can inform, entertain, and inspire. Whether you're creating content for personal projects or aiming to break into the multimedia industry, the skills you develop here will serve as a foundation for future success in any multimedia endeavor.

Figure 10: Video Editing

Part 11: Basic Video Editing Projects

Video editing is a key skill in today's digital world, where videos are used for a wide range of purposes, from social media content and marketing campaigns to educational videos and personal projects. Understanding the fundamentals of video editing can help you create engaging, high-quality videos that capture your audience's attention and convey your message effectively. This section will walk you through basic video editing projects, introducing you to essential editing techniques, tools, and tips for creating polished videos.

What Is Video Editing?

Video editing involves the process of manipulating and rearranging video footage to create a cohesive, polished final product. The goal is to improve the quality of the footage, tell a compelling story, and ensure that the video flows seamlessly. This process can include trimming, merging clips, adjusting colors, adding audio, and applying visual effects. Video editing can be as simple as cutting a few clips together or as complex as creating elaborate cinematic sequences.

Why Learn Video Editing?

1. **Increase Engagement**: Well-edited videos are more engaging, helping to keep your audience's attention. Whether it's for YouTube, social media, or business presentations, high-quality video content is more likely to be shared and appreciated.

2. **Improve Storytelling**: Video editing allows you to shape the narrative. Through the selection of the right footage, pacing, and transitions, you can enhance the emotional impact of your story.

3. **Boost Professionalism**: A polished video looks more professional and credible, whether it's for personal branding, educational content, or a marketing campaign.

4. **Create Impactful Marketing**: Businesses and content creators use video to market their products and services. Understanding video editing helps you craft videos that drive conversions and engage your target audience.

Tools for Basic Video Editing

There are many video editing software tools available, ranging from beginner-friendly options to more advanced professional programs. Here are some popular video editing tools you can use:

1. **iMovie (Mac)**: A user-friendly, free video editing software for Mac users. It offers basic video editing tools like cutting, trimming, adding transitions, and text effects.

2. **Windows Movie Maker (Windows)**: A simple, free video editing software for Windows users. It provides basic editing features like trimming clips, adding effects, and inserting text.

3. **Shotcut**: A free and open-source video editor that offers a range of editing tools for both beginners and intermediate users. It's available for Windows, macOS, and Linux.

4. **DaVinci Resolve**: A professional-grade video editing software that is free to use for basic projects. It provides a wide range of tools for color correction, editing, and effects.

5. **Adobe Premiere Pro**: A professional video editing software with extensive features. It's used by filmmakers and content creators worldwide but may have a steeper learning curve for beginners.

6. **Canva**: While Canva is primarily known for design, it also offers basic video editing capabilities that are great for beginners. You can easily add text, music, and transitions to your video clips.

Basic Video Editing Projects

In this section, we will walk you through a few basic video editing projects that will help you develop your skills and create impactful videos. We'll cover essential video editing techniques and the step-by-step process for each project.

1. Creating a Simple Promotional Video

A promotional video is an excellent way to showcase a product, service, or event. This project will teach you how to combine different video clips, images, text, and music to create a compelling promotional video.

Steps:

- **Collect Your Assets**: Gather the video clips, images, and music that you will use in your promotional video. Ensure that the media aligns with your brand or product message.

- **Trim and Arrange Clips**: Use the editing software to cut unnecessary parts of the video and arrange the clips in a logical sequence.

- **Add Text and Graphics**: Insert titles, subtitles, and logos at the appropriate points in the video. You can also add lower-thirds to introduce speakers or highlight key information.

- **Add Music and Sound Effects**: Choose background music that complements the mood of your video. Ensure that the music is not too overpowering and that it flows smoothly with the video's pacing.

- **Transitions and Effects**: Apply transitions between clips to ensure the video flows smoothly. Simple transitions like fades or slides can be effective without distracting from the content.

- **Export**: Once you're satisfied with the edit, export the video in the appropriate format for your platform (e.g., MP4 for social media, MOV for high-quality output).

Tools You'll Use: Trimming, Text, Transitions, Audio Overlay.

2. Editing a Vlog or Personal Video

Vlogging has become one of the most popular ways to share personal stories, experiences, or opinions online. In this project, you'll learn how to edit a vlog, including cutting unnecessary footage, improving sound quality, and adding visual elements.

Steps:

- **Import Your Footage**: Import all the footage you've recorded for your vlog.

- **Cutting and Trimming**: Remove any mistakes or unnecessary content, leaving only the most engaging parts. Ensure that the video flows well and has a good pace.

- **Enhance Audio**: Use audio editing tools to remove background noise or enhance the sound quality. Consider adding background music to set the mood, but make sure it doesn't overpower your voice.

- **Add Intro/Outro**: Include an intro and outro with your vlog's branding. This could be a simple animation or a logo with your channel's name.

- **Text and Captions**: Add captions for important points or to highlight specific details. This will improve accessibility and engagement.

- **Cut to B-Roll**: Use additional footage (B-Roll) to break up talking-head shots and make the video more visually interesting. This could be clips of the environment or scenes related to what you're discussing.

- **Final Polish**: Adjust the color balance, brightness, and contrast to ensure the video   looks professional. Use simple transitions to switch between shots smoothly.

- **Export**: Export the video to a format suitable for uploading to YouTube, Instagram, or another platform.

Tools You'll Use: Cutting, Trimming, Audio Enhancement, B-Roll, Text, Color Correction.

3. Creating a Tutorial or How-to Video

Tutorial videos are incredibly popular for teaching new skills or explaining concepts. Editing a tutorial involves combining instructional footage with explanations, text overlays, and visual aids to ensure clarity.

Steps:

- **Record Footage**: Film your tutorial content, ensuring that each step is captured clearly and from the best angles.

- **Organize Your Clips**: Arrange the footage in the correct sequence. Add breaks between steps if needed, and use text overlays to clarify each part of the process.

- **Insert Callouts and Arrows**: Use callouts, arrows, and shapes to highlight important details in the tutorial. This can be especially useful when demonstrating software or specific actions.

- **Include Voiceover or Subtitles**: Record a voiceover to explain each step in detail. Alternatively, add subtitles or captions to ensure accessibility.

- **Add Background Music**: Light background music can make the video more enjoyable to watch without distracting from the tutorial.

- **Final Adjustments**: Edit for pacing, ensure smooth transitions, and check that the audio levels are balanced.

- **Export**: Export your tutorial in a format that is suitable for the platform where you plan to upload it (e.g., YouTube, educational sites).

Tools You'll Use: Voiceovers, Text Overlays, Callouts, Transitions, Audio Adjustments.

4. Editing a Short Film or Story

Creating a short film allows you to experiment with storytelling techniques, pacing, and visual effects. This project will teach you how to structure a narrative, edit for emotional impact, and use sound design to enhance the experience.

Steps:

- **Develop a Storyboard**: Before editing, create a storyboard that outlines the major scenes, shots, and transitions in the film.

- **Trim and Arrange Scenes**: Trim your footage to focus on the essential scenes and arrange them in the correct order to tell your story.

- **Pacing and Timing**: Pay attention to the pacing of the story. Ensure that each scene flows naturally into the next, and adjust the timing to create suspense or emotional impact.

- **Sound Design**: Use sound effects and music to enhance the mood of the film. The right soundtrack can elevate a scene, while sound effects can add realism and atmosphere.

- **Color Grading**: Apply color grading to give the film a particular look or mood. You might want to make the colors warmer, cooler, or add a vintage tone, depending on the story.

- **Final Touches**: Add credits, sound adjustments, and ensure that all transitions are smooth.

- **Export**: Export the video in a high-quality format suitable for sharing or submission.

Tools You'll Use: Storyboarding, Trimming, Pacing, Sound Design, Color Grading, Titles and Credits.

Conclusion

By the end of this section, you will have learned how to create simple yet powerful video editing projects using a variety of tools and techniques. Whether you're producing a promotional video, editing a vlog, creating a tutorial, or working on a short film, the skills you develop here will serve as the foundation for more advanced video production projects in the future. Video editing is a creative and rewarding process, and mastering these basic techniques will empower you to produce professional-quality videos for any purpose.

Figure 11: Photo slide shows

Part 12: Crafting Photo Slideshows with Effects

Photo slideshows are a popular and engaging way to present visual content in a dynamic, storytelling format. Whether you're creating a memory album, a business presentation, or a promotional video, a well-crafted slideshow can help you communicate your message in a visually appealing and impactful way. Adding effects, transitions, and music to your photos not only enhances the visual experience but also helps convey emotion and context to the audience.

In this section, we will walk you through the process of crafting photo slideshows with effects, providing step-by-step instructions, tips, and tools to help you create stunning slideshows that captivate and engage viewers.

What Is a Photo Slideshow?

A photo slideshow is a presentation of a series of images shown in sequence, often accompanied by music, text, and transitions. Slideshows can be used for various purposes, including:

- **Personal Projects**: Such as wedding albums, family memories, or vacation slideshows.

- **Business Presentations**: Showcasing products, services, or achievements.

- **Promotional Content**: Advertising, marketing campaigns, or event promotions.

- **Educational and Informational Slideshows**: Displaying data, statistics, or step-by-step instructions.

By incorporating effects, transitions, and background music, slideshows become more than just a collection of images— they transform into an immersive storytelling experience.

Why Craft a Photo Slideshow with Effects?

1. **Enhance Visual Appeal**: Effects such as zoom, pan, and animations make your photos more visually dynamic and interesting to watch.

2. **Engage Your Audience**: A photo slideshow with well-timed transitions and effects keeps the viewer's attention by providing a seamless and polished viewing experience.

3. **Set the Tone**: Adding music or audio effects helps set the mood of the slideshow. Whether it's an upbeat track for a celebration or a calm, sentimental tune for a personal project, audio adds an emotional layer to your visuals.

4. **Simplify Complex Information**: When showcasing a large number of photos, effects and transitions can help structure the information and prevent the slideshow from feeling static or overwhelming.

5. **Create Memorable Content**: A well-crafted slideshow with smooth transitions, effects, and a cohesive theme is more memorable and impactful than a basic photo gallery.

Tools for Creating Photo Slideshows with Effects

There are a variety of software tools you can use to create a photo slideshow, each offering a range of features and capabilities. Below are some options to consider:

1. **Microsoft PowerPoint**: A widely used tool for creating simple slideshows. PowerPoint allows you to add transitions, animations, and background music, making it perfect for business presentations and personal projects.

2. **iMovie (Mac)**: A free video editing tool for Mac users that allows you to create photo slideshows with ease. You can add music, effects, and transitions to your photos to make your slideshow more engaging.

3. **Adobe Premiere Pro**: A professional-grade video editing software with advanced features. Ideal for users who want to create high-quality, cinematic slideshows with advanced effects and precise control.

4. **Canva**: Known for its ease of use, Canva allows you to create simple photo slideshows using customizable templates, effects, and transitions. It's an excellent choice for beginners or anyone looking for quick and easy solutions.

5. **Animoto**: A cloud-based service specifically designed for creating photo slideshows with effects. Animoto provides customizable templates, music, and transitions, making it easy for users with minimal experience to create professional-looking slideshows.

6. **Shotcut**: A free and open-source video editor that can be used to create photo slideshows with transitions and effects. Shotcut offers advanced editing features for users who want more control over their slideshow project.

Crafting a Photo Slideshow with Effects: Step-by-Step Process

Creating a photo slideshow with effects can be a fun and creative process. Below, we'll walk you through the basic steps involved in crafting your slideshow, from selecting photos to adding transitions, effects, and music.

Step 1: Select Your Photos

Start by choosing the photos you want to include in your slideshow. Whether it's a set of family memories, vacation highlights, or product images for a business slideshow, selecting the right photos is crucial to setting the tone.

Tips for Selecting Photos:

- Choose high-quality images that are well-lit and clear.

- Select a variety of images that tell a story or capture different perspectives.

- Consider the overall theme or message of your slideshow.

Step 2: Choose a Tool to Create Your Slideshow

Pick a tool that suits your skill level and project needs. If you're looking for something quick and easy, Canva or Animoto might be the best choice. If you're aiming for more complex editing, software like iMovie or Adobe Premiere Pro can provide advanced features.

Step 3: Upload Your Photos

Once you've selected a tool, upload your photos into the software or platform you're using. Most tools have an easy drag-and-drop feature that allows you to add images quickly.

Step 4: Arrange the Photos

Arrange the photos in a sequence that makes sense for your slideshow. For instance, if you're telling a story, you may want to place the images in chronological order. If it's a promotional slideshow, you may want to arrange them according to the flow of the product or message.

Step 5: Add Transitions Between Photos

Transitions help create smooth movement from one photo to the next, making your slideshow more dynamic. Common transitions include:

- **Fade**: Gradual transition between images.

- **Slide**: The photo slides in or out of the frame.

- **Zoom**: The photo zooms in or out to create emphasis.

- **Wipe**: A photo is wiped off the screen by another photo coming in.

Tips for Transitions:

- Use simple transitions to keep the focus on the content.

- Don't overuse flashy transitions, as they can be distracting.

- Match the transitions to the mood of the slideshow (e.g., smooth fades for a sentimental slideshow, sharp cuts for an energetic promo).

Step 6: Apply Effects to Photos

Effects such as zoom, pan, and filters can enhance the visual appeal of your photos and make your slideshow more engaging. Some common photo effects include:

- **Ken Burns Effect**: A slow zoom and pan effect that brings photos to life.

- **Color Filters**: Apply a consistent filter (e.g., sepia, black-and-white) to create a cohesive look.

- **Slow Motion or Fast Motion**: Play with the timing of your slides to add dramatic effect.

Tips for Effects:

- Keep the effects subtle to maintain the slideshow's professionalism.

- Experiment with panning across images to create a sense of movement.

- Use color filters to set the mood of your slideshow (e.g., warm filters for nostalgic moments).

Step 7: Add Music or Voiceover

Music plays a significant role in setting the tone of the slideshow. Choose a song or instrumental piece that complements the content of your slideshow.

- **For Personal Slideshows**: A sentimental or soft background track can add emotional depth.

- **For Business or Promotional Slideshows**: Choose upbeat or corporate tracks that align with the brand.

- **For Educational Slideshows**: A neutral, background instrumental is ideal.

If necessary, you can also record a voiceover to narrate the slideshow and provide additional context or explanations.

Tips for Music:

- Ensure that the music doesn't overpower the visual content.

- Use royalty-free music or create your own to avoid copyright issues.

- Adjust the audio levels so the music blends well with any voiceover or sound effects.

Step 8: Add Text and Captions

Incorporate text to provide context, captions, or titles for each slide. This can be especially useful in a slideshow that tells a story or presents information. Add titles for each section, or include captions to explain what each image represents.

Tips for Text:

- Keep the text concise and readable.

- Choose font styles that match the theme of your slideshow.

- Make sure the text is clearly visible against the background by adjusting font size and color.

Step 9: Review and Fine-Tune

Before exporting your slideshow, review the entire project to ensure everything flows smoothly. Check the transitions, timing, music, and text for consistency. Make sure the audio levels are balanced, and adjust the pacing if necessary.

Step 10: Export and Share

Once you're satisfied with your slideshow, export it in the appropriate format for your intended platform (e.g., MP4 for social media, MOV for high-quality playback). You can now share your slideshow with friends and family, embed it on a website, or present it in a business setting.

Conclusion

Crafting a photo slideshow with effects is a fun and creative way to present your photos and tell a story. Whether you're creating a personal slideshow to showcase memories or designing a business presentation to highlight products or services, adding effects, transitions, and music enhances the visual appeal and emotional impact of your content. By following the steps outlined in this section, you'll be able to produce professional-quality slideshows that engage your audience and communicate your message effectively.

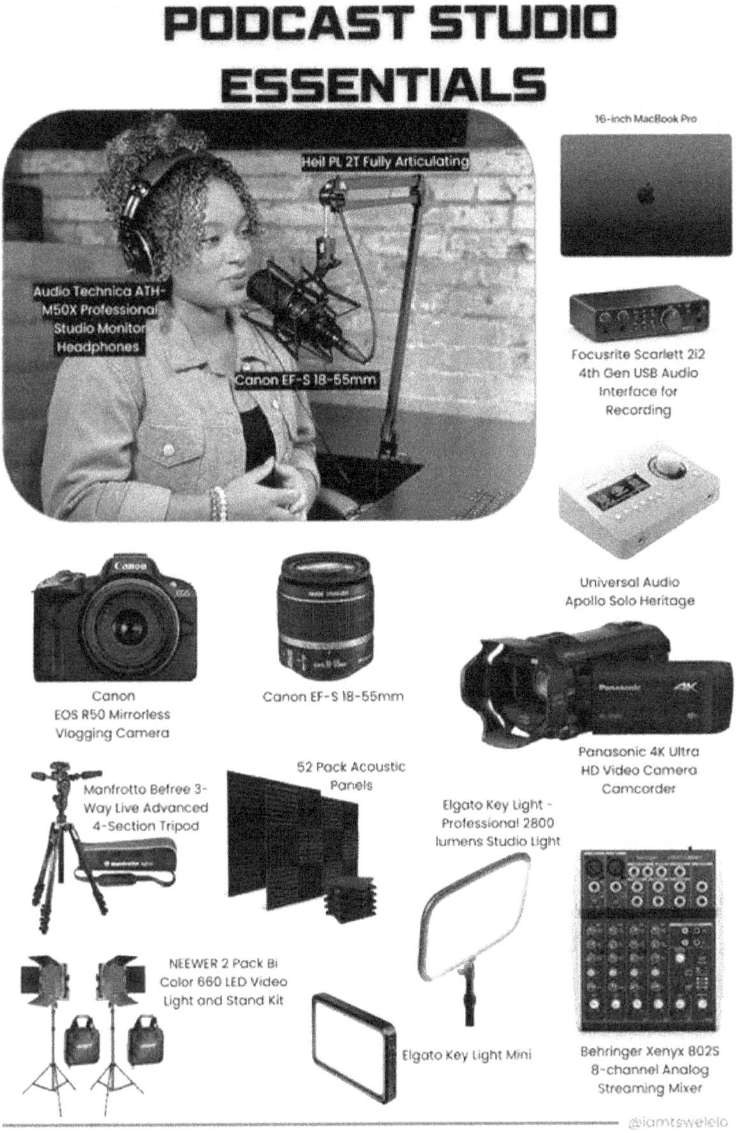

Figure 12: Audio Editing and Podcast Creation

Part 13: Audio Editing and Podcast Creation

In today's digital world, audio content has become a powerful way to communicate, educate, entertain, and engage audiences. Whether it's for a podcast, an audio advertisement, or a voice-over, the ability to create and edit high-quality audio is a skill that can open up many opportunities for creativity and communication. One of the most popular and accessible forms of audio content is podcasting, which has exploded in popularity in recent years. This section will guide you through the process of audio editing and podcast creation, from setting up your equipment to publishing your final episode.

What is Audio Editing and Podcasting?

Audio editing is the process of modifying and enhancing recorded audio to ensure it sounds clear, professional, and polished. This includes tasks like cutting out unwanted noise, adjusting volume levels, adding effects, and fine-tuning the final product. Audio editing is crucial for creating high-quality recordings for podcasts, interviews, soundtracks, and more.

Podcasting is a form of audio broadcasting that allows individuals or businesses to create series of episodes on various topics and share them with an audience. Podcasts are typically distributed via platforms such as Apple Podcasts, Spotify, or Google Podcasts, and can be listened to by anyone with internet access. Podcasts can cover virtually any subject, including news, education, storytelling, entertainment, and more.

Why Audio Editing and Podcast Creation Are Important

111

1. **High-Quality Content**: Whether you're producing a podcast or simply editing an audio file, good audio quality is essential. Poor sound quality can drive listeners away, while clean, crisp, and professionally edited audio keeps the audience engaged.

2. **Professionalism**: Audio editing allows you to remove background noise, smooth out rough spots, and polish your content to a professional standard. This is especially important in podcasting, where the audio is the main medium for communication.

3. **Creativity and Control**: Editing audio gives you the flexibility to shape your content in creative ways, from adding sound effects to adjusting the pacing of a conversation. It lets you craft a narrative and make your podcast or audio content stand out.

4. **Wider Audience Reach**: A well-edited podcast can attract and retain a loyal audience. By offering clear, engaging, and high-quality audio, you're more likely to gain listeners who keep coming back for each episode.

5. **Flexibility and Convenience**: Podcasts can be consumed on-the-go, making them a convenient option for sharing content. Audio editing also allows you to adapt content for different formats or distribution channels (e.g., social media clips, YouTube, etc.).

Tools for Audio Editing and Podcast Creation

There are various software tools available for audio editing and podcast creation, catering to different skill levels and needs. Here are some commonly used tools:

1. **Audacity** (Free): Audacity is a powerful and widely-used open-source audio editing software. It offers a wide range of editing tools, such as cutting, trimming, fading, equalization, and noise reduction. It's perfect for beginners and more advanced users alike and is highly recommended for podcast creators on a budget.

2. **Adobe Audition** (Paid): Adobe Audition is a professional-grade audio editing software used by many in the podcasting industry. It offers advanced features such as multitrack editing, noise reduction, mixing, and effects. It's ideal for users who want to take their audio editing to the next level.

3. **GarageBand** (Free for Mac): GarageBand is a user-friendly audio editing software available on Mac devices. It's great for beginners and casual podcasters, offering basic tools like audio trimming, mixing, and effects.

4. **Reaper** (Paid with Free Trial): Reaper is a full-featured audio production tool with a low-cost licensing structure. It's suitable for both beginners and advanced users, offering everything from basic editing to complex mixing and mastering.

5. **Hindenburg Journalist** (Paid): Hindenburg is another audio editing software that focuses on podcast production. It is particularly popular among journalists and podcasters due to its automated leveling, easy-to-use interface, and streamlined workflow.

6. **Anchor** (Free): Anchor is a free, easy-to-use podcasting platform that allows you to record, edit, and distribute your podcast directly from your phone or

computer. It's a great option for beginners who want a simple, all-in-one solution for creating podcasts.

7. **Auphonic** (Free and Paid Versions): Auphonic is an online tool designed for audio post-production. It helps improve audio quality by reducing noise, adjusting levels, and enhancing clarity, making it a great tool for podcasters who need to refine their audio without much technical expertise.

Steps to Audio Editing and Podcast Creation

Creating and editing a podcast involves several key steps. Here is a step-by-step process to help you get started.

Step 1: Plan Your Podcast

Before you start recording, it's important to plan the content of your podcast. This includes deciding on your podcast's theme, format, target audience, and the length of each episode.

Tips for Planning:

- **Choose a Niche**: Select a specific topic or theme for your podcast. It could be anything from technology to storytelling, interviews, or current events.

- **Create a Script**: While some podcasters prefer to speak without a script, having an outline or bullet points can help you stay on track and avoid rambling.

- **Decide on the Format**: Podcasts can be interviews, monologues, roundtable discussions, or a mix of these formats. Plan the structure of your episodes accordingly.

- **Set a Release Schedule**: Consistency is key in podcasting. Determine how often you will release new episodes—weekly, bi-weekly, or monthly.

Step 2: Gather Your Equipment

To create high-quality podcasts, you'll need some basic equipment:

- **Microphone**: A good microphone is essential for recording clear, professional audio. USB microphones are a popular choice for beginners, while XLR microphones are used by more advanced podcasters.

- **Headphones**: Use headphones to monitor your audio while recording and editing to ensure the best sound quality.

- **Pop Filter**: A pop filter helps reduce unwanted noise caused by hard consonants (e.g., "p" and "b" sounds) during recording.

- **Audio Interface (if using XLR mic)**: If you're using an XLR mic, you'll need an audio interface to connect it to your computer.

- **Recording Space**: Choose a quiet room with minimal background noise for recording. Using blankets, pillows, or foam panels can help improve the sound quality by reducing echo.

Step 3: Record Your Audio

Once you've set up your equipment and planned your content, you're ready to start recording. Here are some recording tips:

- **Speak Clearly and Consistently**: Maintain a steady pace and avoid speaking too fast or too slow.

- **Monitor Your Audio**: Use your headphones to ensure there are no issues with volume levels, background noise, or distortion.

115

- **Record in Segments**: If you're new to podcasting, it's okay to record your podcast in segments. This allows you to take breaks and fix any mistakes during the recording process.

Step 4: Edit Your Audio

After recording, it's time to edit the audio. Audio editing involves:

- **Trimming and Cutting**: Remove any mistakes, pauses, or unwanted sections from the recording.

- **Noise Reduction**: Use noise reduction tools to eliminate background sounds, such as hums, clicks, or echoes.

- **Volume Leveling**: Ensure that your audio levels are consistent throughout the podcast. You can use audio compression and normalization tools to help balance the volume.

- **Adding Music and Effects**: Enhance your podcast with intro and outro music, sound effects, and transitions between segments. Be sure to use royalty-free music or original compositions to avoid copyright issues.

- **Fine-Tuning the Audio**: Use equalization (EQ) to adjust frequencies and enhance the clarity of voices and sounds. You can also apply reverb or compression to improve the overall sound quality.

Step 5: Publish and Distribute

Once your podcast is edited and ready for release, the next step is to publish and distribute it to various podcast platforms.

- **Choose a Hosting Platform**: You can host your podcast on platforms like Anchor, Podbean, or Libsyn, which will provide you with a feed to distribute your podcast.

- **Submit to Directories**: Submit your podcast to popular podcast directories, such as Apple Podcasts, Spotify, and Google Podcasts, to reach a wider audience.

- **Promote Your Podcast**: Share your episodes on social media, your website, or through email newsletters to build your audience and encourage engagement.

Tips for Successful Podcasting

1. **Engage with Your Audience**: Encourage listener feedback and respond to comments. Engaged listeners are more likely to share your podcast with others.

2. **Consistency is Key**: Stick to your publishing schedule and release episodes consistently to build a loyal following.

3. **Invest in Quality Equipment**: High-quality audio equipment goes a long way in improving your podcast's sound. Avoid using built-in microphones or low-quality headsets.

4. **Keep It Short and Sweet**: Unless your podcast has a very niche audience, keep episodes between 20 to 60 minutes. Long episodes can overwhelm listeners, while shorter episodes may be more digestible.

5. **Stay Authentic**: Let your personality shine through. Authenticity helps build a connection with your audience and keeps them coming back.

Conclusion

Audio editing and podcast creation are essential skills for anyone looking to communicate effectively through sound. With the right tools, techniques, and approach, you can produce professional-quality podcasts that engage and inform your audience. Whether you're editing a solo podcast, creating an interview series, or experimenting with sound effects, mastering audio editing will elevate your content and help you connect with listeners around the world.

Figure 13: Animination

Part 14: Making Animations Using Free Software

Animation is a powerful medium that allows creators to bring stories, concepts, and ideas to life in dynamic and visually captivating ways. Whether you want to animate a short story, create educational content, or simply explore your creative potential, animation can add an engaging visual element to your projects. While professional-grade animation tools can be expensive, there are plenty of free software options available for anyone who wants to try their hand at animation without a significant financial investment. This section will explore various free animation tools and guide you through the process of creating animations using these accessible platforms.

What is Animation?

Animation is the process of creating moving images through the manipulation of static images, drawings, or objects. It involves the sequential display of individual frames, each slightly different from the last, which when viewed at a fast rate, creates the illusion of movement. Animation is widely used in fields such as entertainment, advertising, education, and digital media.

There are several types of animation, including:

1. **2D Animation**: This type of animation involves creating images in two dimensions (height and width), and the characters or objects are animated along a 2D plane.

2. **3D Animation**: 3D animation creates the illusion of three-dimensional objects or characters, making use of

120

depth (height, width, and depth) for a more realistic appearance.

3. **Stop-motion Animation**: This technique involves taking photographs of physical objects or puppets, slightly adjusting them between each shot to create movement.

While many professional animators use expensive software like Adobe Animate or Autodesk Maya, free animation software provides an accessible entry point for beginners and hobbyists alike.

Why Use Free Animation Software?

1. **Cost-Effective**: As the name suggests, free software doesn't require a monetary investment. This makes it perfect for people just getting started with animation or those on a tight budget.

2. **Accessible for Beginners**: Free animation software tends to be more user-friendly and designed with beginners in mind. They offer tutorials, guides, and easy-to-understand interfaces that allow anyone to start creating quickly.

3. **Wide Range of Options**: The free software options available today provide a variety of animation techniques, such as 2D, 3D, and stop-motion animation. You can explore different animation styles without worrying about licensing fees or subscriptions.

4. **Community Support**: Free software often has large user communities where you can ask questions, share your work, and learn from others. Many of these tools also offer built-in tutorials, helping you get the most out of the software.

5. **Learning Experience**: Using free tools allows you to develop animation skills and techniques before committing to professional-grade software. Once you feel comfortable, you can then decide if you'd like to upgrade to paid software for more advanced features.

Free Animation Software Options

There are a variety of free animation software options that can help you bring your animation ideas to life. Below are some of the best and most popular free animation programs.

1. **Pencil2D** (Best for 2D Animation)

   o **Overview**: Pencil2D is an open-source animation tool that is ideal for hand-drawn 2D animation. It's simple, lightweight, and perfect for beginners who want to start with traditional frame-by-frame animation.

   o **Key Features**:

     ▪ Easy-to-use interface

     ▪ Bitmap and vector drawing tools

     ▪ Layering for complex animations

     ▪ Supports both raster and vector graphics

     ▪ Compatible with Windows, Mac, and Linux

   o **Why Use It**: Pencil2D is great for artists who want to create 2D animations without needing complex features. It's free, intuitive, and efficient for beginners.

2. **Blender** (Best for 3D Animation)

- o **Overview**: Blender is one of the most popular free and open-source software programs for creating 3D animations. It offers a complete suite of tools for modeling, sculpting, texturing, rigging, and animating 3D characters and objects.

- o **Key Features**:

  - Advanced 3D modeling and sculpting tools

  - Animation rigging and keyframe animation

  - Real-time rendering with Eevee engine

  - Physics simulations (cloth, smoke, fire, etc.)

  - VFX, compositing, and video editing

- o **Why Use It**: Blender is a powerful tool for anyone looking to explore 3D animation. Though it has a steeper learning curve, it offers professional-quality features for free.

3. **Synfig Studio** (Best for Vector-Based 2D Animation)

  - o **Overview**: Synfig Studio is an open-source 2D animation software that focuses on vector-based animation. It allows you to create high-quality animations without needing to draw every frame by hand.

  - o **Key Features**:

    - Vector-based drawing tools

    - Keyframe animation

123

- Advanced rigging for character animation

- Supports sound synchronization

- Compatible with Windows, Mac, and Linux

o **Why Use It**: Synfig is great for creating smooth animations and cartoon-style work without needing to manually draw each frame, which saves time and effort.

4. **Krita** (Best for Frame-by-Frame Animation)

o **Overview**: Krita is a free and open-source digital painting software that also includes animation capabilities. While it is primarily known as a painting tool, it offers frame-by-frame animation for 2D artists.

o **Key Features**:

- Brush engines and painting tools

- Onion skinning for smooth animation transitions

- Timeline-based animation tools

- Supports layers and frame-by-frame animation

- Compatible with Windows, Mac, and Linux

o **Why Use It**: Krita is ideal for artists who prefer drawing and painting their animations frame by frame. It's perfect for traditional 2D

124

animation and offers powerful brushes and paint tools.

5. **TupiTube** (Best for Kids and Beginners)

   o **Overview**: TupiTube is a simple, user-friendly animation software designed with children and beginners in mind. It allows users to create 2D vector animations with ease.

   o **Key Features**:

      ▪ User-friendly interface

      ▪ Vector and bitmap drawing tools

      ▪ Easy-to-follow animation timeline

      ▪ Onion skinning feature

      ▪ Compatible with Windows, Mac, and Linux

   o **Why Use It**: TupiTube is great for those just starting with animation. It's simple and easy to use, making it a good choice for young learners or absolute beginners.

6. **OpenToonz** (Best for Studio-Style 2D Animation)

   o **Overview**: OpenToonz is a professional-grade 2D animation software that's been used by major animation studios. It's open-source and free, making it a great choice for independent animators who want studio-level quality.

   o **Key Features**:

      ▪ Traditional hand-drawn animation tools

- Rigging and bone animation system

- Effects creation and compositing

- Digital ink and paint tools

- Compatible with Windows and Mac

- **Why Use It**: OpenToonz is ideal for animators who want to take their 2D animation to a professional level. It's feature-packed and used by studios, making it a powerful tool for serious animation projects.

7. **Animaker** (Best for Web-Based Animation)

   - **Overview**: Animaker is a web-based animation tool that lets you create animations using drag-and-drop features and templates. It's great for beginners and those who need to create quick animations for presentations or marketing.

   - **Key Features**:

     - Pre-made templates and characters

     - Drag-and-drop interface

     - Voiceover integration

     - 2D and 2.5D animations

     - Compatible with all major browsers

   - **Why Use It**: Animaker is a great option for those who need to create simple animations quickly. It offers ready-made assets and an easy interface for non-animators.

Steps to Make Animations Using Free Software

1. **Choose Your Animation Software**: Based on your project requirements, select the software that best fits your animation style (2D, 3D, stop-motion). Download and install the software if necessary.

2. **Create or Import Your Assets**: Depending on your animation type, you can either create characters, backgrounds, and objects from scratch, or import pre-made assets. For 2D animations, this might include drawing in your software, while for 3D animations, you may need to model the objects in Blender.

3. **Set Up Your Timeline**: The timeline is where you'll arrange the frames or keyframes of your animation. Organize your assets on different layers and adjust the timing of your frames to ensure smooth motion.

4. **Animate Your Assets**: Use tools like keyframes, rigging, and motion paths to animate your assets. For 2D animations, you'll draw the transition from one frame to the next, while 3D animations may require you to manipulate objects and set their movement.

5. **Add Effects and Sounds**: Enhance your animation with special effects, background music, and sound effects. Many free animation tools support the addition of audio tracks and visual effects that can make your animation more dynamic.

6. **Preview and Refine**: Preview your animation regularly to check for any mistakes or rough transitions. Refine your work by adjusting frames, smoothing motion, and making corrections.

7. **Export Your Animation**: Once you're satisfied with your animation, export it in the desired format. This

could be an animated GIF, video file, or image sequence, depending on the software you're using.

Conclusion

Creating animations doesn't have to be expensive or difficult. With the wide range of free software available, anyone can start experimenting with animation and turn their ideas into moving images. Whether you're working on 2D or 3D animations, stop-motion, or motion graphics, these free tools offer powerful features that allow you to unleash your creativity. By mastering free animation software, you can produce high-quality animations that can be used for films, advertisements, educational content, or personal projects, all while gaining valuable skills in the process.

Figure 14: Digital Story Telling

Part 15: Digital Storytelling Techniques

Digital storytelling is the art of using digital media tools and platforms to tell a story. Unlike traditional storytelling, which relies primarily on oral or written words, digital storytelling incorporates visuals, sounds, animations, music, and interactivity to engage audiences in unique and powerful ways. The fusion of narrative with technology has revolutionized the way we communicate stories, allowing creators to enhance the emotional and intellectual impact of their messages. Whether you're sharing personal experiences, teaching concepts, or promoting a brand, digital storytelling is a dynamic and versatile method for crafting compelling narratives.

In this section, we'll explore the fundamental techniques behind digital storytelling, offer practical examples of how to use them, and introduce the various tools available for aspiring storytellers to master their craft.

What is Digital Storytelling?

Digital storytelling blends traditional storytelling elements with digital tools to create engaging, multimedia narratives. It involves combining different forms of media such as:

1. **Text**: Written words that form the core narrative.

2. **Images**: Visual elements like photographs, illustrations, and infographics that complement the story.

3. **Audio**: Voiceovers, music, sound effects, and ambient sounds that enhance the mood and atmosphere.

4. **Video**: Moving visuals or animations that illustrate the story in action.

5. **Interactivity**: Interactive elements like clickable maps, quizzes, or user choices that allow the audience to engage with the content.

The power of digital storytelling lies in its ability to create a fully immersive experience that resonates with audiences on multiple sensory levels.

Why is Digital Storytelling Important?

1. **Engagement**: Digital stories are interactive and visually stimulating, keeping audiences engaged for longer periods than traditional text-based content.

2. **Emotional Connection**: Combining visuals and sounds helps to evoke emotions more effectively, creating a deeper connection between the storyteller and the audience.

3. **Accessibility**: With online platforms and social media, digital stories can be shared with a global audience, enabling wider reach and impact.

4. **Versatility**: Digital stories can be used across various mediums, including websites, social media, apps, presentations, and more, making it a flexible tool for marketing, education, entertainment, and personal expression.

5. **Memorability**: By using visuals and audio in conjunction with the story, digital stories are often

more memorable, as they appeal to both auditory and visual learners.

Key Techniques for Effective Digital Storytelling

1. **Develop a Strong Narrative Structure**

    o   **Clear Story Arc**: Like any good story, a digital story should have a clear beginning, middle, and end. Establish a narrative structure that introduces the characters, sets the scene, develops the conflict, and leads to a resolution.

    o   **Focus on a Central Theme**: Identify the key message or theme you want to convey through your story. Whether it's a personal experience, a business idea, or an educational topic, staying focused on the central theme will help guide the narrative and keep your story cohesive.

2. **Use Visuals to Complement the Story**

    o   **Images**: Visuals help tell the story by illustrating important scenes, settings, and emotions. High-quality images, such as photos, illustrations, or even abstract graphics, can enhance the audience's understanding and emotional connection.

    o   **Video**: Video clips or animations can be used to show real-life events or bring a story to life. Whether it's a simple video montage or an animated sequence, incorporating moving visuals adds depth to your narrative.

    o   **Infographics**: Use infographics to visualize complex information, statistics, or timelines in a way that's easy for the audience to digest and relate to.

3. **Incorporate Audio for Mood and Impact**

   o **Narration**: A voiceover can be a powerful tool for telling your story. Whether it's a casual, conversational tone or a more formal delivery, narration allows you to guide the audience through the content and bring your words to life.

   o **Music**: Background music can set the tone for your story. Whether it's upbeat, calming, dramatic, or somber, music reinforces the emotions of your narrative and creates an immersive experience.

   o **Sound Effects**: Subtle sound effects, such as nature sounds, city noise, or door creaks, can help convey the atmosphere of a particular scene and draw the audience further into the story.

4. **Add Interactivity to Engage the Audience**

   o **Clickable Elements**: Enhance the user experience by adding interactive elements to your digital story, such as clickable links, hotspots, or navigation buttons. These elements can allow the audience to explore the content at their own pace or make decisions that alter the direction of the story.

   o **User Input**: Incorporating interactive elements like polls, quizzes, or feedback forms allows users to engage with the story directly, making it more participatory and personal.

- o **Branching Narratives**: Interactive storytelling is a form of non-linear storytelling where the user can choose different paths or outcomes. Video games, educational content, and some marketing campaigns often employ this technique to increase engagement and replayability.

5. **Pacing and Timing**

- o **Rhythm of the Story**: Just like in any form of storytelling, pacing plays a crucial role in digital stories. Balancing moments of tension with moments of relief keeps the audience engaged without overwhelming them. Use music, visual transitions, and narration to pace the story appropriately.

- o **Timing with Media**: Ensure that the visuals and audio elements align with the rhythm of the narrative. A slow scene might need softer, slower music, while an action-packed moment could benefit from faster-paced visuals and intense sound effects.

Tools for Creating Digital Stories

Digital storytelling requires a blend of multimedia tools to create a seamless and engaging experience. Here are some of the best free tools you can use to craft your digital story:

1. **Adobe Spark**: This versatile online tool allows you to create stunning visual stories, combining text, images,

and video. Adobe Spark is user-friendly and ideal for beginners.

2. **Canva**: Canva is a graphic design platform that offers a wide variety of templates for creating images, infographics, and slideshows. It also features simple tools for video and animation creation.

3. **Storybird**: Storybird helps you create digital picture books by combining your text with professionally illustrated images. This tool is perfect for beginners looking to share personal stories or educational content.

4. **iMovie**: For Mac users, iMovie is a free video editing tool that offers basic editing functions like trimming, transitions, and voiceover recording to create compelling video-based digital stories.

5. **Powtoon**: Powtoon lets you create animated video stories. It's great for business or educational storytelling and provides many pre-made templates that you can customize.

6. **Animoto**: This web-based tool allows you to create video slideshows by uploading photos and videos and combining them with music and text. It's great for creating personal or marketing digital stories quickly.

7. **WeVideo**: An online video editing tool that offers cloud-based storage and easy editing options. With WeVideo, you can combine video, audio, images, and text to tell your story in an engaging way.

Examples of Digital Storytelling Applications

1. **Personal Stories and Memoirs**: Digital storytelling can be used to create personal stories or family

memoirs, using a combination of photos, home videos, and voice narration to preserve and share important memories.

2. **Educational Content**: Teachers and educators can use digital storytelling to present lessons or explain complex subjects in a more engaging and interactive way. You can use visuals, sound, and animation to make abstract concepts more understandable.

3. **Business Marketing**: Companies use digital storytelling to craft compelling brand narratives. Whether through explainer videos, client testimonials, or promotional content, storytelling allows businesses to connect emotionally with their audience.

4. **Social Advocacy**: Activists and nonprofits use digital storytelling to share powerful messages about social issues. By combining compelling visuals with emotional narratives, these organizations can raise awareness and inspire action.

Conclusion

Digital storytelling is a versatile and engaging way to communicate ideas, concepts, and emotions to an audience. By combining text, images, audio, and interactivity, digital storytellers can create rich, multimedia experiences that captivate and inform. Whether you're creating a personal story, an educational project, or a marketing campaign, mastering digital storytelling techniques will help you craft compelling narratives that resonate with your audience. With the right tools and a bit of creativity, the possibilities for digital storytelling are endless.

Figure 15: Music Studio

Part 16: Composing Music with Computer Software

In the digital age, music composition has transcended traditional methods, opening up vast opportunities for musicians, producers, and hobbyists to create music with the power of computer software. Composing music with computer software allows for endless creativity, flexibility, and control, making it accessible to everyone from beginners to seasoned professionals. This section explores the essential tools and techniques for composing music, focusing on software applications that are designed to help users bring their musical ideas to life.

The Role of Computer Software in Music Composition

Computer software has revolutionized how music is created, edited, and shared. Where musicians once relied on physical instruments, pen and paper, or rudimentary recording equipment, today's technology offers an array of digital tools that allow for the creation of professional-quality music without requiring extensive knowledge of traditional music theory or sound engineering.

Some of the key advantages of composing music with software include:

- **Multi-track Recording**: You can layer different instruments and sounds, creating complex compositions without the need for a large band or studio setup.

- **Editing and Arrangement**: You can easily edit, cut, copy, paste, and move around musical sections to experiment with different arrangements.

- **Sound Libraries**: Access to vast libraries of virtual instruments and sound effects, enabling you to create music in any genre and style.

- **Real-time Playback**: Hear your composition in real time, making it easier to tweak notes, harmonies, and rhythms until you achieve your desired sound.

- **Accessibility**: Many music software programs cater to beginners and professionals alike, offering easy-to-understand interfaces for novices and advanced features for experienced composers.

Key Software for Music Composition

Several powerful and accessible music composition software options are available today, each catering to different levels of expertise and types of music creation. Below are some popular programs:

1. **GarageBand (Mac): Ideal for Beginners**
   GarageBand is a highly user-friendly software that allows for easy composition and recording of music. With built-in instruments, loops, and effects, it's perfect for those new to digital music creation. You can record live instruments, create beats, mix audio, and experiment with virtual instruments—all on one platform.

2. **FL Studio (Windows/Mac): Ideal for Electronic Music and Beat Production**
   FL Studio is a widely popular program known for its intuitive interface and powerful features for producing electronic music. It includes a range of pre-installed sounds, synthesizers, and drum kits, making it a go-to choice for many music producers. Its advanced features, such as piano roll editing and automation tools, allow for precise manipulation of musical elements.

3. **Ableton Live (Windows/Mac): Ideal for Live Performance and Studio Production**
   Ableton Live is well-suited for musicians who want to compose and perform live. With a real-time interface and non-linear workflow, it allows users to experiment and create music fluidly. Whether you're composing electronic beats, live-looping, or arranging full compositions, Ableton offers the tools you need.

139

4. **Logic Pro X (Mac):
   Ideal for Advanced Composers**
   Logic Pro X is an industry-standard digital audio workstation (DAW) that offers powerful music composition tools for advanced users. With a comprehensive suite of virtual instruments, sound libraries, and professional-grade features, Logic Pro X is used by professional musicians, producers, and composers across various genres.

5. **MuseScore (Windows/Mac/Linux):
   Ideal for Classical and Orchestral Composition**
   MuseScore is a free, open-source music notation software ideal for classical and orchestral composers. It allows you to write music in standard notation, making it perfect for musicians who prefer traditional sheet music while also providing playback capabilities. MuseScore is a great choice for anyone who wants to compose music in a formal, notational format.

6. **Cubase (Windows/Mac):
   Ideal for Studio Production and Composition**
   Cubase is a comprehensive DAW widely used for professional music production. It offers sophisticated features for both MIDI and audio composition, including advanced sound manipulation, mixing tools, and effects. Whether you're working with virtual instruments or recording live musicians, Cubase provides the tools to achieve polished compositions.

7. **Soundtrap (Web-based):
   Ideal for Collaboration and Remote Music Creation**
   Soundtrap is a web-based music composition tool that offers a simple interface for users of all levels. Its collaborative features allow multiple people to work on

the same project from different locations in real time, making it perfect for group music creation or remote projects.

Composing Music: The Process

Composing music with computer software is a highly customizable and creative process that depends on the software you're using and the type of music you want to create. Below is a general process you can follow, whether you're working on a simple melody or a full orchestral composition.

1. Set Up Your Project

- **Choose Your Software**: Select the music composition software that best suits your needs and skill level.

- **Start a New Project**: Open your software and create a new project. Depending on the software, you may need to choose the type of project, such as a MIDI-based composition, audio recording, or mixed-media project.

2. Create a Basic Structure

- **Choose Your Tempo and Key Signature**: Set the tempo (speed) and key signature (the scale of your composition). This provides the foundation for your piece.

- **Create a Basic Melody or Chord Progression**: Start by composing a simple melody or chord progression. This forms the core of your composition and gives it direction.

3. Layer Your Music

- **Add Tracks**: Add different tracks to represent different instruments or sections of your music. You might add a melody track, a rhythm section, a bass line, and accompaniment.

- **Use Virtual Instruments**: Many music composition software programs come with virtual instruments, such as pianos, strings, and synthesizers. Choose instruments that match the style of music you're composing.

- **Create MIDI Patterns**: If you're composing electronic music, use MIDI (Musical Instrument Digital Interface) patterns to create and manipulate beats, melodies, and effects. These patterns allow you to fine-tune each note, adjust timing, and experiment with sounds.

4. Add Harmonies and Layers

- **Create Harmonies**: Once you have your basic melody, you can add harmonies, counter-melodies, and additional layers to enrich the sound. Virtual orchestras, choirs, and synthesizers can help add depth and complexity to your piece.

- **Arrange Your Tracks**: Arrange the different sections of your music (intro, verse, chorus, bridge, outro) using your software's timeline. Move elements around to explore different song structures and experiment with transitions between sections.

5. Refine and Edit

- **Editing Notes and Timing**: Once the basic composition is laid out, fine-tune each note's pitch, length, and timing. Most software allows for easy manipulation of MIDI data, so you can adjust each note to make the melody and rhythm feel just right.

142

- **Quantize**: Quantizing is a technique used to correct timing errors in MIDI performance, ensuring that your notes are perfectly aligned to the beat and rhythm.

6. Add Effects and Polish

- **Mixing and Effects**: Use the mixing tools within your software to balance the volume, panning, and effects (such as reverb or EQ) of each track. Mixing is an essential step in the music composition process that ensures all elements sound cohesive.

- **Mastering**: Once you're satisfied with your track, use mastering tools to enhance the overall sound quality and prepare your music for distribution. Mastering may involve adjusting volume levels, equalizing the sound, and applying dynamic range compression.

7. Export Your Music

- **Export as Audio File**: Once your composition is complete, export the project as an audio file (such as an MP3 or WAV file) for sharing, uploading, or distribution.

- **Share and Publish**: You can share your music with the world by uploading it to platforms like SoundCloud, YouTube, or streaming services, or you may want to distribute it commercially through music stores like iTunes or Spotify.

Tips for Composing Music with Computer Software

1. **Start Simple**: Don't be overwhelmed by the software. Begin with a simple melody or chord progression and gradually build from there.

2. **Learn the Basics of Music Theory**: A basic understanding of music theory (such as scales, intervals, and chord progressions) will help you create more coherent and engaging compositions.

3. **Experiment with Different Sounds**: Don't hesitate to try out new instruments, sound effects, or genres. Software offers endless possibilities for creating unique compositions.

4. **Use Templates and Loops**: Many music software programs include pre-made loops and templates that can serve as a foundation for your music. These can be particularly helpful if you're new to composing.

5. **Collaborate with Others**: Many music software platforms, such as Soundtrap, allow you to collaborate with others in real time. Working with other musicians can inspire creativity and help you learn new techniques.

Conclusion

Composing music with computer software is a rewarding and highly creative process that allows anyone to create professional-quality music, regardless of their musical background. By utilizing the right tools, techniques, and a bit of imagination, you can compose music for any genre, project, or platform. Whether you're a hobbyist, a professional musician, or a budding composer, computer software opens up a world of possibilities for bringing your musical ideas to life.

Figure 16:Card Design

Part 17: Designing E-Cards with Sound and Motion

In the world of digital communication, e-cards have become a popular and creative way to send greetings, share messages, and celebrate special occasions. E-cards, or electronic greeting cards, are typically sent via email or through online platforms and often include dynamic elements such as sound, animation, and interactivity. In this section, we will explore how to design e-cards that incorporate both sound and motion, creating a more immersive and personalized experience for recipients.

145

The Power of Sound and Motion in E-Cards

While traditional greeting cards rely on text and imagery to convey emotion and intent, e-cards have the added benefit of using sound and motion to enhance their impact. The inclusion of sound and animation makes e-cards more engaging and entertaining, providing a more memorable experience for the recipient.

Benefits of Adding Sound and Motion:

- **Enhanced Emotional Impact**: Music, sound effects, and animation can amplify the mood of the message, whether it's a cheerful birthday greeting, a romantic gesture, or a heartfelt thank you.

- **Personalization**: Adding a customized voice message or a favorite song can make the e-card feel more personal and meaningful.

- **Engagement**: Motion captures attention, and sound adds an auditory layer to the visual experience, making the card more likely to be noticed and appreciated.

- **Interactivity**: With the right tools, e-cards can be made interactive, allowing recipients to click, explore, and even create a dynamic experience that responds to their actions.

Tools for Designing E-Cards with Sound and Motion

Creating e-cards with sound and motion requires a combination of graphic design and multimedia tools. Below are some of the best tools to help you design and animate e-cards, incorporating both visual elements and audio.

1. **Canva** **(Web-based)**
   Ideal for Beginners and Quick Designs

Canva is a versatile design tool that allows users to create e-cards with ease. While Canva is known for its simplicity, it also includes a range of features that allow you to add animations, transitions, and music to your designs. You can choose from ready-made templates and add your own audio files or select from their stock library. Canva also allows you to export the finished design as a video or GIF, making it easy to send as an e-card.

2. **Adobe   Spark   (Web-based) Ideal for Animation and Video Integration** Adobe Spark is a user-friendly platform for creating visually engaging e-cards with motion. With Spark, you can add animations, transitions, and even voiceovers to your e-card designs. It also supports video and music integration, which is essential for adding both sound and motion to the card. Spark's intuitive interface makes it easy to create professional-looking animated e-cards without needing advanced design skills.

3. **Adobe   Animate   (Windows/Mac) Ideal for Professional-Level Animation** For more complex and detailed e-cards, Adobe Animate is a powerful software that offers precise control over animation. It allows you to create vector-based animations with sound, making it perfect for crafting custom animated e-cards. You can animate characters, backgrounds, and text, and sync them with your chosen sound effects or music. Adobe Animate also allows for exporting your creations as HTML5, which is ideal for interactive e-cards.

4. **Animaker   (Web-based) Ideal for Quick Animation and Interactive E-Cards**

Animaker is an easy-to-use animation tool that enables you to create animated e-cards with sound. It comes with a wide selection of templates, and you can easily add sound effects, background music, and animated elements to your designs. Animaker's drag-and-drop interface allows you to customize animations, adding movement to text and images. This tool is perfect for creating interactive, fun, and dynamic e-cards for any occasion.

5. **Piktochart   (Web-based) Ideal for Interactive E-Cards and Infographics** Piktochart is traditionally used for creating infographics, but it's also a great tool for designing e-cards with sound and motion. While it may not be as animation-focused as other tools, Piktochart offers excellent interactive features. You can embed sound, include motion graphics, and export your designs as interactive web cards. It's an excellent tool for creating informative e-cards, such as invitations or announcements, with a bit of animation and sound.

Designing the E-Card: A Step-by-Step Guide

Creating an engaging e-card that combines sound and motion involves a blend of creativity and technical knowledge. Below is a step-by-step guide to designing a custom e-card that is visually appealing, interactive, and memorable.

1. Choose a Purpose and Occasion for the E-Card

- **Determine the Theme**: The first step in designing your e-card is deciding on its purpose and theme. Whether it's for a birthday, holiday, wedding, thank-you note, or any other special occasion, the design should match the tone of the message.

148

- **Define the Message**: What message do you want to convey? Keep it concise and clear. Decide if you want to include a personal message or if the focus will be on visuals, sounds, and animations.

2. Select Your Design Tools

- **Pick the Right Tool**: Depending on your skill level and the complexity of the animation you want to create, choose one of the tools mentioned earlier (Canva, Adobe Spark, etc.). For beginners, Canva and Adobe Spark are excellent choices, while more experienced users may prefer Adobe Animate.

3. Design the Visuals

- **Background**: Start by choosing a background that complements the occasion. For example, a celebratory birthday card might have colorful confetti or balloons in the background.

- **Images and Graphics**: Add images, illustrations, or icons that enhance the theme of your card. For instance, a holiday card might feature snowflakes or a Christmas tree, while a romantic card might feature hearts or flowers.

- **Typography**: Choose a font style that suits the message and occasion. Play around with the size and color of the text to ensure it's legible and visually appealing.

4. Incorporate Motion (Animation)

- **Animate Text and Graphics**: Use your chosen design tool to add animations to text, images, or backgrounds. For example, you can make text fade in, slide, or bounce onto the screen. Graphics can move across the screen or appear with special effects like zoom or spin.

- **Timing and Transitions**: Set the duration for each animation, making sure they flow naturally with the overall message. Avoid too many fast-moving elements, as it may overwhelm the recipient.

5. Add Sound and Music

- **Select Audio**: Choose appropriate background music, sound effects, or even a voiceover. For a cheerful greeting, you might use upbeat music, while a heartfelt message might include a soft, instrumental background track.

- **Sync Sound with Animation**: Ensure that your sound and animation are in sync. For instance, a birthday e-card with confetti falling might have celebratory music playing in the background. If you include voiceovers, time the audio to match the visual transitions.

6. Test the Interactivity (Optional)

- **Add Interactive Elements**: If you're using a platform that supports interactivity, consider adding clickable areas, animations that respond to mouse movements, or areas that reveal hidden messages when clicked. Interactive e-cards can add a fun and personalized touch.

7. Export and Share

- **Choose the Right Format**: Depending on the platform where you'll share the e-card, choose the right export format. If it's for social media, a video or GIF file may work best. If it's for email, you might want to export as a small file (such as MP4 or MOV) to avoid loading issues.

- **Test Before Sending**: Before sending your e-card, test it on different devices to make sure it displays correctly, and the sound and animations work as intended.

- **Send or Share**: Once satisfied with your creation, send your e-card to the recipient via email, messaging apps, or social media.

Tips for Designing Engaging E-Cards

1. **Keep it Short and Sweet**: E-cards are meant to be quick, engaging, and visually stimulating. Avoid making them too long, as they should be easy to enjoy in a few seconds.

2. **Be Mindful of File Size**: Large e-cards with animations and sound can take longer to load. Ensure your final file size is optimized for easy sharing and quick loading times.

3. **Consider Accessibility**: Make sure your e-card is accessible to all. Use clear, easy-to-read fonts, provide captions for audio, and ensure the design is visually easy to navigate.

4. **Match the Sound to the Mood**: The sound should enhance the overall experience of the e-card, not overpower it. Make sure your audio choice matches the tone and style of the visuals.

Conclusion

Designing e-cards with sound and motion opens up a world of creative possibilities. By combining visual elements with dynamic audio and animation, you can create highly engaging, personalized greetings for any occasion. Whether you're sending a quick birthday wish or a special holiday greeting, adding these multimedia elements will ensure your message stands out and leaves a lasting impression on the recipient. With the right tools and techniques, designing e-cards can be an enjoyable and rewarding creative endeavor.

Figure 17: Photo Editing

Part 18: Enhancing Photographs with Editing Tools

In today's digital world, photography has become a powerful tool for storytelling, branding, and artistic expression. With the availability of sophisticated photo editing software, anyone with basic computer skills can enhance their photographs and turn them into professional-looking images. Whether you're a hobbyist photographer, a social media influencer, a business owner, or a creative artist, the ability to enhance your photos with editing tools can make a significant difference in how your images are perceived.

In this section, we will explore the different ways you can enhance photographs using editing tools. We'll cover the basics of photo editing, including color correction, cropping, retouching, and adding effects. We'll also introduce some of the most popular photo editing tools that will help you transform your photos into stunning works of art.

Why Edit Photographs?

While modern cameras and smartphones come equipped with high-quality lenses and sophisticated sensors, raw photographs often require enhancement to reach their full potential. Editing allows you to correct imperfections, highlight key elements, and add creative flair. Here are some reasons why editing your photos is important:

1. **Improve Image Quality**: Enhance sharpness, adjust brightness, and correct exposure to ensure your photo looks its best.

2. **Fix Imperfections**: Remove unwanted elements, smooth out skin, or correct red-eye.

3. **Creative Expression**: Add effects, filters, and overlays to give your photos a unique and personalized look.

4. **Highlight the Message**: Enhance colors, focus, and contrast to draw attention to the subject and convey a specific mood or message.

5. **Sharpen Professionalism**: Editing can elevate your photos to a professional level, whether for business, social media, or personal projects

Basic Editing Techniques

Before diving into more advanced techniques, it's important to understand the foundational editing skills. These essential steps can drastically improve the quality of any photo.

1. Cropping and Straightening

- **Cropping**: Cropping removes unwanted areas of an image to improve composition, create focus, or resize an image. The most important aspect is adhering to the rule of thirds, which divides the photo into three equal parts both horizontally and vertically. Cropping helps you eliminate distractions and center the most important subject.

- **Straightening**: Sometimes photos can come out slightly tilted or askew. Use the straightening tool to adjust the horizon and level the image for a more professional look.

2. Adjusting Exposure and Contrast

- **Exposure**: Exposure controls the brightness of the image. If a photo is too dark or too bright, adjusting the exposure can help restore detail and improve visibility.

- **Contrast**: Contrast affects the difference between light and dark areas of the photo. Increasing the contrast makes colors pop and adds more depth, while decreasing the contrast can create a softer, more muted effect.

3. Color Correction

- **White Balance**: White balance adjusts the color temperature of the photo to make it appear more natural. A photo with poor white balance might have a blue or yellow tint. Correcting it can make the photo look more lifelike.

- **Saturation**: Saturation affects the intensity of colors in a photo. Increasing saturation makes colors more vibrant, while decreasing it leads to a more subdued and elegant look.

- **Tint and Hue Adjustments**: Tuning specific colors can help correct or enhance particular tones in the image, especially if you're looking to achieve a specific look or feel.

4. Sharpening

- **Sharpening** enhances fine details and edges in the photograph, making the image appear crisper and more defined. Be careful not to overdo it, as too much sharpening can cause noise and make the image look artificial.

Advanced Editing Techniques

Once you've mastered the basics, you can explore more advanced photo editing techniques that offer greater control over your images.

1. Retouching and Removing Imperfections

- **Clone Stamp/Healing Brush**: These tools allow you to remove blemishes, unwanted objects, or distractions in the background. The clone stamp duplicates part of the image and applies it over the unwanted areas, while the healing brush blends it seamlessly with the surrounding area.

- **Skin Smoothing**: For portrait photography, skin smoothing tools can make the skin appear softer by reducing blemishes and wrinkles. This technique is especially useful in beauty and fashion photography.

2. Applying Filters and Effects

- **Filters**: Filters are pre-designed effects that can dramatically alter the appearance of a photo with just one click. They can create vintage, cinematic, or stylized looks, making your photos more visually striking.

- **Gradients and Textures**: Gradients are gradual color changes that can add depth to an image. Textures, such as overlays or bokeh effects, can add artistic flair and creativity to your images.

3. Adding Layers and Masks

- **Layering**: Layers allow you to manipulate different elements of the image independently. You can add new images, text, or graphics on top of the existing photo, keeping the original image intact while experimenting with various changes.

- **Masks**: Masks are used to hide or reveal parts of an image. They allow for more precise control over adjustments, helping to create professional-looking composites and edits without affecting the entire image.

4. Adjusting Focus and Depth of Field

- **Blur Effects**: Adding a blur to the background or foreground can help create a shallow depth of field, drawing focus to the main subject. This is especially popular in portrait and product photography.

- **Vignetting**: Vignetting darkens the corners and edges of the image, which helps to bring focus to the center of the photograph.

5. Creating Panoramas and Collages

- **Panoramas**: By stitching multiple images together, you can create wide-angle photos of landscapes or cityscapes. Photo editing tools allow you to blend these images smoothly and ensure the edges match perfectly.

- **Collages**: Collages combine multiple photos into a single image, perfect for creating visual stories or displaying a series of related images, such as family events or travel adventures.

Popular Photo Editing Tools

There are numerous software programs and applications available for photo enhancement, ranging from beginner-friendly tools to more advanced editing suites. Here are some of the most widely used photo editing tools:

1. **Adobe Photoshop (Windows/Mac) Ideal for Professional Photo Editing**
Adobe Photoshop is the industry standard for photo editing, offering a comprehensive set of tools for everything from basic adjustments to advanced manipulation. Photoshop's capabilities are vast, with features like layers, retouching, and color correction, making it ideal for professional photographers and designers.

2. **Lightroom (Windows/Mac) Ideal for Batch Editing and Lightroom Presets**
Adobe Lightroom is a popular choice for photographers who need to edit large batches of photos quickly. It offers powerful color correction, exposure adjustments, and editing features, all organized within an intuitive interface. Lightroom is

especially useful for those who specialize in RAW image editing and need precise control over details.

3. **GIMP** **(Windows/Mac/Linux)**
   Free and Open-Source Option
   GIMP (GNU Image Manipulation Program) is a free alternative to Photoshop. While it may not have all the advanced features of Photoshop, it still offers a wide range of tools for editing, retouching, and creating artwork. GIMP is an excellent choice for those who want a powerful editing tool without the expense.

4. **Canva** **(Web-based)**
   Ideal for Quick and Simple Edits
   Canva is a simple and intuitive design tool with robust photo editing features. While it's not as advanced as Photoshop or Lightroom, Canva is perfect for beginners who want to perform quick edits, apply filters, and create social media graphics, posters, or invitations. It also includes a large library of templates and design elements.

5. **Snapseed** **(Mobile)**
   Ideal for On-the-Go Editing
   Snapseed is a free mobile photo editing app developed by Google. It offers a variety of professional tools for editing photos on your smartphone or tablet, including filters, color adjustments, and retouching tools. Snapseed is great for quick edits, especially for social media posts or travel photography.

Conclusion

Enhancing photographs with editing tools is an essential skill in today's visually-driven world. Whether you're capturing memories, creating content for social media, or working on professional projects, knowing how to enhance your photos can dramatically improve their visual appeal and storytelling power. By mastering basic editing techniques and exploring advanced features like retouching, layering, and special effects, you can take your photography to new heights and create images that captivate and inspire.

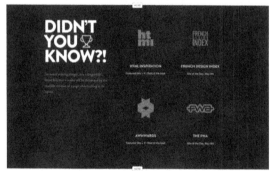

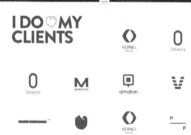

Figure 18: Creating a Virtual Portfolio

Part 19: Creating a Virtual Portfolio

A virtual portfolio is a powerful tool for showcasing your work, building your personal brand, and attracting potential clients or employers. In today's digital age, having an online portfolio is essential for anyone in a creative or professional field, such as graphic design, photography, web development, writing, or any other skill-based profession. Whether you are a freelancer, a job seeker, or a hobbyist looking to share your work, a well-curated virtual portfolio can make a significant impact and open up many opportunities.

In this section, we will explore the importance of having a virtual portfolio, how to create one, and the key elements that make a portfolio stand out. Additionally, we'll walk through some popular platforms and tools that can help you build a stunning virtual portfolio, as well as tips for maintaining and updating it regularly.

Why Create a Virtual Portfolio?

A virtual portfolio serves as an online showcase of your skills, experience, and creative abilities. It is a comprehensive collection of your best work, which can be shared with potential employers, clients, or collaborators. Here are several reasons why a virtual portfolio is important:

1. **Visibility and Accessibility**: A virtual portfolio is accessible to anyone with an internet connection, allowing you to share your work with a global audience. It's easier for prospective clients or employers to view your portfolio than searching through physical documents or email attachments.

2. **Professional Presentation**: A portfolio is a professional way to present your skills and expertise. A polished, well-organized portfolio demonstrates that you take your work seriously and can present it in a way that reflects your attention to detail and creativity.

3. **Showcase Your Best Work**: Unlike a resume or cover letter, a portfolio allows you to showcase actual samples of your work. By curating a collection of your best and most relevant pieces, you can highlight the skills and experiences that make you unique.

4. **Create an Online Presence**: A virtual portfolio can help you build your online presence and personal brand. With the right tools, you can not only display your work but also incorporate your personality, style, and philosophy, making it easier for others to connect with you.

5. **Expand Opportunities**: An online portfolio can be a direct marketing tool for your services, especially for freelancers and creatives. It can lead to new projects, clients, and collaborations, ultimately expanding your career opportunities.

Key Elements of a Virtual Portfolio

Creating a virtual portfolio involves more than just uploading some photos or documents. A well-thought-out portfolio must be carefully structured to make a lasting impression. Here are the essential elements you should include:

1. Homepage (Introduction)

The homepage of your portfolio serves as the first impression and introduction to who you are and what you do. It should be visually appealing, clear, and concise. The homepage should include:

- **Your Name or Business Name**: Make sure your name or business name is prominently displayed to make it easy for visitors to know who you are.

- **Tagline or Professional Statement**: Include a short, compelling statement that describes your area of expertise or what you offer. For example, "Creative Graphic Designer Specializing in Brand Identity" or "Freelance Web Developer Building User-Centric Websites."

- **Navigation Menu**: Make sure that visitors can easily navigate through your portfolio by including a clear and simple menu (e.g., About Me, Work Samples, Contact).

- **Call to Action**: Encourage visitors to take action by including a clear call to action, such as "Contact Me for Collaborations" or "View My Work."

2. About Me / Bio

The About Me page provides visitors with information about your background, skills, experience, and what drives you. This is your opportunity to tell your story and connect with potential clients or employers. Include:

- **Personal Background**: Share a brief introduction to who you are, including your education, career journey, and interests.

- **Skills and Expertise**: Highlight your key skills and areas of expertise that are relevant to your portfolio.

- **Professional Philosophy or Approach**: Share your values, philosophy, or approach to your work, which can help differentiate you from others in your field.

- **Professional Experience**: If relevant, include a summary of your professional work experience, freelance projects, or collaborations.

- **Photo**: Including a professional headshot adds a personal touch to your bio and helps create a stronger connection with your audience.

3. Work Samples (Portfolio Gallery)

The heart of your portfolio lies in your work samples. This section should include a curated selection of your best work, with each piece showcasing your skills, creativity, and ability to meet clients' needs. Here's how to present your work:

- **High-Quality Images/Files**: Ensure that your work is presented in high resolution, free from pixelation or distortion. This reflects the quality of your work and demonstrates professionalism.

- **Project Descriptions**: For each work sample, provide a brief description outlining the project's objectives, your role, the tools or techniques you used, and the outcome. This helps visitors understand the context of your work.

- **Categories/Tags**: Organize your work into categories or tags (e.g., Branding, Web Design, Photography, Illustration) to make it easier for viewers to navigate and find the work they're interested in.

4. Testimonials and Reviews

Including testimonials or reviews from previous clients or employers is a great way to build trust and credibility. Positive feedback can help potential clients feel more confident about working with you. If you don't have formal testimonials yet, consider asking previous collaborators to write a few words about their experience working with you.

5. Contact Information

Make it easy for visitors to reach you by providing clear contact information. Include:

- **Email Address**: A professional email address where potential clients can contact you.

- **Social Media Links**: If relevant, include links to your social media profiles (e.g., LinkedIn, Instagram, Twitter) to give visitors more ways to connect with you.

- **Contact Form**: A simple contact form allows visitors to send you messages directly from your portfolio site.

- **Phone Number**: If you're comfortable sharing it, including a phone number is another way to make yourself accessible.

6. Resume or CV

If applicable, include a section where visitors can download your resume or CV. This is especially useful for job seekers or freelancers who may want to include a detailed summary of their experience, education, and professional achievements.

Popular Platforms to Create Your Virtual Portfolio

Building a virtual portfolio has never been easier thanks to the many platforms and tools available today. Below are some popular options for creating an online portfolio:

1. WordPress

WordPress is one of the most popular website-building platforms, offering customizable themes and plugins for creating a professional portfolio. Many themes are designed specifically for portfolios and include features like image galleries, project showcases, and customizable layouts.

2. Wix

Wix is a user-friendly website builder that allows you to create a stunning portfolio with no coding skills required. It offers drag-and-drop functionality, customizable templates, and a range of design options to help you create a personalized portfolio.

3. Behance

Behance is a popular platform for creative professionals to showcase their work. It is part of Adobe and provides a global community where you can post and share your work, get feedback, and connect with potential clients or employers.

4. Squarespace

Squarespace is another great option for building an online portfolio, with beautiful templates designed for creative professionals. It's known for its modern designs, user-friendly interface, and robust features.

5. Dribbble

Dribbble is a platform for designers, illustrators, and other creatives to showcase their work and connect with other professionals. Dribbble is particularly useful for design portfolios, offering an engaging community where people can discover and share design inspiration.

6. Adobe Portfolio

Adobe Portfolio is included with Adobe Creative Cloud and allows you to easily create a personalized portfolio website. It integrates seamlessly with other Adobe products, making it an ideal option for photographers, graphic designers, and other creatives who use Adobe tools.

Tips for Maintaining and Updating Your Virtual Portfolio

Once you've created your virtual portfolio, it's important to keep it updated and relevant. Here are some tips for maintaining your portfolio:

- **Update Regularly**: Add new projects, remove outdated work, and update your bio or contact information regularly.

- **Optimize for Mobile**: Ensure that your portfolio looks good on mobile devices since many potential clients will view it on their phones.

- **Focus on Quality, Not Quantity**: Choose your best work to showcase. It's better to have a smaller number of high-quality projects than a large number of average pieces.

- **Show Your Growth**: Over time, include newer projects that demonstrate your skill progression. Your portfolio should evolve along with your career.

Conclusion

A virtual portfolio is an indispensable tool for showcasing your creativity, skills, and professional achievements. Whether you are a freelancer, a job seeker, or someone looking to connect with potential clients, a well-crafted online portfolio will help you stand out and open up new opportunities. By carefully curating your work, providing detailed descriptions, and keeping your portfolio updated, you can create a digital presence that reflects your talents and makes a lasting impression.

Figure 19: Producing Educational Materials

Part 20: Producing Educational Videos

Creating educational videos has become one of the most effective ways to engage audiences and share knowledge. With the rise of online learning platforms, social media, and digital content, producing educational videos offers a unique opportunity to explain complex topics in a simple, visual, and engaging manner. Whether you are a teacher, trainer, content creator, or business professional, mastering the art of producing educational videos can help you communicate your ideas more effectively and reach a larger audience.

In this section, we will explore the key steps involved in creating high-quality educational videos, from pre-production to post-production, and introduce tools and tips to make the process smoother and more efficient.

Why Educational Videos Are Important

Educational videos offer a dynamic way to present information, making learning more engaging and accessible. Here are several reasons why educational videos are an invaluable tool:

1. **Visual and Interactive Learning**: Videos combine visuals, audio, and text, catering to different learning styles. This makes it easier for viewers to understand and retain information.

2. **Engagement**: Compared to traditional text-based content, videos tend to capture attention more effectively. Dynamic visuals, animation, and storytelling elements help keep viewers engaged.

3. **Accessibility**: Videos can be accessed anytime and anywhere, making it easier for learners to review material at their own pace, leading to better retention.

4. **Clarity**: Some topics or concepts are best explained through visual demonstrations. Videos allow you to break down complex ideas step-by-step, enhancing understanding.

5. **Shareability**: Educational videos can be easily shared across social media platforms, online communities, and websites, reaching a wider audience and promoting a sense of community around learning.

Steps to Produce Educational Videos

Producing high-quality educational videos involves several stages, from planning and scripting to filming and editing. Below is a step-by-step guide on how to create engaging and effective educational videos.

1. Plan Your Content

The first step in creating an educational video is to plan your content. A solid plan ensures that the video is focused, clear, and valuable to the audience. Here's how to plan:

- **Identify Your Audience**: Understand who your target audience is. Are they beginners, intermediate learners, or experts? Tailor your content to their needs and skill level.

- **Define the Learning Objective**: What do you want your viewers to learn by the end of the video? Clearly define the goal of your video, whether it's explaining a concept, teaching a skill, or providing a step-by-step tutorial.

- **Research and Gather Information**: Ensure that the information you present is accurate and up-to-date. Conduct thorough research to support your content, and gather any resources (e.g., images, charts, diagrams) you may need.

- **Outline and Structure**: Create an outline of the video's structure. Break down the content into sections to ensure it flows logically. For instance, an introduction, main body, and conclusion are essential elements to cover.

2. Script Your Video

Writing a script for your video is crucial for maintaining a clear and concise flow. A script helps you stay on track, avoid unnecessary tangents, and ensure that you are delivering your message effectively. Here's what to include in your script:

- **Introduction**: Introduce yourself and the topic. Briefly explain what the viewers will learn and why it's important.

- **Main Content**: Divide the core of your content into sections. Use clear, simple language and explain complex ideas step-by-step. Include any visuals, demonstrations, or examples that will enhance understanding.

- **Call to Action**: At the end of the video, encourage viewers to take some action, such as subscribing, following a link for more information, or practicing the skills taught in the video.

- **Timing**: Keep the script concise. An educational video should be long enough to explain the material without losing the viewer's attention. Typically, videos between 5 and 15 minutes are optimal, depending on the complexity of the topic.

3. Gather the Necessary Equipment

To produce high-quality educational videos, you need the right tools and equipment. The quality of your video, audio, and visuals is crucial to engaging your audience. Here's a list of basic equipment you'll need:

- **Camera**: A good camera is essential for recording high-quality video. A DSLR or mirrorless camera is ideal, but if you're on a budget, a high-quality smartphone camera can also work. Ensure your camera has good resolution and a stable frame rate.

- **Microphone**: Clear audio is just as important as video quality. Invest in an external microphone (such as a lapel mic or condenser mic) to improve sound quality. Avoid using built-in microphones as they may result in poor sound.

- **Lighting**: Proper lighting is essential for clear, professional-looking videos. Use natural light or invest in affordable lighting kits (e.g., softbox lights or ring lights) to brighten up your setup and eliminate shadows.

- **Screen Recording Software**: If you're creating educational content related to computer skills or software tutorials, consider using screen recording software like OBS Studio, Camtasia, or ScreenFlow to capture your screen while explaining processes.

- **Editing Software**: After filming, you'll need video editing software to cut, arrange, and polish your footage. Popular options include Adobe Premiere Pro, Final Cut Pro, and more beginner-friendly software like iMovie or DaVinci Resolve.

4. Film the Video

Now that you've planned and scripted your content, it's time to film your video. Follow these tips to ensure smooth and efficient filming:

- **Set Up Your Space**: Ensure your filming environment is quiet, well-lit, and free from distractions. If you're using a background, make sure it is tidy and not distracting.

- **Use a Tripod or Stabilizer**: To avoid shaky footage, use a tripod or a stabilizer for your camera. This will help maintain a steady shot throughout the video.

- **Engage with Your Audience**: Speak clearly and at a steady pace. Engage with your viewers by making eye contact with the camera and using natural body language. Be enthusiastic about the topic to keep the audience interested.

- **Follow Your Script**: Stick to the script, but don't be afraid to improvise if it feels more natural. Make sure to capture all necessary shots, and if you make any mistakes, you can always retake parts later.

- **Record Multiple Takes**: If needed, film multiple takes to get the best performance. It's better to have extra footage to work with during editing than to realize later that something important was missed.

5. Edit the Video

Video editing is where your educational video comes to life. Editing helps you remove mistakes, add visuals, and create a polished final product. Here's what to focus on during editing:

- **Trim Unnecessary Footage**: Remove any sections where you've made mistakes or gone off-topic. Keep the video concise and to the point.

- **Add Visual Aids**: Insert graphics, slides, charts, or animations to support your explanations. Visual aids help clarify complex concepts and make the video more engaging.

- **Incorporate Music and Sound Effects**: Adding background music or sound effects can enhance the overall viewer experience. Make sure the music doesn't overpower the narration and is appropriate for the topic.

- **Subtitles and Captions**: Adding subtitles or captions can make your video more accessible to a wider audience, including those with hearing impairments. It also makes your video more appealing to non-native speakers.

- **Transitions and Effects**: Use smooth transitions between sections of the video to maintain a logical flow. Avoid overusing flashy effects that could distract from the content.

6. Upload and Promote the Video

Once your video is edited, it's time to upload and share it with the world. Choose a platform that aligns with your audience and goals, such as YouTube, Vimeo, or educational platforms like Teachable or Udemy. Make sure your video is easy to find by:

- **Creating an Engaging Title and Description**: Choose a title that is both descriptive and catchy. Use relevant keywords in the description to make the video searchable.

- **Promoting on Social Media**: Share your video on platforms like Facebook, Instagram, Twitter, and LinkedIn to reach a broader audience. Engage with viewers by responding to comments and asking for feedback.

- **Encouraging Engagement**: Ask viewers to like, comment, and share your video, and invite them to subscribe for more educational content. This helps build a community around your educational videos.

Conclusion

Producing educational videos is an effective way to engage, educate, and inspire your audience. By following the steps outlined above, you can create high-quality videos that make learning enjoyable and accessible. Whether you're teaching a skill, explaining a concept, or sharing insights, a well-produced educational video can elevate your content and increase your reach. Embrace the power of video and start creating content that will leave a lasting impact on your audience.

Figure 20: Building A Personal Website

Part 21: Building a Personal Website Using HTML/CSS

In today's digital world, having an online presence is essential. A personal website can serve as a digital portfolio, a resume, a blog, or a hub for showcasing your skills and achievements. While there are many website-building platforms available, learning how to build your own website using HTML (Hypertext Markup Language) and CSS (Cascading Style Sheets) can give you more control, flexibility, and a deeper understanding of web design.

In this part of the book, we will guide you through the process of building a basic personal website from scratch using HTML and CSS. We will cover everything from setting up your project to creating a structured layout, styling your pages, and adding essential features.

What Are HTML and CSS?

Before we dive into the practical steps, it's important to understand the roles of HTML and CSS:

- **HTML (Hypertext Markup Language)**: HTML is the fundamental language for structuring content on the web. It defines the structure of web pages by using elements such as headings, paragraphs, lists, links, and images.

- **CSS (Cascading Style Sheets)**: CSS is used to style the content created with HTML. It controls the appearance of the website, including the layout, fonts, colors, spacing, and positioning. CSS enables you to create visually appealing and user-friendly websites.

Together, HTML and CSS form the backbone of every website on the internet. HTML provides the structure, while CSS enhances the design and layout.

Step 1: Setting Up Your Project

Before you start writing any code, it's important to set up your project files and organize your workspace. Here's how you can do that:

1. **Create a New Folder**: Create a new folder on your computer where all your website files will be stored. Name it something like "MyPersonalWebsite."

2. **Create HTML and CSS Files**: Inside the folder, create two files:

   o index.html: This file will contain the HTML structure of your website's homepage.

   o style.css: This file will contain the CSS code to style the elements in your HTML file.

3. **Text Editor**: Open the files in a text editor or integrated development environment (IDE). Popular options include:

   o **Visual Studio Code** (free and highly recommended)

   o **Sublime Text**

   o **Notepad++**

These editors provide helpful features like syntax highlighting, auto-completion, and error checking.

Step 2: Basic HTML Structure

Now, let's start with the fundamental structure of your website. Open your index.html file and enter the following code:

```
<!DOCTYPE html>

<html lang="en">

<head>

  <meta charset="UTF-8">

  <meta name="viewport" content="width=device-width, initial-scale=1.0">

  <title>Your Name - Personal Website</title>

  <link rel="stylesheet" href="style.css">

</head>

<body>

  <header>

    <h1>Welcome to My Personal Website</h1>

    <nav>

      <ul>

        <li><a href="#about">About Me</a></li>

        <li><a href="#projects">Projects</a></li>

        <li><a href="#contact">Contact</a></li>

      </ul>

    </nav>

  </header>

  <section id="about">
```

```
<h2>About Me</h2>

<p>This is where you introduce yourself. Talk about
your background, skills, and interests.</p>

</section>


<section id="projects">

<h2>Projects</h2>

<p>Here you can showcase your work, including links to
your GitHub, portfolio, or examples of projects you've worked
on.</p>

</section>


<section id="contact">

<h2>Contact</h2>

<p>Provide details on how people can contact you, such
as an email address, social media links, or a contact form.</p>

</section>


<footer>

<p>&copy; 2025 Your Name. All Rights Reserved.</p>

</footer>
</body>
</html>
```

Explanation of HTML Structure:

- **<!DOCTYPE html>**: This declaration tells the browser that the document is written in HTML5.

- **<html lang="en">**: This element represents the root of your HTML document. The lang="en" attribute specifies that the content is in English.

- **<head>**: The head section contains meta-information about the document, such as character encoding, viewport settings, and the title of the page.

- **<link rel="stylesheet" href="style.css">**: This line links your HTML file to the CSS file, allowing you to style your page.

- **<header>**: This section usually contains the main title of the website and navigation links.

- **<section>**: Sections are used to group content logically. In this case, we have three sections: About Me, Projects, and Contact.

- **<footer>**: The footer typically contains copyright information or other relevant details.

Step 3: Adding Basic CSS Styling

Now, let's add some simple CSS styles to make your website look visually appealing. Open your style.css file and add the following code:

```
/* Reset default margins and padding */
* {
  margin: 0;
  padding: 0;
```

```css
    box-sizing: border-box;
}


/* Set a background color and font for the entire page */
body {
    font-family: Arial, sans-serif;
    background-color: #f4f4f4;
    color: #333;
    line-height: 1.6;
}


/* Style the header section */
header {
    background-color: #333;
    color: white;
    padding: 20px;
    text-align: center;
}


header h1 {
    font-size: 2.5em;
}
```

```
nav ul {
    list-style-type: none;
    padding: 0;
}

nav ul li {
    display: inline;
    margin-right: 20px;
}

nav ul li a {
    color: white;
    text-decoration: none;
    font-size: 1.2em;
}

nav ul li a:hover {
    color: #4CAF50; /* Change to green on hover */
}

/* Style the sections */
```

```css
section {

    padding: 20px;

    margin: 20px;

    background-color: white;

    border-radius: 8px;

    box-shadow: 0 2px 4px rgba(0, 0, 0, 0.1);

}


/* Style the footer */

footer {

    text-align: center;

    padding: 10px;

    background-color: #333;

    color: white;

    margin-top: 20px;

}
```

Explanation of CSS Code:

- **Universal Selector (*)**: This selector applies a reset to remove default margins and padding, ensuring consistent styling across browsers.

- **Body Styling**: Sets the font, background color, text color, and line height for the body of the page.

- **Header Styling**: The header section has a dark background, white text, and padding for spacing. The text-align: center; centers the header content.

- **Navigation Styling**: The nav ul removes the default list styling, and the list items (li) are displayed inline with some margin between them. The links (a) are styled to look clean, and the hover effect changes their color to green.

- **Section Styling**: Each section has padding, a white background, rounded corners, and a subtle box shadow to make it visually distinct.

- **Footer Styling**: The footer is styled similarly to the header, with centered text and padding.

Step 4: Testing Your Website

Once you've written your HTML and CSS, it's time to test your website:

1. **Open the index.html file** in a browser (double-click the file). You should see your website displayed with the content and styling you added.

2. **Check Responsiveness**: Resize the browser window to make sure the layout adjusts well on different screen sizes. You can also test it on your mobile device.

Step 5: Expanding Your Website

Once you've built the basic structure of your personal website, you can expand it further:

- **Add More Pages**: You can create additional pages (e.g., a blog or portfolio) by creating new HTML files and linking them in the navigation menu.

- **Enhance Styling**: Use more advanced CSS techniques such as Flexbox, Grid, and animations to make your website more interactive and visually appealing.

- **Add Interactivity**: Learn basic JavaScript to add interactivity to your website, such as form validation or animations triggered by user actions.

- **Publish Your Website**: To make your website live on the internet, you'll need a hosting service. Platforms like GitHub Pages, Netlify, and paid services like Bluehost or SiteGround can host your website for free or for a small fee.

Conclusion

Building a personal website using HTML and CSS is a rewarding experience that allows you to express your creativity while gaining valuable web development skills. By following the steps outlined in this chapter, you can create a functional, visually appealing website that reflects your personal style and interests. As you gain more experience, you can experiment with advanced features and design techniques to make your website even more dynamic and interactive. Happy coding!

Figure 21: A Writing a Computer Code

Part 22: Writing Your First Python Script

Python is one of the most versatile and beginner-friendly programming languages. Writing your first Python script is an exciting step into the world of programming. Here's a detailed guide to help you create and execute your first Python program, whether you're aiming for a simple task or laying the foundation for more advanced projects.

What is a Python Script?

A Python script is simply a file containing Python code. These scripts can automate tasks, perform calculations, process data, or even create games. Unlike using the interactive Python shell, where you type and execute one line at a time, a script allows you to save your code in a file and run it repeatedly.

Step 1: Setting Up Your Environment

Before writing a Python script, ensure your environment is ready:

1. **Install Python**:
   - Download and install the latest version of Python from https://www.python.org.
   - Verify installation by opening a terminal or command prompt and typing:
   - python --version

or

python3 --version

2. **Choose a Code Editor or IDE**:
   - **Text Editors**: Use a simple text editor like Notepad++ (Windows) or TextEdit (macOS in plain text mode).
   - **Integrated Development Environments (IDEs)**: Popular IDEs like PyCharm, VS Code, or IDLE provide helpful features like syntax highlighting and error checking.

Step 2: Writing Your Script

1. **Create a New File**: Open your chosen editor and create a new file. Save it with a .py extension, e.g., first_script.py.

2. **Write Your Code**: Let's start with a simple script to print "Hello, World!" — a tradition in programming.

3. # This is your first Python script

4. print("Hello, World!")

5. **Add Comments**: Comments (lines beginning with #) explain the code for readers and yourself later.

Step 3: Running Your Script

1. **Via Command Line or Terminal**:

   o Navigate to the directory where you saved your file.

   o Run the script by typing:

   o python first_script.py

or

python3 first_script.py

   o The output will display:

   o Hello, World!

2. **Using an IDE**:

   o Open your script in the IDE and press the "Run" button.

> o The output should appear in the IDE's terminal.

Step 4: Expanding Your Script

After mastering the basics, try adding more functionality to your script. Here are a few examples:

1. **Perform Simple Calculations**:

2. # Adding two numbers

3. num1 = 10

4. num2 = 20

5. result = num1 + num2

6. print("The sum of", num1, "and", num2, "is", result)

7. **Using Input**:

8. # Greeting the user

9. name = input("What is your name? ")

10. print("Hello, " + name + "! Welcome to Python programming.")

11. **Using Conditional Statements**:

12. # Check if a number is even or odd

13. num = int(input("Enter a number: "))

14. if num % 2 == 0:

15.   print(num, "is even.")

16. else:

17.   print(num, "is odd.")

192

18. **Loops for Repetition**:

19. # Print numbers from 1 to 5

20. for i in range(1, 6):

21.   print(i)

Step 5: Debugging and Testing

Debugging is an essential skill when writing scripts:

- **Check for Syntax Errors**: Python will display error messages if there's an issue with your code.

- **Test Incrementally**: Test your code in small chunks to identify problems easily.

- **Use Print Statements**: Printing variables and results at different stages can help debug logic errors.

Step 6: Saving and Sharing Your Script

- **Save Your Work**: Keep your scripts organized in folders with meaningful names.

- **Share Your Code**: Share your Python files with others or upload them to platforms like GitHub for collaboration.

Step 7: Advancing Beyond Basics

Once you're comfortable with basic scripts, explore these topics to level up:

1. **Modules and Libraries**: Use Python's built-in libraries, like math for calculations or random for generating random numbers.

2. **Data Structures**: Learn about lists, dictionaries, and tuples to manage data efficiently.

3. **Object-Oriented Programming (OOP)**: Use classes and objects to structure complex programs.

4. **Advanced Tools**: Explore libraries like pandas for data analysis, flask for web development, or pygame for game creation.

Practice Project: A Simple Calculator

Here's a mini-project to solidify your learning:

```
# Simple Calculator
def add(x, y):
    return x + y


def subtract(x, y):
    return x - y


def multiply(x, y):
    return x * y


def divide(x, y):
    if y != 0:
        return x / y
    else:
        return "Cannot divide by zero!"
```

```python
print("Select operation:")
print("1. Add")
print("2. Subtract")
print("3. Multiply")
print("4. Divide")

choice = input("Enter choice (1/2/3/4): ")
num1 = float(input("Enter first number: "))
num2 = float(input("Enter second number: "))

if choice == '1':
    print("Result:", add(num1, num2))
elif choice == '2':
    print("Result:", subtract(num1, num2))
elif choice == '3':
    print("Result:", multiply(num1, num2))
elif choice == '4':
    print("Result:", divide(num1, num2))
else:
    print("Invalid input!")
```

Conclusion

Writing your first Python script is a gateway to endless possibilities in programming. With practice, you'll move from simple scripts to creating complex software, games, or even AI systems. Remember, Python's strength lies in its simplicity and vast community support. Take the first step, explore, and enjoy the journey of programming!

Figure 22: Designing a Mobile App

Part 23: Developing a Basic Mobile App

In the modern digital age, mobile applications (apps) have become an integral part of everyday life, helping us perform various tasks—from communication and entertainment to productivity and health. Creating a mobile app is a fantastic way to explore computer technology and expand your technical skills. In this section, we will walk you through the essential steps for developing a basic mobile app, from planning the app idea to writing code and testing your app on mobile devices.

By the end of this section, you will have a foundational understanding of mobile app development and be able to create your first basic app.

What Is Mobile App Development?

Mobile app development is the process of creating software applications that run on mobile devices such as smartphones and tablets. These apps can be designed for specific platforms, like Android and iOS, and serve various functions, such as social networking, entertainment, education, or productivity.

There are two main types of mobile apps:

1. **Native Apps**: These apps are developed specifically for one platform (iOS or Android) using platform-specific programming languages (e.g., Swift for iOS or Java for Android).

2. **Cross-Platform Apps**: These apps are built to work on multiple platforms using a single codebase, often

through frameworks like Flutter, React Native, or Xamarin.

For beginners, we'll focus on **cross-platform development** using **Flutter** and **Dart**—a popular, easy-to-learn framework that allows you to create mobile apps for both Android and iOS with one codebase.

Step 1: Setting Up Your Development Environment

Before you start building your app, you need to set up the development environment. Here's how you can do that:

1. **Install Flutter:**

    o Flutter is a free, open-source SDK (software development kit) that helps you build natively compiled applications for mobile, web, and desktop from a single codebase.

    o Go to Flutter's official website and follow the installation guide to install Flutter on your operating system (Windows, macOS, or Linux).

2. **Install Dart:**

    o Dart is the programming language used by Flutter. It is designed for front-end development and allows you to create fast, reliable, and scalable applications.

    o Dart is included with Flutter, so once you install Flutter, you already have Dart set up.

3. **Install an IDE (Integrated Development Environment):**

o   Popular choices for Flutter development are **Visual Studio Code** and **Android Studio**. Both are free and provide powerful features like code completion, debugging, and performance analysis.

o   Install one of these IDEs and then add the Flutter and Dart plugins.

4. **Set Up an Emulator/Simulator**:

o   To test your app, you'll need a virtual device or an emulator. Both Android Studio and Visual Studio Code offer built-in emulators for Android devices, or you can use Xcode's simulator if you're building for iOS.

o   Create a virtual device through the IDE to simulate a mobile device and run your app.

Step 2: Planning Your Mobile App

Before jumping into writing code, it's essential to plan your app. Here's how you can do it:

1. **Define the App's Purpose**: What will your app do? Start by defining a simple purpose for your app. For example, your app could be a to-do list app, a photo gallery, or a simple calculator.

2. **Design the User Interface (UI)**: Think about the layout of your app. Sketch out the different screens your app will have and how users will interact with them. For a beginner app, aim for simplicity. For example:

o   A **home screen** with a button to navigate to another screen.

- o   A **settings screen** for adjusting preferences or adding content.

3. **Identify Core Features**: Identify the core features of your app that are essential for its functionality. For instance, if you're building a to-do list app, the core features could include adding tasks, marking tasks as completed, and removing tasks.

Step 3: Writing Your First Flutter Code

Once you have everything set up and planned out, it's time to start coding. Below is an example of a simple to-do list app written in Flutter:

1. **Create a New Flutter Project**:

   - o   Open your IDE and create a new Flutter project by selecting the "New Project" option.

   - o   Choose "Flutter Application" and provide a project name (e.g., todo_app).

   - o   The IDE will generate some starter code for you.

2. **Building the Main Screen**: Open the lib/main.dart file, which contains the main logic of your app. The following code snippet shows a basic Flutter app structure for a simple to-do list:

import 'package:flutter/material.dart';

void main() {

  runApp(MyApp());

}

```
class MyApp extends StatelessWidget {
  @override
  Widget build(BuildContext context) {
    return MaterialApp(
      home: TodoScreen(),
    );
  }
}


class TodoScreen extends StatefulWidget {
  @override
  _TodoScreenState createState() => _TodoScreenState();
}


class _TodoScreenState extends State<TodoScreen> {
  List<String> todos = [];


  final    TextEditingController    controller    =
TextEditingController();

  void addTodo() {
    setState(() {
```

```
      todos.add(controller.text);

      controller.clear();

    });
  }


  @override
  Widget build(BuildContext context) {
    return Scaffold(
      appBar: AppBar(
        title: Text('Simple Todo List'),
      ),
      body: Padding(
        padding: const EdgeInsets.all(16.0),
        child: Column(
          children: [
            TextField(
              controller: controller,
              decoration: InputDecoration(hintText: 'Enter task'),
            ),
            ElevatedButton(
              onPressed: addTodo,
              child: Text('Add Task'),
```

```
      ),
      Expanded(
        child: ListView.builder(
          itemCount: todos.length,
          itemBuilder: (context, index) {
            return ListTile(
              title: Text(todos[index]),
              trailing: IconButton(
                icon: Icon(Icons.delete),
                onPressed: () {
                  setState(() {
                    todos.removeAt(index);
                  });
                },
              ),
            );
          },
        ),
      ),
    ],
  ),
),
```

```
  );
 }
}
```

Explanation of Code:

- **MaterialApp**: This widget is the root of the application, providing basic material design elements like buttons and text fields.

- **StatefulWidget**: This widget allows the app to maintain dynamic content. In this case, we are managing the state of the to-do list.

- **TextField**: This is where users can input tasks.

- **ListView.builder**: This widget dynamically generates the list of tasks, allowing users to see all tasks added.

- **IconButton**: This button allows users to delete tasks from the list.

Step 4: Testing Your App

After writing the code, it's important to test your app to ensure everything works as expected. Here's how to test it:

1. **Run the App**: Click the "Run" button in your IDE or use the terminal command flutter run to launch the app on your emulator or physical device.

2. **Check for Errors**: Ensure that the app loads correctly and performs as expected. If you see errors in the console, read them carefully and make adjustments to your code.

3. **Interact with the App**: Test all the features of your app, including adding and deleting tasks. Make sure the

app is responsive and that the UI looks good on different screen sizes.

Step 5: Enhancing the App

Now that you have built a basic app, you can add more features to enhance its functionality, such as:

- **Saving Data**: Use local storage (like SharedPreferences) to save the tasks even after the app is closed.

- **Adding Due Dates**: Include a feature that allows users to set due dates for tasks.

- **Notifications**: Implement push notifications to remind users about tasks.

Step 6: Publishing Your App

Once your app is complete and thoroughly tested, you can publish it to the Google Play Store or Apple App Store.

1. **For Android**: You can publish your app to the Google Play Store by creating a developer account and submitting your app through the Google Play Console.

2. **For iOS**: To publish on the Apple App Store, you'll need an Apple Developer account, and you can submit your app via Xcode.

Conclusion

Developing a basic mobile app is a rewarding and educational experience. By following the steps outlined in this part, you have learned the essentials of mobile app development using Flutter and Dart. While building a simple app is a great start, mobile app development is a vast field that allows you to explore advanced features, design patterns, and user interactions. As you continue learning and experimenting with different ideas, you'll be able to create more sophisticated apps. Happy coding!

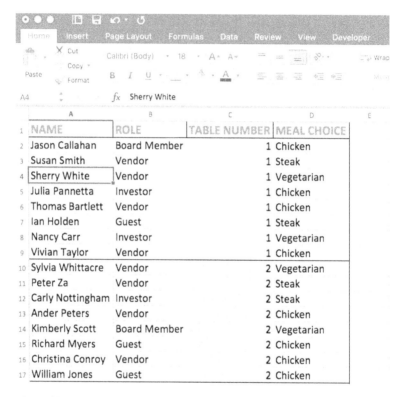

Figure 23: Automating Tasks With Macros in Excel

Part 24: Automating Tasks with Macros in Excel

Microsoft Excel is one of the most powerful tools for data management, analysis, and visualization. While Excel offers a wide range of functions and features for organizing data, it can become tedious to repeat the same tasks over and over. This is where **macros** come in. Macros are an invaluable feature that allows you to automate repetitive tasks, saving you time and effort while improving accuracy. In this part, we will explore how you can use macros in Excel to automate tasks and boost your productivity.

By the end of this section, you will have a comprehensive understanding of macros, how to create and use them, and how they can simplify your workflow in Excel.

What is a Macro in Excel?

A **macro** is a sequence of instructions or actions that can be recorded or written in Visual Basic for Applications (VBA) to automate repetitive tasks in Excel. Essentially, a macro allows you to program Excel to perform a set of actions with a single click or shortcut.

Why Use Macros?

- **Time-saving**: Automating tasks that are repeated frequently can save you hours of manual work.

- **Accuracy**: Macros eliminate human error by ensuring that the same set of actions is performed consistently.

- **Efficiency**: Macros allow you to perform complex tasks quickly, without the need for manual data entry or manipulation.

- **Customization**: You can tailor macros to suit your specific needs and workflow.

Step 1: Enabling Macros in Excel

Before you start creating macros, you need to ensure that macros are enabled in Excel. By default, macros are often disabled for security reasons. To enable them, follow these steps:

1. **Open Excel** and click on the **File** tab.

2. Select **Options** from the menu.

3. In the Excel Options window, choose **Trust Center** from the list on the left.

4. Click on the **Trust Center Settings** button.

5. In the Trust Center, select **Macro Settings**.

6. Choose **Enable all macros** (you can also select **Disable all macros with notification** to get a prompt before enabling macros).

7. Click **OK** to confirm your settings.

Step 2: Recording a Macro

One of the easiest ways to create a macro in Excel is by recording your actions. The **Record Macro** feature allows you to perform a series of tasks in Excel, and Excel will automatically generate the necessary code behind the scenes. Here's how you can record a macro:

1. **Open Excel** and go to the **View** tab on the Ribbon.

2. Click on **Macros** in the Macros group, then select **Record Macro**.

3. In the **Record Macro** dialog box:

   o **Name your macro**: Choose a name for your macro (e.g., "SumColumn" for a macro that sums a column of data).

   o **Assign a shortcut key** (optional): You can assign a keyboard shortcut for easy access to the macro (e.g., Ctrl + Shift + S).

o **Choose where to store the macro**:

- **This Workbook**: Stores the macro in the current workbook.

- **New Workbook**: Stores the macro in a new Excel workbook.

- **Personal Macro Workbook**: Saves the macro in a hidden workbook that opens whenever Excel starts, making the macro available across all workbooks.

o **Description**: Optionally, you can add a description for the macro.

4. Click **OK** to start recording the macro.

5. **Perform the actions** you want to automate in Excel. For example, you might format a table, apply filters, or calculate the sum of a column.

6. Once you have completed the tasks, click **Stop Recording** in the **Macros** group on the Ribbon.

Excel will now have a macro that performs all the tasks you recorded. You can run this macro at any time by using the shortcut key you assigned or by navigating to **Macros > View Macros**.

Step 3: Running a Macro

To run a macro in Excel, follow these steps:

1. Go to the **View** tab and click on **Macros**.

2. Select **View Macros** from the drop-down menu.

3. In the **Macro** dialog box, you will see a list of all macros available in the workbook or personal macro workbook.

4. Select the macro you want to run and click **Run**. Alternatively, if you assigned a shortcut key, press that key combination to run the macro instantly.

Step 4: Editing a Macro

While recording macros is straightforward, sometimes you may want to modify the code to make the macro more flexible or efficient. Macros are written in **Visual Basic for Applications (VBA),** a programming language built into Excel. Here's how to edit a macro:

1. Go to the **View** tab and click on **Macros**.

2. Select **View Macros** and choose the macro you want to edit.

3. Click **Edit**. This opens the **VBA editor,** where you can see the code behind the macro.

Here's an example of a simple VBA code generated when you record a macro that sums the values in a column:

```
Sub SumColumn()

    Range("A1:A10").Select

    Selection.Copy

    Range("B1").Select

    ActiveSheet.Paste

    Application.CutCopyMode = False

End Sub
```

You can edit the code to adjust it for different ranges or customize it further. For example, you could change Range("A1:A10") to Range("B1:B10") if you want the macro to sum data in a different column.

Step 5: Writing a Macro from Scratch

While recording macros is easy, sometimes you may want to write a macro from scratch. Writing VBA code allows for more advanced functionality and flexibility. Here's a simple example of a macro that sums a range of numbers and displays the result in a message box:

1. Open the **VBA editor** (Alt + F11).

2. In the editor, go to **Insert** > **Module** to create a new module.

3. Write the following code in the module:

Sub SumRange()

Dim total As Double

total = Application.WorksheetFunction.Sum(Range("A1:A10"))

MsgBox "The sum of the range is " & total

End Sub

4. Close the editor and run the macro as described earlier. The result will appear in a message box showing the sum of the values in the range A1:A10.

Step 6: Managing Macros

Over time, you might accumulate several macros in your workbook. Excel provides tools to manage, delete, or rename macros:

1. **View Macros**: Go to the **View** tab and click on **Macros** > **View Macros** to see all macros in the workbook.

2. **Delete or Rename Macros**: From the **View Macros** dialog box, select a macro and click **Delete** or **Rename** as needed.

Step 7: Common Uses of Macros in Excel

There are countless ways you can use macros to automate tasks in Excel. Some common applications include:

- **Formatting**: Automate repetitive formatting tasks such as changing fonts, applying borders, or adjusting cell sizes.

- **Data Cleaning**: Use macros to clean up data by removing duplicates, converting text to proper case, or splitting data into columns.

- **Reporting**: Automate the process of creating reports, such as summarizing data, applying formulas, or generating charts.

- **Email Automation**: Use macros to send email reports or notifications directly from Excel (using Outlook).

Step 8: Sharing and Distributing Macros

If you want to share your Excel workbook with others and allow them to use your macros, make sure to save the file in a format that supports macros, such as the **Excel Macro-Enabled Workbook** (.xlsm).

To share your macro-enabled file:

1. Go to **File** > **Save As**.

2. Choose **Excel Macro-Enabled Workbook (.xlsm)** as the file type.

3. Save and share the file with your colleagues or clients.

Conclusion

Automating tasks with macros in Excel is a powerful way to save time and reduce the risk of errors. By recording or writing custom macros, you can streamline your workflow and focus on more important aspects of your work. Whether you are formatting data, cleaning up spreadsheets, or generating reports, macros can help you accomplish these tasks efficiently and accurately. As you become more familiar with VBA, you will be able to create more complex macros to tackle even more advanced automation tasks in Excel.

Part 25: Creating Custom Keyboard Shortcuts

In the world of productivity, efficiency is paramount. One of the best ways to increase your efficiency while working on a computer is by using keyboard shortcuts. They allow you to perform tasks quickly, without the need for excessive mouse clicks or navigating through multiple menus. While many programs come with predefined keyboard shortcuts, creating your own custom shortcuts can provide even greater control and adaptability, ensuring that your workflow is optimized for your needs. In this part, we will explore how to create custom keyboard shortcuts in different programs and operating systems, making your computing experience faster and more seamless.

What are Keyboard Shortcuts?

A **keyboard shortcut** is a combination of keys that provides a quick way to perform a specific action or command within a program or operating system. Instead of using the mouse or navigating through menus, a keyboard shortcut lets you perform actions with just a few key presses. Common keyboard shortcuts include:

- **Ctrl + C**: Copy
- **Ctrl + V**: Paste
- **Ctrl + Z**: Undo
- **Ctrl + S**: Save

While these shortcuts are built into most applications, many programs and operating systems allow users to create custom shortcuts to suit their specific tasks and preferences.

Why Create Custom Keyboard Shortcuts?

Custom keyboard shortcuts provide several benefits:

1. **Speed**: With custom shortcuts, you can perform your most-used actions faster and more efficiently, reducing the time spent navigating menus or clicking buttons.

2. **Ergonomics**: Using keyboard shortcuts can reduce strain on your hands and wrists by minimizing the need to use the mouse.

3. **Personalization**: Custom shortcuts let you tailor your computer experience to fit your unique workflow, increasing productivity.

4. **Streamlining Complex Tasks**: You can combine multiple actions into a single shortcut, automating repetitive tasks and improving your overall efficiency.

Creating Custom Keyboard Shortcuts in Windows

Windows operating systems allow you to create custom shortcuts for programs and tasks, which can be especially useful for quickly accessing your favorite programs, files, and folders.

Creating Custom Shortcuts for Programs

To create a custom keyboard shortcut for a program in Windows, follow these steps:

1. **Right-click on the program's shortcut** on your desktop or in the Start menu.

2. Select **Properties** from the context menu.

3. In the **Shortcut** tab, locate the **Shortcut key** field.

4. Click in the **Shortcut key** field and press the keys you want to assign as the shortcut. Windows automatically adds **Ctrl + Alt** to the combination. For example, if you press the **S** key, your shortcut will become **Ctrl + Alt + S**.

5. Click **Apply** and then **OK** to save the changes.

6. Now, whenever you press the custom keyboard shortcut, the program will open.

Creating Custom Shortcuts for Files or Folders

If you want to create custom shortcuts for specific files or folders:

1. Right-click on the file or folder you want to create a shortcut for.

2. Select **Create Shortcut** from the context menu.

3. Once the shortcut is created, follow the same steps as above to assign a custom keyboard shortcut.

Creating Custom Keyboard Shortcuts in macOS

On macOS, you can create custom keyboard shortcuts for any app that supports them, including built-in apps like Safari, Finder, and Mail, as well as third-party apps like Microsoft Office or Adobe Creative Cloud. Here's how you can set up custom shortcuts:

1. **Open System Preferences** and click on **Keyboard**.

2. In the **Keyboard** settings, select the **Shortcuts** tab.

3. In the left pane, choose the type of shortcut you want to create (e.g., **App Shortcuts**).

4. Click the **+** button to add a new shortcut.

5. In the dialog box that appears, select the application for which you want to create a custom shortcut from the drop-down list.

6. Enter the exact menu title of the command you want to assign a shortcut to. This must be the precise wording as it appears in the app's menu (e.g., **Save As** in Word).

7. In the **Keyboard Shortcut** field, type the key combination you want to use. For example, you might choose **Command + Shift + S**.

8. Click **Add** to save your custom shortcut.

Now, whenever you press your new custom shortcut in the designated app, the action will be triggered.

Creating Custom Keyboard Shortcuts in Software Applications

Many software applications, such as Microsoft Office, Adobe Photoshop, and Visual Studio Code, allow users to define custom keyboard shortcuts for specific tasks. These applications often come with default shortcuts, but they also provide customization options. Below are some examples of popular applications and how to create custom shortcuts within them:

Microsoft Office (Word, Excel, PowerPoint)

1. Open the **Word**, **Excel**, or **PowerPoint** application.

2. Click on the **File** tab and select **Options**.

3. In the **Word Options** (or Excel Options/PowerPoint Options) window, select **Customize Ribbon**.

4. Click on the **Customize** button next to **Keyboard Shortcuts**.

5. In the **Customize Keyboard** dialog box, scroll through the list of commands or use the **Categories** and **Commands** fields to find the action you want to assign a shortcut to.

6. Click in the **Press new shortcut key** field and press the key combination you want to assign.

7. Click **Assign** and then **Close** to save the shortcut.

Adobe Photoshop

1. Open **Photoshop.**

2. Go to **Edit > Keyboard Shortcuts**.

3. In the **Keyboard Shortcuts** dialog box, you'll see different categories (e.g., **Application Menus, Panel Menus, Tools**).

4. Select the category and then choose the command you want to assign a shortcut to.

5. Click the field next to the command and press the key combination you want to use.

6. If the shortcut is already assigned to another action, Photoshop will alert you and allow you to change it.

7. Click **OK** to save your changes.

Creating Custom Keyboard Shortcuts for Web Browsers

Web browsers such as Google Chrome and Mozilla Firefox also allow you to create custom shortcuts for navigating to specific websites or activating browser extensions.

Google Chrome

1. Open **Chrome** and type chrome://extensions/ in the address bar.

2. Scroll down to the **Keyboard Shortcuts** section and click on it.

3. You will see a list of extensions installed in Chrome. For each extension, you can assign a keyboard shortcut for specific actions (e.g., opening a new tab or activating a particular extension).

4. Click on the field next to the action you want to assign a shortcut to and press your desired key combination.

5. Your custom shortcuts will now work within Chrome.

Mozilla Firefox

1. Open **Firefox** and type about:addons in the address bar.

2. Click on **Extensions** in the left panel.

3. Find the extension you want to create a shortcut for and click the **Options** button.

4. Look for the **Keyboard Shortcuts** settings, if available, and assign your preferred keyboard shortcut.

Best Practices for Creating Custom Keyboard Shortcuts

While creating custom keyboard shortcuts can be extremely beneficial, it's important to keep a few best practices in mind to avoid conflicts and ensure efficiency:

1. **Consistency**: Keep your shortcuts consistent across applications to avoid confusion. For example, use **Ctrl + S** for saving in every program.

2. **Avoid Conflicts**: Check if the shortcut you want to assign is already used by another command. If so, either choose a different combination or modify the existing shortcut.

3. **Use Modifier Keys**: Modifier keys like **Ctrl, Shift, Alt**, and **Command** allow you to create a wider range of shortcut combinations.

4. **Make It Easy to Remember**: Choose shortcuts that are easy to remember based on the task you're automating. For example, **Ctrl + N** for opening a new file is intuitive.

5. **Limit the Number of Custom Shortcuts**: While custom shortcuts are useful, having too many can become overwhelming. Use them for the most critical tasks that will save you the most time.

Conclusion

Creating custom keyboard shortcuts can significantly enhance your productivity and streamline your workflow, whether you're using your computer for work, creative projects, or daily tasks. By customizing shortcuts in your operating system and software applications, you can reduce the time spent navigating menus, increase efficiency, and create a more personalized computing experience. With practice, these custom shortcuts will become second nature, allowing you to work faster and more intuitively. Start creating your own shortcuts today and experience the power of personalized productivity.

Part 26: Building a Chatbot for Customer Service

In today's fast-paced digital world, businesses are increasingly relying on technology to provide faster and more efficient customer service. One of the most innovative and effective ways to streamline customer interactions is by integrating a chatbot into your service systems. A **chatbot** is an AI-driven tool that can simulate human conversation and assist users in real-time, providing quick responses, answering questions, and even guiding them through processes. In this part of the book, we will explore how to build a basic chatbot specifically for customer service, the tools needed, and best practices to make it effective and user-friendly.

What is a Chatbot?

A **chatbot** is a software application that uses AI (Artificial Intelligence), natural language processing (NLP), and predefined rules to interact with users via text or voice. In a customer service context, chatbots are designed to simulate human conversation, answer frequently asked questions (FAQs), troubleshoot common issues, and even assist with product or service recommendations.

Chatbots can be found on websites, social media platforms, messaging apps, and within mobile applications. They save time, reduce the workload on human agents, and provide customers with instant responses.

Why Build a Chatbot for Customer Service?

There are numerous reasons why businesses are turning to chatbots for customer service:

1. **24/7 Availability**: Chatbots can provide support at any time of day or night, ensuring that customers always have access to assistance, regardless of time zone or business hours.

2. **Cost-Efficiency**: With a chatbot handling common inquiries, human agents can focus on more complex and higher-value tasks, thus reducing labor costs and improving the efficiency of the customer service team.

3. **Improved Customer Experience**: Chatbots can offer immediate responses, leading to quicker resolution of issues, which can boost customer satisfaction and loyalty.

4. **Scalability**: As businesses grow, chatbots can handle a larger volume of inquiries simultaneously, without the need to expand the support team.

5. **Data Collection and Insights**: Chatbots can track interactions and customer behavior, providing valuable insights that can inform business decisions and improve services.

Key Components of a Chatbot for Customer Service

To build an effective customer service chatbot, several key components need to be considered:

1. **Natural Language Processing (NLP)**: NLP is a branch of AI that helps chatbots understand human language. It allows the chatbot to process and analyze the text provided by the user and respond appropriately.

2. **Intuitive User Interface**: A well-designed, easy-to-navigate interface is critical. This may include buttons,

quick replies, or menus that help users interact with the bot smoothly.

3. **Predefined Responses**: A chatbot should be able to handle common questions and provide predefined responses to ensure fast and accurate communication. This involves creating a database of frequently asked questions (FAQs) and their answers.

4. **Escalation to Human Agents**: While chatbots can handle simple queries, there will always be situations that require human intervention. The chatbot should be able to detect when an issue needs to be escalated to a live agent and make the transition as seamless as possible.

5. **Machine Learning**: For more advanced chatbots, machine learning allows the bot to continuously improve and provide better responses over time by learning from past conversations.

Step-by-Step Guide to Building a Chatbot for Customer Service

Building a basic chatbot involves several steps, from planning the scope of the bot's capabilities to deploying it across platforms. Below is a comprehensive guide on how to create a customer service chatbot.

Step 1: Define Your Chatbot's Purpose

Before you start building the chatbot, you need to determine its goals. Ask yourself questions like:

- What types of customer inquiries will the bot handle? (e.g., FAQs, order status, troubleshooting, product recommendations)

- Will the chatbot be integrated with other systems such as CRM, email, or ticketing systems?

- How will the bot escalate issues to human agents when necessary?

- What platforms will the chatbot be deployed on? (e.g., website, Facebook Messenger, WhatsApp)

Defining these parameters will help you design a chatbot that meets the specific needs of your business and customers.

Step 2: Choose the Right Tools and Platforms

Several platforms and tools are available to help you build a chatbot without extensive coding knowledge. Some popular chatbot-building platforms include:

- **Dialogflow (Google)**: Offers powerful natural language understanding and integrates easily with Google services, as well as other platforms like Facebook Messenger and Slack.

- **Microsoft Bot Framework**: A comprehensive platform to create, test, and deploy intelligent bots using Microsoft technologies.

- **ManyChat**: Focuses on creating bots for Facebook Messenger, but also supports SMS and email integration.

- **Chatfuel**: Great for building bots for Facebook Messenger with an easy drag-and-drop interface.

- **TARS**: A no-code platform that allows businesses to create conversational landing pages and lead generation forms.

When selecting a tool, consider your technical skill level, the platforms you want to deploy on, and the features that are important for your business (e.g., integration with CRM, ticketing systems, etc.).

Step 3: Build the Conversation Flow

The conversation flow defines how the chatbot will interact with users. This is where you map out the entire user journey and the possible questions users might ask. Start by:

1. **Listing Common Questions**: Identify the most common inquiries or issues that customers face. For example:

    o "What are your business hours?"

    o "How can I track my order?"

    o "What is your return policy?"

2. **Creating Responses**: Write clear, concise, and helpful responses for each common question.

3. **Designing Menus**: Provide options for users to choose from, such as "Track my order" or "Speak with an agent."

4. **Handling Escalation**: Design the process of escalating issues to human agents. The bot should recognize when it cannot assist a customer and offer an option to connect to a live representative.

You can use flowchart tools like **Lucidchart** or **Draw.io** to visualize the conversation flow.

Step 4: Implement Natural Language Processing (NLP)

NLP allows the chatbot to understand user input that may be phrased in various ways. Using an NLP tool like **Dialogflow**

226

or **Rasa**, you can train your chatbot to recognize different intents and entities. For example:

- If a user types "Where is my order?" or "Can I track my package?", both questions express the same intent: tracking an order.

- You can teach the chatbot to identify key phrases, such as "order" or "tracking," and provide the appropriate response based on that context.

This helps make your chatbot more flexible and capable of handling various user inputs in a natural way.

Step 5: Test and Train the Chatbot

Testing is a critical step in chatbot development. You should thoroughly test the bot to ensure it provides correct responses and handles various edge cases effectively. During the testing phase:

- **Simulate Real Conversations**: Test the bot's responses by asking a variety of questions, both common and uncommon.

- **Analyze the Bot's Performance**: Identify any areas where the chatbot struggles or misunderstands user input.

- **Refine the Responses**: Adjust the responses or the conversation flow based on the results of your tests.

If your chatbot includes machine learning, it will continue to improve over time as it processes more interactions.

Step 6: Deploy and Monitor the Chatbot

Once the chatbot is ready and thoroughly tested, deploy it across your chosen platforms (e.g., website, Facebook

Messenger, or WhatsApp). Most chatbot platforms offer easy integration with websites and messaging apps.

After deployment, it's important to monitor the chatbot's performance:

- **Track Metrics**: Monitor key metrics such as user engagement, conversation completion rates, and satisfaction levels.

- **Refine and Improve**: Continuously refine the chatbot by reviewing feedback and conversations. Use machine learning to improve its responses and performance.

- **Monitor Escalations**: Ensure that any issues requiring human intervention are handled promptly and smoothly.

Best Practices for Building a Successful Customer Service Chatbot

To make your chatbot as effective as possible, keep the following best practices in mind:

1. **Keep It Simple**: Ensure that your chatbot is easy to interact with. Avoid making the conversation too complex or overwhelming for users.

2. **Personalize the Experience**: Where possible, personalize the responses based on customer data (e.g., their name or order history) to create a more engaging experience.

3. **Provide Clear Options**: Offer users clear choices and options to guide them through the conversation, rather than leaving them to figure out what to ask.

4. **Use a Friendly Tone**: Ensure your chatbot has a friendly, conversational tone that mirrors your brand's voice.

5. **Always Have a Human Backup**: Make it easy for users to transition to a live agent whenever necessary.

Conclusion

Building a chatbot for customer service can greatly enhance your ability to provide efficient, timely support to customers while reducing the burden on your support team. By following the steps outlined in this chapter, you can create a chatbot that provides useful and personalized assistance to your customers. Whether you use pre-built tools or build one from scratch, chatbots can play a pivotal role in improving customer satisfaction and streamlining your business's operations. With constant improvement and monitoring, your chatbot will continue to evolve and serve as a valuable asset to your customer service strategy.

Figure 24: Video Game

Part 27: Designing a Simple Game

Creating a simple game is an exciting and rewarding project that can introduce you to game development concepts, programming, and creative design. Designing a game doesn't require extensive experience or complex tools—many free platforms and beginner-friendly game engines are available that allow you to create your own fun, interactive experiences. Whether you are building a basic mobile game, a desktop game, or a web-based game, the process can be an excellent way to explore the world of game development.

In this section, we will walk you through the essential steps of designing a simple game, from conceptualization and design to implementation and testing. You will learn how to use game development platforms and basic programming techniques to bring your ideas to life.

What is Game Design?

Game design is the process of creating the content, rules, gameplay, and mechanics for a game. It includes planning the user experience (UX), creating visuals, implementing sound, and integrating all these elements into a functioning interactive system. The goal of game design is to create an enjoyable, engaging, and challenging experience for the player.

Why Design a Simple Game?

Designing a simple game offers numerous benefits, including:

1. **Learning Game Development Basics**: Game design teaches you essential skills such as programming, logic, user interface (UI) design, and testing.

231

2. **Creativity**: You can express yourself creatively through the storyline, characters, art, and music.

3. **Problem-Solving Skills**: Game development challenges you to think critically and solve complex problems, from game mechanics to bug fixes.

4. **Portfolio Building**: A simple game can be a great addition to your portfolio if you are interested in pursuing a career in game development or design.

5. **Fun and Satisfaction**: There's a great sense of accomplishment in seeing your own game come to life and providing entertainment for others.

Steps to Design a Simple Game

Step 1: Define the Concept

Before jumping into coding or artwork, start with a clear concept for your game. Ask yourself the following questions:

- **What is the genre?** Decide on the type of game you want to create. Popular genres for simple games include:

    o Puzzle games (e.g., match-3 games, Sudoku)

    o Platformers (e.g., side-scrolling games like Mario)

    o Arcade games (e.g., endless runners, shooting games)

    o Strategy games (e.g., tower defense)

    o Text-based games (e.g., interactive fiction)

- **What is the goal of the game?** What should the player aim to achieve? This could be completing levels, solving puzzles, or defeating enemies.

- **Who is the target audience?** Understanding who will play your game will help you make design decisions, such as difficulty level, visuals, and theme.

- **How does the game work?** Outline the basic mechanics—what the player does, how they interact with the game world, and how they win or lose. What actions can the player take (e.g., move, jump, shoot, interact with objects)?

Example: A simple game concept could be a puzzle where players move blocks to clear a path and reach the exit.

Step 2: Choose a Game Development Platform

There are several game development platforms that cater to beginners. Depending on your skill level and preferred programming language, you can choose the best tool for your project. Here are a few popular game engines that are ideal for creating simple games:

- **Scratch:** Scratch is a free, beginner-friendly platform that lets you create interactive games using visual coding blocks. It's great for young learners and absolute beginners who don't know how to program but want to understand game logic.

- **Unity:** Unity is one of the most popular game engines and is ideal for both 2D and 3D games. It uses C# as its programming language and has a vast community, tutorials, and resources to help you get started.

- **Godot:** Godot is an open-source game engine with a focus on 2D and 3D game development. It has its own scripting language (GDScript), which is similar to Python, making it easy for beginners to learn.

- **GameMaker Studio**: GameMaker Studio allows you to create 2D games with its simple drag-and-drop interface and scripting features. It's beginner-friendly and supports a wide range of platforms, including mobile, desktop, and web.

- **Construct**: Construct is another drag-and-drop game engine that is ideal for 2D games. It's accessible for beginners and doesn't require prior coding knowledge, but it still allows for powerful game mechanics.

Step 3: Plan the Game Mechanics

Now that you have a concept in mind, it's time to break down the core mechanics and structure of your game. The mechanics define how the player interacts with the game, and they are the foundation of the gameplay experience.

- **Controls**: How does the player control the character or objects in the game? For example, in a platformer, the player might use arrow keys or WASD to move and spacebar to jump.

- **Levels/Challenges**: Will the game have levels? If so, how do they increase in difficulty? You could have progressively more challenging puzzles, faster enemies, or new obstacles.

- **Player Progression**: How does the player progress? This could include collecting items, earning points, or unlocking new areas or abilities.

- **Win/Loss Conditions**: How does the game end? Does the player win after completing a level, or does the game end when a player runs out of lives or time?

234

Step 4: Create the Art and Sound

Even a simple game benefits from good design and sound. Art and sound help set the mood, create immersion, and provide feedback to the player.

- **Art**: For simple games, you don't need to create elaborate, high-definition graphics. Focus on clean, clear visuals that make the game easy to understand. You can use free or affordable assets from sites like **OpenGameArt.org**, or create your own with tools like **Piskel** (for pixel art) or **Aseprite**.

- **Sound**: Audio can significantly enhance the player's experience. You can add background music, sound effects for actions (like jumping or shooting), and ambient sounds for atmosphere. Websites like **freesound.org** offer free sound clips, or you can create your own using tools like **Audacity** or **FL Studio**.

Step 5: Code the Game

If you're using a beginner-friendly engine like Scratch or Construct, you can implement your game mechanics without any coding knowledge. However, if you're using platforms like Unity, Godot, or GameMaker, you will need to write some code.

- **Programming Basics**: Start with simple code structures like variables (e.g., keeping track of score or player health), loops (e.g., for game flow or animations), and conditionals (e.g., checking if the player won or lost).

- **Player Movement**: In a simple 2D platformer, you would code the movement of the player character, such as using arrow keys to move left or right and spacebar to jump.

- **Game Logic**: Code the game's win/loss conditions, progression, and obstacles. For instance, if the player's score exceeds a certain number, they move to the next level.

- **Collisions and Interactions**: Program interactions, such as collecting items, avoiding enemies, or interacting with objects in the environment.

Step 6: Test and Debug the Game

After coding, it's crucial to test the game to make sure everything works as intended. Playtest the game several times, looking for:

- **Bugs**: Is there any unexpected behavior, like the character getting stuck, the score not updating, or levels not loading properly?

- **Difficulty Balance**: Is the game too easy or too hard? Adjust the difficulty level to make sure it's challenging but fair.

- **Feedback**: Does the game provide appropriate feedback to the player? For example, do they know when they've collected an item, completed a level, or lost a life?

After fixing any issues, you should test the game again to ensure that everything works smoothly.

Step 7: Publish and Share Your Game

Once you're satisfied with the game, it's time to share it with others. Depending on the platform you're using, you can export your game to:

- **Web**: You can upload your game to platforms like **itch.io** or **Kongregate**, where players can play your game directly in their browser.

- **Mobile**: If you built your game using a platform like Unity, you can export it to Android or iOS.

- **Desktop**: Games made with engines like Unity or GameMaker can also be exported to desktop platforms like Windows, Mac, or Linux.

Share your game with friends, family, or the gaming community and get feedback to improve it further.

Conclusion

Designing a simple game is a fun and educational project that allows you to learn about game development, programming, and creative design. Whether you're making a simple puzzle, platformer, or interactive experience, you'll gain valuable skills in coding, art creation, and problem-solving. By following the steps outlined in this section, you'll be able to design and create your own game that you can proudly share with others. Start small, and as you gain experience, you can work on more complex games and develop your skills further.

Figure 25:Raspberry Pi

Part 28: Learning to Work with Raspberry Pi

Raspberry Pi is a low-cost, credit-card-sized computer that has revolutionized the way people approach electronics, programming, and hardware projects. Originally designed to teach basic computer science and programming in schools, the Raspberry Pi has evolved into a versatile tool for hobbyists, educators, engineers, and anyone interested in learning more about technology. It allows users to create a wide range of projects, from home automation and robotics to weather stations and gaming systems.

In this section, we'll introduce you to the world of Raspberry Pi, its components, how to get started with it, and how you can leverage it for your own projects, regardless of whether you're a beginner or an experienced maker. Whether you want to build a simple gadget, automate tasks, or explore the world of electronics, Raspberry Pi offers a perfect starting point.

What is Raspberry Pi?

Raspberry Pi is a small, affordable single-board computer designed to enable learning and experimentation. The board includes all the components necessary to make it functional, such as a CPU, memory, USB ports, HDMI output, and GPIO (General Purpose Input/Output) pins. This versatility makes Raspberry Pi an excellent platform for building various types of projects.

There are different models of Raspberry Pi, with the most popular being:

- **Raspberry Pi 4 Model B**: This is the most powerful model, offering up to 8GB of RAM, a quad-core processor, and support for 4K video output.

- **Raspberry Pi 3 Model B+**: An older but still very capable model with a 1.4 GHz processor and built-in Wi-Fi and Bluetooth.

- **Raspberry Pi Zero**: A smaller, cheaper version, ideal for minimalistic projects or portable applications.

Each model has different processing power, memory, and connectivity options, but all Raspberry Pi devices are flexible and support a variety of operating systems, including **Raspberry Pi OS** (formerly Raspbian), **Ubuntu**, and others.

Why Use Raspberry Pi?

Raspberry Pi offers several compelling advantages:

1. **Affordability**: Raspberry Pi is very affordable, with prices ranging from $5 to $55 depending on the model. This makes it accessible to a broad range of people, from students to hobbyists.

2. **Learning and Experimentation**: Raspberry Pi is an excellent tool for learning programming (Python, Scratch, etc.), electronics, and computer science in general. It supports various programming languages and development environments.

3. **Versatility**: Raspberry Pi can be used in various applications, such as:

   o Home automation and IoT projects

   o Robotics and automation

   o Building media centers

- o Creating custom servers (e.g., web servers, file servers)

- o Gaming (retro game consoles with emulation)

- o Weather stations, cameras, and more

4. **Open-Source Ecosystem**: Raspberry Pi has a large, active community that contributes to open-source software and hardware projects. You can find numerous tutorials, projects, and software libraries to help you get started.

5. **Customization**: Raspberry Pi can be easily customized with accessories like cameras, sensors, motors, and other external devices, making it an ideal platform for hands-on, interactive projects.

Getting Started with Raspberry Pi

Step 1: Purchase the Raspberry Pi Kit

To get started with Raspberry Pi, you'll need the following essential components:

- **Raspberry Pi board** (Model 4, 3, or Zero depending on your needs)

- **Power supply** (5V/3A USB-C for Raspberry Pi 4, or 5V/2.5A micro-USB for older models)

- **MicroSD card** (at least 16GB, to store the operating system and files)

- **HDMI cable** (for connecting to a monitor)

- **Monitor** (for display output)

- **Keyboard and Mouse** (for input)

- **Case** (to protect your Raspberry Pi from dust and damage)

Some kits come with all the necessary accessories, while others might require you to purchase certain components separately. You can find Raspberry Pi starter kits online, which often include the board, power supply, case, and pre-loaded microSD card.

Step 2: Set Up the Raspberry Pi

Once you have all your components, follow these steps to set up your Raspberry Pi:

1. **Insert the MicroSD Card**: The microSD card acts as the storage for your Raspberry Pi and needs to have an operating system installed. Raspberry Pi OS (formerly Raspbian) is the recommended choice, but other Linux-based operating systems, such as Ubuntu, are also available.

2. **Connect the Monitor, Keyboard, and Mouse**: Plug your monitor into the HDMI port and connect the keyboard and mouse via USB.

3. **Power Up the Pi**: Connect the power supply to the Raspberry Pi, and it will automatically boot up.

4. **Complete the Initial Setup**: The first time you boot up, you'll be prompted to complete a basic configuration (language, Wi-Fi setup, etc.). After this, you're ready to start exploring!

Step 3: Install Software and Explore

Once your Raspberry Pi is up and running, you can start exploring its capabilities. Raspberry Pi OS comes with a suite of pre-installed software, including:

- **Python**: A popular programming language for beginners and professionals alike.

- **Scratch**: A visual programming language that helps you learn basic programming concepts.

- **LibreOffice**: A free office suite for word processing, spreadsheets, and presentations.

- **Web Browser**: Chromium is the default browser for browsing the web.

You can also install additional software and tools by using the **Raspberry Pi OS Software Center** or the **command-line terminal**.

Building Projects with Raspberry Pi

Once you've become familiar with your Raspberry Pi, the next step is to start building projects. Below are some project ideas to get you started:

1. Build a Weather Station

With the help of sensors (temperature, humidity, pressure, etc.), you can turn your Raspberry Pi into a weather station that collects and displays weather data. This can be done by connecting various sensors via the GPIO pins and programming the Pi to read data and display it on the screen.

2. Home Automation System

Raspberry Pi is a great platform for controlling smart home devices like lights, fans, and security systems. Using **Node-RED** (a flow-based programming tool) or **Home Assistant**, you can create automation tasks that control various devices through your phone or computer.

3. Retro Gaming Console

243

With software like **RetroPie**, you can turn your Raspberry Pi into a retro gaming console capable of emulating classic video game systems such as NES, SNES, Sega Genesis, and more. Connect your Raspberry Pi to a TV and use USB controllers to play your favorite retro games.

4. Media Center

Using software like **Kodi**, you can transform your Raspberry Pi into a media center for streaming movies, music, and other media from local storage or the internet. Connect it to your TV for a complete home theater setup.

5. DIY Robot

With the addition of motors, sensors, and other components, you can build a simple robot that moves, avoids obstacles, or responds to commands. You can control it through the GPIO pins or even connect it to the internet and control it remotely via Wi-Fi.

Programming with Raspberry Pi

Raspberry Pi supports various programming languages and can be used to learn and practice coding. Here are a few languages and tools that are commonly used with Raspberry Pi:

- **Python**: Python is the most popular language for Raspberry Pi programming. It's simple to learn, has extensive libraries, and is great for beginners. Python is commonly used for automation, hardware control (via GPIO), and web development on Raspberry Pi.

- **Scratch**: A beginner-friendly, drag-and-drop programming language. Scratch is ideal for introducing programming concepts to younger audiences or absolute beginners.

- **C/C++**: For more advanced users, C or C++ can be used for high-performance applications or low-level control of the Raspberry Pi hardware.

- **JavaScript**: For web-based projects, JavaScript (along with Node.js) is great for creating interactive websites or server-based applications.

Conclusion

Raspberry Pi is an incredibly powerful tool that opens up numerous possibilities for learning and experimentation. Whether you're looking to dive into programming, electronics, or even robotics, Raspberry Pi provides an affordable and accessible platform to start building your own projects. By learning to work with Raspberry Pi, you'll develop valuable skills that can be applied to a wide variety of real-world applications. Start small, experiment, and let your creativity guide you through the world of Raspberry Pi!

Part 29: Coding Interactive Quizzes

Interactive quizzes are a fantastic way to engage users, test their knowledge, and create fun and educational content. With the increasing importance of online learning, interactive quizzes are now a staple in many educational platforms, websites, and even mobile apps. Creating an interactive quiz can be a rewarding project that combines creativity, coding skills, and logic. Whether you want to build quizzes for a website, mobile app, or educational platform, the process of developing them can be both fun and educational.

In this part, we will dive into the world of interactive quizzes, exploring how to code a basic quiz from scratch using HTML, CSS, and JavaScript. We'll cover the key components of an interactive quiz, step-by-step instructions for creating one, and ways to enhance the user experience with additional features.

Why Build Interactive Quizzes?

Before diving into the coding aspect, let's understand why interactive quizzes are so popular and how they can be valuable:

1. **Engagement**: Quizzes are highly engaging and can capture the attention of users. Whether for educational purposes or entertainment, people love to test their knowledge in a fun and interactive way.

2. **Feedback and Learning**: Interactive quizzes allow for immediate feedback, which is crucial for the learning process. Correct and incorrect answers can trigger explanations or further learning resources, helping users improve their knowledge on the topic.

3. **User Experience**: A well-designed quiz can provide an excellent user experience by offering a personalized, interactive environment. You can design quizzes with different styles, levels of difficulty, and even score tracking.

4. **Versatility**: Quizzes can be used in various fields, such as education (e.g., testing knowledge), marketing (e.g., customer feedback), entertainment (e.g., personality tests), and even recruitment (e.g., screening candidates).

Components of an Interactive Quiz

An interactive quiz generally consists of the following components:

1. **Question Display**: The quiz shows a question to the user along with multiple answer choices.

2. **Answer Selection**: The user selects an answer by clicking or tapping on one of the choices.

3. **Feedback**: After submitting an answer, the quiz provides immediate feedback (correct/incorrect) and sometimes an explanation.

4. **Score Calculation**: The quiz tracks the user's score, either in real-time or at the end of the quiz.

5. **Timer (Optional)**: Some quizzes include a countdown timer to increase the challenge.

6. **Progress Bar (Optional)**: A visual indicator that shows the user's progress through the quiz.

7. **Results**: At the end of the quiz, the results are displayed, including the total score and perhaps a message based on the score achieved.

Getting Started with Coding an Interactive Quiz

We will use HTML, CSS, and JavaScript to create an interactive quiz. Here is a step-by-step guide for building a basic quiz:

Step 1: Set up the HTML Structure

The HTML part is responsible for structuring the content of the quiz. Below is the basic structure of an interactive quiz:

```
<!DOCTYPE html>

<html lang="en">

<head>

   <meta charset="UTF-8">

   <meta name="viewport" content="width=device-width, initial-scale=1.0">

   <title>Interactive Quiz</title>

   <link rel="stylesheet" href="style.css">

</head>

<body>

   <div id="quiz-container">

      <h2>Quiz Title</h2>

      <div id="question-container">

         <!-- Question and answers will go here -->

      </div>

      <button id="next-button">Next Question</button>

      <div id="result-container">
```

```
    <!-- Results will be shown here -->
  </div>
</div>
<script src="quiz.js"></script>
</body>
</html>
```

Explanation:

- The <div id="quiz-container"> holds the entire quiz.

- The <div id="question-container"> will display the current question and its multiple choices.

- The "Next Question" button lets users move on to the next question after answering.

- The results container will display the quiz score and a message at the end.

Step 2: Style the Quiz with CSS

CSS will be used to style the quiz to make it visually appealing and user-friendly. Here's a basic CSS structure to make the quiz more attractive:

```
body {
    font-family: Arial, sans-serif;
    background-color: #f4f4f9;
    display: flex;
    justify-content: center;
    align-items: center;
```

```
    height: 100vh;

    margin: 0;

}


#quiz-container {

    background-color: white;

    border-radius: 8px;

    box-shadow: 0 4px 8px rgba(0, 0, 0, 0.1);

    padding: 20px;

    width: 300px;

}


#question-container {

    margin-bottom: 20px;

}


button {

    padding: 10px 20px;

    background-color: #4CAF50;

    color: white;

    border: none;

    border-radius: 4px;
```

```
  cursor: pointer;

}


button:hover {

  background-color: #45a049;

}


#result-container {

  margin-top: 20px;

  font-size: 1.2em;

  text-align: center;

}
```

Explanation:

- The body of the page is styled to center the quiz container on the screen.

- The #quiz-container holds the quiz and is styled with padding, a white background, and a subtle box shadow to make it stand out.

- Buttons are styled for better interactivity and visual appeal.

- The results section will show the score with a larger font and center-aligned text.

Step 3: Add Functionality with JavaScript

The JavaScript code will handle the quiz logic, including showing questions, checking answers, calculating the score, and moving between questions. Below is a basic example of the JavaScript required to power the quiz:

```
// Define the questions and answers

const questions = [
    {
        question: "What is the capital of France?",
        options: ["Berlin", "Madrid", "Paris", "Rome"],
        answer: "Paris"
    },
    {
        question: "Which planet is known as the Red Planet?",
        options: ["Earth", "Mars", "Venus", "Jupiter"],
        answer: "Mars"
    },
    {
        question: "Who wrote 'Romeo and Juliet'?",
        options: ["Shakespeare", "Dickens", "Hemingway", "Austen"],
        answer: "Shakespeare"
    }
];
```

```
let currentQuestionIndex = 0;

let score = 0;


// Function to display a question

function displayQuestion() {

    const question = questions[currentQuestionIndex];

    const               questionContainer               =
document.getElementById('question-container');

    questionContainer.innerHTML = `

        <p>${question.question}</p>

        <ul>

            ${question.options.map(option => `

                <li><button
onclick="checkAnswer('${option}')">${option}</button>
</li>

            `).join('')}

        </ul>

    `;

}


// Function to check the selected answer

function checkAnswer(selectedAnswer) {

    const               correctAnswer               =
questions[currentQuestionIndex].answer;
```

```javascript
if (selectedAnswer === correctAnswer) {

  score++;

}

currentQuestionIndex++;

if (currentQuestionIndex < questions.length) {

  displayQuestion();

} else {

  showResults();

}

}


// Function to display the results

function showResults() {

  const resultContainer = document.getElementById('result-container');

  resultContainer.innerHTML = `

    <p>Your score: ${score} out of ${questions.length}</p>

    <button onclick="restartQuiz()">Restart Quiz</button>

  `;

}
```

254

```
// Function to restart the quiz

function restartQuiz() {

    score = 0;

    currentQuestionIndex = 0;

    showResults();

}


// Initialize the quiz

displayQuestion();
```

Explanation:

- The quiz data (questions, options, and answers) is stored in an array of objects.

- The displayQuestion function updates the DOM to show the current question and its options.

- When the user selects an answer, the checkAnswer function compares it to the correct answer, increments the score if correct, and moves to the next question.

- Once all questions are answered, the showResults function displays the final score and gives the user an option to restart the quiz.

Enhancing the Quiz

Once you've built the basic structure of your quiz, here are a few ways to enhance its functionality:

1. **Timer**: Add a countdown timer to each question, creating a sense of urgency. You can use JavaScript's setInterval() to track time.

2. **Randomize Questions and Answers**: You can shuffle the questions and answer options to make each quiz attempt unique.

3. **User Profiles**: Allow users to create a profile, save scores, and track their progress across multiple quiz attempts.

4. **Feedback and Explanations**: After each answer, provide a short explanation of why the answer is correct or incorrect, which helps users learn more effectively.

5. **Design and Animation**: Make the quiz more visually appealing by adding CSS animations, progress bars, and transitions between questions.

Conclusion

Coding interactive quizzes is an excellent way to combine your programming skills with creativity. By learning how to build a simple interactive quiz with HTML, CSS, and JavaScript, you unlock the potential to create engaging educational tools, entertainment applications, and even interactive marketing content. The possibilities are endless, and with a little practice, you can turn your quizzes into dynamic, fun, and valuable experiences for your users.

Part 30: Creating an AI-Driven Tool

Artificial Intelligence (AI) has revolutionized the way we interact with technology, creating opportunities to build smarter, more efficient tools that can understand, learn, and adapt. With AI becoming an integral part of modern applications, creating your own AI-driven tool can be an exciting and rewarding project. Whether you're looking to develop an AI-powered chatbot, a recommendation system, or an intelligent assistant, understanding the fundamentals of AI development will help you build innovative tools that can make tasks easier and more efficient.

In this part, we will guide you through the process of creating a simple AI-driven tool from scratch. We will cover everything from the basics of AI, tools and libraries required, and how to integrate AI functionality into your application. By the end of this section, you will have a solid foundation to begin developing AI tools for various purposes.

Understanding AI and Its Applications

Before diving into the development of AI tools, it's important to understand what AI is and how it can be applied. AI is the simulation of human intelligence processes by machines, especially computer systems. These processes include learning (the ability to improve performance based on experience), reasoning (solving problems), and self-correction.

AI-driven tools can serve a variety of purposes and industries, including:

- **Chatbots and Virtual Assistants**: Automated systems that simulate conversation with users,

257

handling customer queries, providing support, and even making recommendations.

- **Recommendation Systems**: Tools that suggest products, content, or services based on user preferences, behavior, and past interactions (e.g., Netflix, Amazon).

- **Image and Speech Recognition**: AI that can analyze images or process natural language to extract meaningful information.

- **Predictive Analytics**: AI tools that predict future outcomes based on historical data, such as forecasting sales, analyzing stock trends, or predicting customer behavior.

Key Components of an AI-Driven Tool

Building an AI-driven tool typically involves several key components:

1. **Data Collection**: AI systems need data to learn from. This data could be anything from text, images, numerical data, or user interactions, depending on the type of AI tool you're building.

2. **Model Training**: AI systems learn from data. Machine learning models are trained on large datasets to make predictions, recognize patterns, or generate outputs. Depending on your tool, you might need to train models for classification, regression, or clustering.

3. **Machine Learning Libraries**: There are various libraries and frameworks that help simplify the process of building AI-driven tools. Popular libraries include TensorFlow, PyTorch, Scikit-learn, and Keras, which

provide pre-built models and algorithms for different types of tasks.

4. **Integration**: Once the model is trained, it can be integrated into your application. For web and mobile apps, you can use APIs or frameworks like Flask (Python), TensorFlow.js, or PyTorch mobile to embed AI functionality into your tool.

5. **Deployment**: After building and testing your tool, you need to deploy it for use. This could involve hosting the tool on a server, building a mobile app, or integrating it with an existing system.

Step-by-Step Guide to Building an AI-Driven Tool

Step 1: Define Your Tool's Purpose

Before you begin coding, it's important to define what kind of AI-driven tool you want to build. Consider the following questions:

- What problem will your tool solve?

- Who will use the tool?

- What data will you need to train the AI model?

- What type of AI (e.g., Natural Language Processing, Computer Vision, Recommendation Systems) does your tool need?

For example, you might want to create a recommendation system for a shopping website or a chatbot for customer service.

Step 2: Choose the Right AI Technology and Tools

Next, you need to choose the AI technology that suits your tool's requirements. Here are some popular AI technologies and their use cases:

- **Natural Language Processing (NLP)**: Used for tasks involving human language, such as chatbots, sentiment analysis, or translation.

  - o Libraries: spaCy, NLTK, Hugging Face Transformers

- **Computer Vision**: Used for image recognition, object detection, facial recognition, and more.

  - o Libraries: OpenCV, TensorFlow, Keras, PyTorch

- **Reinforcement Learning**: Used for tasks like game-playing bots and robots.

  - o Libraries: OpenAI Gym, Ray Rllib

- **Recommendation Systems**: Used to provide personalized suggestions.

  - o Libraries: Surprise, Scikit-learn, TensorFlow Recommenders

Step 3: Data Collection and Preprocessing

For your AI tool to learn and make predictions, you'll need to collect data relevant to your tool's purpose. This data could be:

- Text data for chatbots or sentiment analysis

- Image data for object detection

- User interaction data for recommendation systems

Once you have your data, it must be preprocessed to remove noise, handle missing values, and transform it into a format suitable for training AI models. Common preprocessing steps include:

- **Cleaning**: Removing irrelevant or missing data.

- **Normalization**: Scaling numerical values to a standard range.

- **Tokenization**: Breaking text data into individual words or sentences.

- **Vectorization**: Converting words into numerical representations (for NLP tasks).

Step 4: Train the AI Model

Once you have your data ready, you can start training your machine learning model. Here's an example of how you might train a simple classification model using Scikit-learn:

from sklearn.model_selection import train_test_split

from sklearn.ensemble import RandomForestClassifier

from sklearn.metrics import accuracy_score

Example data (features and labels)

X = [[1, 2], [2, 3], [3, 4], [4, 5]] # features

y = [0, 1, 0, 1] # labels

Split data into training and testing sets

```
X_train, X_test, y_train, y_test = train_test_split(X, y,
test_size=0.2, random_state=42)


# Initialize and train the model

model = RandomForestClassifier()

model.fit(X_train, y_train)


# Make predictions and evaluate the model

predictions = model.predict(X_test)

print("Accuracy:", accuracy_score(y_test, predictions))
```

For complex tasks like image recognition or NLP, you can use frameworks like TensorFlow or PyTorch to define and train deep learning models.

Step 5: Integrate AI into Your Tool

Once your AI model is trained, it's time to integrate it into your tool. For a web application, you can use Flask or Django to build an API that serves your AI model. Here's an example using Flask:

```
from flask import Flask, request, jsonify

import joblib


# Load trained model

model = joblib.load('model.pkl')
```

```
app = Flask(__name__)


@app.route('/predict', methods=['POST'])

def predict():

    data = request.get_json()

    prediction = model.predict([data['input']])

    return jsonify(prediction=prediction[0])


if __name__ == '__main__':

    app.run(debug=True)
```

For a mobile app, you can use TensorFlow Lite (for Android) or CoreML (for iOS) to deploy your AI model and integrate it into your app.

Step 6: Test and Deploy Your Tool

Before launching your tool, thoroughly test it to ensure it works as expected. You can test it by running multiple scenarios, ensuring the AI performs well under different conditions. After successful testing, deploy your AI-driven tool on the desired platform (website, mobile app, or server).

For cloud deployment, you can use services like AWS, Google Cloud, or Microsoft Azure to host your tool and manage scalability.

Enhancing the AI Tool

After building the basic version of your AI tool, there are many ways to enhance its functionality:

1. **Continuous Learning**: Implement a feedback loop where the tool learns from user interactions to improve over time (e.g., improving chatbot responses based on feedback).

2. **User Personalization**: For tools like recommendation systems, personalize recommendations based on user behavior, location, or preferences.

3. **Integrate AI Models**: Integrate multiple AI models to create a more sophisticated tool. For example, combining NLP for understanding text with machine learning for classification.

4. **Improve Performance**: Optimize the tool for speed, scalability, and accuracy. You can use techniques like model quantization for smaller models or distributed processing for large-scale AI.

Conclusion

Creating an AI-driven tool involves multiple stages, from understanding the problem you're trying to solve to collecting data, building and training the model, integrating it into your application, and finally deploying it. The power of AI lies in its ability to learn, adapt, and provide intelligent solutions to real-world problems. By mastering the basics of AI development, you can build tools that are not only functional but also smart and scalable.

Whether you're building a chatbot, recommendation system, or predictive model, AI-driven tools have the potential to transform your ideas into powerful, user-centric applications that can evolve and improve over time.

Section 4: Business and Productivity

In today's fast-paced world, where competition is fierce and time is a precious resource, leveraging technology to boost business efficiency and productivity has become more important than ever. Computers and software tools have revolutionized how businesses operate, enabling entrepreneurs, managers, and employees to accomplish more in less time. The ability to automate tasks, manage projects, analyze data, and streamline communication has transformed the workplace into a dynamic environment where businesses can scale, grow, and succeed like never before.

In this section, we will delve into how you can harness the power of computers to enhance business operations and productivity. Whether you're running a small startup, managing a team, or handling personal projects, mastering the use of technology can lead to smarter decision-making, more efficient workflows, and a significant boost to overall productivity. From managing finances and conducting market research to automating repetitive tasks and building a brand, computers offer a wide array of tools that can help you excel in the modern business landscape.

This section will provide practical insights and hands-on strategies for using computers in various aspects of business, including:

- **Organizational Tools**: Learn how to use project management software, communication tools, and task automation to stay organized and optimize your workflow.

- **Data Management and Analysis**: Understand the importance of data in decision-making and explore tools for storing, analyzing, and visualizing data to make informed business choices.

265

- **Digital Marketing and Branding**: Discover how to build a strong online presence, create marketing campaigns, and use analytics to track the success of your efforts.

- **E-Commerce**: Learn how to establish an online store and manage it efficiently, from setting up an e-commerce platform to integrating payment systems and inventory management.

- **Financial Management**: Understand how to manage business finances, track expenses, and budget using powerful accounting tools and software.

By the end of this section, you'll have the skills to leverage computer technology to drive efficiency, improve productivity, and make smarter business decisions that can lead to sustained growth and success. Whether you're a business owner, a freelancer, or a professional looking to streamline your work, this section will empower you to use technology in ways that were once reserved for large corporations, giving you the edge you need in the modern business world.

Part 31: Creating a Business Plan Template

A business plan is an essential tool for anyone starting or managing a business. It serves as a roadmap, helping entrepreneurs define their goals, outline their strategies, and anticipate challenges. Having a solid business plan not only helps you stay focused but also provides clarity to investors, lenders, and potential partners about the vision and potential of your business.

Creating a business plan template is a practical and efficient way to ensure consistency and ease of use, especially for individuals or teams creating multiple business plans over time. A well-designed template allows you to quickly draft plans while ensuring that all the critical components are included, making the process faster and more organized.

In this part, we will guide you through creating a customizable business plan template that you can use for various types of businesses. Whether you are a startup, an expanding business, or seeking to revise an existing plan, this template will help you structure your ideas, goals, and strategies effectively.

Key Components of a Business Plan Template

1. **Executive Summary**

   o **Overview**: Provide a brief summary of the business, including its mission, vision, and primary objectives. This section is meant to capture the reader's attention and convey the business's value proposition.

- o **Goals**: State the short-term and long-term goals of the business. Include measurable milestones to gauge progress.

- o **Market Opportunity**: Highlight the gap your business is filling in the market and why there is a demand for your product or service.

- o **Financial Snapshot**: Include an outline of expected revenue, expenses, and funding requirements (if applicable).

2. **Business Description**

- o **Business Structure**: Define the type of business (e.g., sole proprietorship, partnership, corporation) and outline the organizational structure.

- o **Business Model**: Detail the business's operational model—how the business will make money (e.g., product sales, services, subscriptions).

- o **Mission Statement**: A concise description of the business's core purpose and values.

- o **Industry Overview**: Provide context by discussing the industry in which the business operates, key trends, and the competitive landscape.

3. **Market Research**

- o **Target Audience**: Define the target market, including demographics, psychographics, and buying behaviors.

- o **Market Analysis**: Identify key competitors and analyze their strengths and weaknesses. Show how your business will differentiate itself and what gives it a competitive edge.

- o **Market Trends**: Analyze industry trends and predict how they might impact your business in the future.

- o **Marketing Strategy**: Describe how you plan to reach your audience (e.g., digital marketing, traditional advertising, partnerships).

4. **Organization and Management**

- o **Leadership Team**: Outline key team members, their roles, and their relevant experience. Include brief bios and an overview of their responsibilities within the business.

- o **Legal Structure**: Specify the legal structure of your business (LLC, corporation, etc.) and any key legal considerations.

- o **External Support**: Mention any consultants, advisors, or partners who play a role in the business.

5. **Products or Services**

- o **Product/Service Offering**: Provide a detailed description of the products or services your business will offer. Explain how these will meet the needs of your target market.

- o **Development**: Discuss any ongoing development or innovation processes to improve or expand your offerings.

- o **Pricing Strategy**: Outline how you plan to price your products/services based on market research, competition, and perceived value.

- o **Unique Selling Proposition (USP)**: Explain what makes your product or service unique and why customers will choose your business over competitors.

6. **Sales and Marketing Plan**

- o **Sales Strategy**: Define how you plan to sell your product or service. This could include retail, online sales, direct sales, or through distributors.

- o **Marketing Strategy**: Detail the methods you'll use to attract and retain customers. This may include digital marketing, content marketing, social media, influencer partnerships, and more.

- o **Promotions and Advertising**: Identify specific promotional campaigns, advertising channels, and strategies you will use to generate awareness and drive sales.

7. **Financial Plan**

- o **Revenue Model**: Outline the revenue sources for your business, such as product sales, subscriptions, or licensing fees.

- o **Funding Requirements**: Specify the amount of capital you need to launch or expand your business, including how the funds will be used.

- o **Financial Projections**: Include forecasts for income, expenses, cash flow, and profitability for the first few years of business.

- o **Break-even Analysis**: Calculate when your business will break even and begin generating profits.

- o **Risks and Contingencies**: Identify potential risks (economic downturns, competitor actions, etc.) and outline contingency plans to address them.

8. **Appendix**

- o Include any supporting documents that help reinforce your business plan, such as charts, graphs, legal documents, licenses, or patents. This is where you can add detailed financial statements or resumes of the leadership team.

Designing Your Template

When designing your business plan template, consider the following tips:

- • **Organize for Readability**: Use clear headings, bullet points, and concise language to ensure your business plan is easy to navigate and read.

- • **Include a Table of Contents**: For longer plans, a table of contents will help readers find the information they need quickly.

- • **Utilize Spreadsheets for Financials**: For sections like the financial plan, it's best to use spreadsheets for calculations and projections. You can embed these directly in your template or provide links to external documents.

- **Visuals**: Use charts, graphs, and infographics where applicable to enhance the visual appeal and make data easier to understand.

Tools for Creating the Template

- **Microsoft Word or Google Docs**: These are great for creating a text-based business plan with structured formatting.

- **Canva or Adobe InDesign**: Use these graphic design tools to create visually appealing business plans, especially if you want to add branding elements or create a polished, professional look.

- **Google Sheets or Excel**: These are perfect for including detailed financial projections, cash flow analysis, and other calculations in your business plan.

Conclusion

A well-crafted business plan template not only helps streamline the process of drafting a business plan but also ensures that you cover all essential components. With a solid plan in place, you're better equipped to secure funding, attract partners, and effectively manage your business as it grows. Whether you're planning for a new venture or seeking to refine an existing one, a structured business plan template will serve as a powerful tool in helping you succeed.

Part 32: Designing Marketing Materials

Marketing materials are the backbone of any business's promotional strategy. They serve as the visual representation of your brand, communicating key messages to your audience in an engaging, memorable, and persuasive way. Whether you're running a small startup or a large corporation, well-designed marketing materials can elevate your business, improve brand recognition, and drive customer engagement.

In this part, we will explore the process of designing effective marketing materials. You'll learn how to create materials that are not only visually appealing but also aligned with your brand's identity and business objectives. From brochures and flyers to digital ads and email templates, the right marketing materials can significantly impact your business's success.

Key Marketing Materials to Design

1. **Business Cards**

    o **Why Business Cards Matter**: Business cards are one of the most fundamental marketing tools. They provide potential customers, clients, or partners with a tangible representation of your business. A well-designed business card can leave a lasting impression and serve as a reminder of your services or products.

    o **Design Tips**: Keep the design simple and clear. Include your business logo, contact details (email, phone number, website), and social media handles if relevant. Use your

273

brand colors and fonts to maintain consistency with other materials. A unique design element, like a die-cut or embossed detail, can also make your business card stand out.

- o **Tools to Create**: Software like **Canva**, **Adobe Spark**, or **Microsoft Publisher** is great for designing business cards with templates available for quick customization.

2. **Brochures**

- o **Why Brochures Are Important**: Brochures are effective in providing detailed information about your products or services. Whether printed or digital, brochures help convey your business's message in an organized and visually appealing format.

- o **Design Tips**: Use a clear, concise layout that guides the reader through the content. Include a brief introduction, the main body with detailed descriptions or offers, and a call to action. Use high-quality images and bold headings to highlight important information. Make sure your contact details and business website are easy to find.

- o **Tools to Create**: **Adobe InDesign**, **Canva**, and **Microsoft Publisher** offer templates for creating professional brochures.

3. **Flyers**

- o **Why Flyers Work**: Flyers are an effective way to promote events, sales, or special offers. Due to their compact size, they can be distributed easily and are perfect for grabbing attention in busy locations.

- o **Design Tips**: Keep it simple yet striking. Your flyer should have a headline that grabs attention, a clear message explaining what's being offered, and a strong call to action. Use bold typography and eye-catching graphics. Avoid overcrowding the flyer with too much text.

- o **Tools to Create**: **Canva**, **Adobe Spark**, and **Crello** are user-friendly platforms for creating flyers with pre-designed templates.

4. **Posters**

- o **Why Posters Are Effective**: Posters are ideal for promoting larger events or building brand awareness in a variety of locations. They have the power to draw attention in crowded environments, whether it's a retail store, a conference, or an outdoor setting.

- o **Design Tips**: Use bold colors and large fonts for easy readability from a distance. Keep the message short and impactful. Include your logo, website, and any other necessary details like dates, times, and locations for events. Focus on high-quality images that reflect your brand's style and tone.

- o **Tools to Create**: **Adobe Photoshop**, **Canva**, and **Microsoft Publisher** are ideal for poster creation.

5. **Email Templates**

o **Why Email Marketing Matters**: Email is one of the most effective digital marketing channels. A well-designed email template can help you maintain brand consistency and create compelling messages that engage your audience.

o **Design Tips**: Ensure your email design is mobile-friendly, as a large portion of users will read emails on their phones. Use clear headings, attractive imagery, and a call to action that stands out. Personalize the email where possible to make the recipient feel engaged. Maintain a balance between visuals and text— too many images can trigger spam filters.

o **Tools to Create**: **Mailchimp**, **Constant Contact**, and **HubSpot** provide customizable email templates with drag-and-drop features.

6. **Social Media Graphics**

o **Why Social Media Visuals Are Key**: Social media is a platform where businesses can interact with their audience directly. Well-designed graphics are crucial for driving engagement and increasing followers. Whether it's for a post, story, or ad, visually appealing content gets shared and recognized.

o **Design Tips**: Ensure consistency with your brand's colors, fonts, and logo. Create posts with clear messaging that encourage likes, shares, or comments. Use high-quality visuals, animations, and even infographics to convey information quickly and effectively.

    o **Tools to Create**: **Canva**, **Adobe Spark**, and **Crello** offer easy-to-use templates for social media platforms like Facebook, Instagram, Twitter, and LinkedIn.

7. **Banners and Signage**

    o **Why Banners Are Important**: Banners are often used for exhibitions, trade shows, and events to draw attention to a booth or display. They help build brand recognition and can convey messages in a large, easily visible format.

    o **Design Tips**: Banners need to be bold, clear, and easy to read from a distance. Use large, high-contrast fonts, and make sure your logo and brand colors are prominent. Keep the text short and focused on the key message or offer.

    o **Tools to Create**: **Canva**, **Adobe InDesign**, and **PosterMyWall** are useful tools for banner creation.

Design Principles for Effective Marketing Materials

When designing marketing materials, it's crucial to follow basic design principles to ensure your materials are effective:

- **Consistency**: Maintain consistent branding across all marketing materials (logos, fonts, colors) to create a strong, unified brand image.

- **Simplicity**: Avoid cluttering your materials with excessive information or visuals. Clear, simple designs are more effective at conveying the message.

- **Target Audience**: Understand who your audience is and tailor your design to appeal to them. The colors, fonts, and tone should reflect your audience's preferences and values.

- **Call to Action**: Every marketing material should have a clear call to action (CTA), whether it's visiting your website, signing up for a newsletter, or calling your business.

- **High-Quality Visuals**: Use high-quality images and graphics. Blurry or low-resolution visuals can damage your brand's credibility.

- **Alignment and Balance**: Ensure that text and visuals are well-aligned and balanced. This helps improve readability and aesthetic appeal.

Tools for Designing Marketing Materials

- **Canva**: A highly accessible tool for creating a wide variety of marketing materials, from business cards to social media graphics, with drag-and-drop simplicity and templates.

- **Adobe Illustrator**: Best for creating vector-based designs such as logos, posters, and business cards. A more advanced tool suited for professionals.

- **Adobe InDesign**: Ideal for print materials like brochures, flyers, and magazines due to its powerful layout tools.

- **Microsoft Publisher**: A more user-friendly alternative to InDesign for creating flyers, brochures, and newsletters.

- **Crello**: Similar to Canva, it provides easy-to-use templates and tools for designing marketing materials with a range of pre-made designs.

Conclusion

Designing marketing materials is about communicating your business's message in a visually appealing and effective way. Whether you are creating print materials like business cards and flyers or digital assets like email templates and social media graphics, the goal is to engage your audience, build brand recognition, and encourage action. With the right tools, design principles, and creativity, you can produce marketing materials that elevate your brand and help grow your business.

Part 33: Making a Financial Budget Tracker

A financial budget tracker is a vital tool for managing personal or business finances. It allows individuals or organizations to monitor their income and expenses, track spending patterns, and ensure they stay within their financial limits. Whether you are looking to save for a major purchase, reduce debt, or achieve long-term financial goals, a budget tracker is a fundamental component of financial planning.

In this part, we will walk through the process of creating a financial budget tracker. You'll learn how to set up your budget tracker, what categories to include, and how to keep it updated. We will also explore various tools that make the process easier and more efficient, including software options like Microsoft Excel, Google Sheets, and specialized apps.

Why a Financial Budget Tracker is Important

- **Increased Financial Awareness**: A budget tracker helps you gain a deeper understanding of your financial habits. You can easily see where your money is going and identify areas where you might be overspending.

- **Goal Achievement**: By tracking your budget, you can set financial goals (such as saving for an emergency fund or paying off debt) and monitor your progress towards achieving them.

- **Improved Savings**: With a clear view of your income and expenses, you can adjust your spending habits to increase savings. A budget tracker can help you ensure that you consistently save a portion of your income.

- **Debt Management**: Tracking your spending and income helps you identify how much you owe, the interest rates, and prioritize paying off high-interest debts. By allocating specific amounts to debt repayment, you can work toward becoming debt-free.

- **Peace of Mind**: Having control over your finances reduces financial stress. With a budget tracker, you'll always know where you stand, whether you're on track to meet your goals or need to make adjustments.

Steps to Create a Financial Budget Tracker

1. **Determine Your Financial Goals**

   o Before you begin tracking your finances, identify your financial goals. These could range from saving for a vacation, setting aside money for retirement, paying off credit cards, or building an emergency fund. Defining clear goals will help you stay focused and motivated as you track your spending.

2. **Choose the Right Tool**

   o You can choose to create a financial budget tracker using several tools:

     ▪ **Excel or Google Sheets**: Both platforms allow you to create highly customizable budget trackers. They come with templates, but you can also design your own spreadsheet to suit your needs.

     ▪ **Budgeting Apps**: If you prefer mobile apps, options like **Mint, YNAB (You Need A Budget), PocketGuard**, or

GoodBudget offer features like automatic tracking and categorization of expenses.

- **Accounting Software**: For businesses, more advanced tools like **QuickBooks** or **Wave** provide financial tracking capabilities and allow for budgeting and financial planning in one platform.

3. **Create Income and Expense Categories**

   o Organize your tracker into categories that reflect your sources of income and types of expenses. Common categories include:

   - **Income**: Salary, business income, rental income, investment income, etc.

   - **Fixed Expenses**: Rent/mortgage, utilities, subscriptions, insurance premiums, etc.

   - **Variable Expenses**: Groceries, entertainment, dining out, personal care, etc.

   - **Savings**: Emergency fund, retirement savings, or any other savings goals.

   - **Debt Repayment**: Credit card payments, loan repayments, etc.

   o **Tip**: Make sure to have a separate category for discretionary spending (things like entertainment, dining out, hobbies) so you can easily track non-essential expenses.

4. **Set Up Your Budget Tracker Spreadsheet (Excel or Google Sheets)**

   o **Step-by-Step Setup in Excel/Google Sheets:**

1. **Create Columns**: Set up columns for "Date," "Category," "Description," "Amount," "Income/Expense," and "Balance."

2. **Set Income Categories**: List your income sources (salary, additional income, etc.) and add the monthly expected amounts.

3. **Expense Categories**: Create rows for each type of expense (e.g., rent, utilities, groceries, etc.), and leave space to track actual spending.

4. **Calculate Differences**: Use formulas to subtract expenses from income, showing you whether you are overspending or staying within your budget. For example, you can use formulas like =SUM(B2:B10) to total your expenses and =B1-SUM(B2:B10) to calculate your remaining balance.

5. **Track Savings and Debt Repayment**: Add sections for savings and debt repayment, so you can monitor progress towards financial goals.

Example of a simple budget layout:

Date	Category	Description	Amount	Income/ Expense	Balance
01/01 /2025	Salar y	Monthl y Pay	$300 0	Income	$300 0

Date	Category	Description	Amount	Income/ Expense	Balance
01/01 /2025	Rent	Apartment	$1000	Expense	$2000
02/01 /2025	Groceries	Weekly Shop	$150	Expense	$1850

5. **Track Expenses Regularly**

   o Consistency is key when it comes to tracking your budget. Record your expenses daily or weekly. Regular updates will help you avoid overspending and stay on top of your financial goals.

   o **Tip**: Make it a habit to check your bank or credit card statements and input the transactions into your tracker to ensure accuracy.

6. **Review and Adjust Your Budget**

   o At the end of each month or week, review your budget tracker to see how well you've adhered to your budget. Did you exceed your spending on certain categories? Did you save as much as you intended? If necessary, make adjustments for the upcoming period.

   o **Tip**: If you find you consistently overspend in certain categories (like dining out or entertainment), consider cutting back or reallocating those funds to savings or debt repayment.

7. **Monitor Your Financial Goals**

- o Your budget tracker should not only track income and expenses but also keep you focused on your financial goals. For example, you can create a section that shows how much you've saved toward your emergency fund or how much you've paid off your credit card balance.

- o Regularly assessing your progress toward your goals helps you stay motivated and make necessary adjustments to achieve them.

Advanced Budgeting Features

Once you have mastered the basics of creating a financial budget tracker, you can add advanced features to make your tracker more powerful:

1. **Automated Data Entry**: Use budgeting apps like **Mint** or **YNAB**, which automatically link to your bank accounts and credit cards to track your spending. This eliminates the need for manual entry, saving time and reducing errors.

2. **Expense Forecasting**: In Excel or Google Sheets, you can set up formulas to forecast future spending. For example, you can calculate how much you expect to spend on utilities next month by averaging the past three months' bills.

3. **Graphs and Charts**: For visual learners, adding graphs or pie charts to your tracker can help illustrate where your money is going. For example, a pie chart of your expenses can show you how much of your budget goes toward fixed versus variable costs.

4. **Debt Repayment Tracker**: Include a section to track how much you owe on credit cards, loans, and other debts, and visualize how much progress you've made each month. You can even create a debt snowball or debt avalanche strategy to prioritize paying off high-interest debts.

Conclusion

Creating and maintaining a financial budget tracker is a crucial step towards financial health and security. By organizing your income and expenses, setting goals, and regularly reviewing your progress, you can make informed decisions about how to allocate your resources effectively. Whether you choose to use a spreadsheet, budgeting software, or a mobile app, the key is to stay consistent and use the tracker as a tool to achieve your financial goals. By doing so, you'll not only gain control over your finances but also build a solid foundation for long-term financial success.

Part 34: Planning Projects Using Software

Project planning is a critical component of ensuring the success of any endeavor, whether it's a personal project, a business initiative, or a large-scale team effort. Traditional project planning methods often relied on pen-and-paper lists and manual schedules, but today, various software tools have transformed the way we organize and manage tasks, timelines, resources, and goals.

In this section, we will explore how to effectively use project management software to plan and execute projects. We'll cover a range of tools—from simple to advanced—and how you can apply them to manage projects in various fields such as business, construction, events, software development, and more.

Why Use Software for Project Planning?

The use of software for project planning offers several advantages over traditional methods:

1. **Efficiency**: Project management software allows for quick task creation, easy delegation, and seamless tracking. Automation features can help reduce manual work and repetitive tasks, saving time.

2. **Real-time Collaboration**: Many project management tools offer real-time collaboration, allowing team members to work together, share updates, and provide feedback from different locations.

3. **Clear Organization**: Software tools help organize projects in a structured manner with clear task lists,

timelines, and workflows. This ensures nothing is overlooked, and progress can be easily tracked.

4. **Centralized Information**: Project planning software consolidates all project-related information in one place, making it easier to manage resources, monitor progress, and maintain clarity across teams.

5. **Improved Communication**: Integrated messaging systems, notifications, and comment threads enhance communication among project stakeholders and ensure all parties are aligned.

6. **Data Tracking and Reporting**: Most tools offer reporting features that allow you to track key metrics such as project progress, budget, time spent, and resource allocation. This data is useful for making informed decisions and for reporting to stakeholders.

7. **Scalability**: Whether you are working on a small personal project or a large corporate initiative, project planning software can scale to meet your needs. It's easy to manage small, simple tasks or complex workflows with multiple dependencies.

Steps for Planning Projects Using Software

1. **Define Your Project's Scope and Goals**

   o Before jumping into the software, clearly define the goals, objectives, and scope of your project. What are you aiming to achieve? What are the deliverables and deadlines? Establishing clear parameters at the outset helps you choose the appropriate tools and ensures that all subsequent planning is aligned with your project's purpose.

288

○ Example: In a website development project, the goals could include launching the site within three months, improving user experience, and ensuring it's mobile-friendly.

2. **Choose the Right Project Management Software**

○ Selecting the right project planning tool depends on the complexity of your project, your team size, and your specific needs. Here are some popular project management tools:

- **Trello**: A user-friendly tool for managing simple projects with boards, lists, and cards. Ideal for small teams and personal projects.

- **Asana**: A flexible tool for both small and large teams. It offers task management, timelines, workflows, and project tracking.

- **Microsoft Project**: A comprehensive project management tool suitable for large, complex projects. It provides features like Gantt charts, resource allocation, and budget management.

- **Monday.com**: Known for its visually appealing interface and versatility, Monday.com is suitable for projects of all sizes and industries.

- **Basecamp**: An easy-to-use tool for team collaboration, task management, and document sharing.

- **Smartsheet**: A tool for managing projects with a spreadsheet-like interface that integrates project management features, ideal for teams familiar with Excel.

3. **Create a Task List or Workflow**

   o Break down your project into manageable tasks. This could include everything from research and design to implementation and testing. The more detailed your tasks, the easier it will be to track progress and stay on top of deadlines.

   o Organize tasks by category (e.g., marketing, development, research) and assign priority levels to ensure essential tasks are completed first. Many tools allow you to create sub-tasks, assign due dates, and set dependencies (tasks that cannot begin until another task is completed).

Example (in Asana):

   o Create a task list with the main categories: Research, Design, Development, Testing, Launch.

   o Under Research, break it down into smaller tasks: Market research, competitor analysis, gather user feedback.

   o Add due dates and assign responsible team members to each task.

4. **Assign Roles and Responsibilities**

o Assign each task to the appropriate team member. This ensures accountability and clarity regarding who is responsible for what. With project management software, you can easily track who is working on which tasks and hold them accountable for completing them on time.

Example: In Microsoft Project, you can assign specific resources (team members, tools, or equipment) to each task and adjust work schedules accordingly. This is helpful for managing team capacity and avoiding over-assigning individuals.

5. **Set Deadlines and Milestones**

o Establish deadlines for each task, as well as key milestones for the project. Milestones represent significant achievements within the project (e.g., completing a prototype, securing funding, finishing testing). These checkpoints help you stay on track and measure the progress of the project.

o **Tip**: Use Gantt charts (available in tools like Microsoft Project and Smartsheet) to visualize the timeline of tasks and milestones. Gantt charts offer a visual representation of your project schedule and task dependencies.

6. **Monitor and Track Progress**

o As your project moves forward, consistently monitor progress and ensure that tasks are being completed on time. Many project management tools offer dashboards that display project status, overdue tasks, and completed milestones in one central location.

o **Tip**: Regularly update your project plan. If tasks are delayed or budgets are exceeded, adjust timelines or reallocate resources to ensure project success.

7. **Collaborate and Communicate**

o Use communication features built into project management tools, such as messaging, file sharing, and comment threads. This ensures that everyone involved in the project stays informed and can easily address issues or provide updates.

o **Example**: In Monday.com, you can tag team members in comments, attach files, and set notifications for important updates. This keeps everyone in the loop.

8. **Manage Resources and Budget**

o Keep track of resources (people, equipment, tools) and their allocation throughout the project. Budget management features, often included in advanced tools like Microsoft Project, help ensure that the project remains financially on track. Monitoring resources ensures that no team member is overloaded and that you have what you need to meet deadlines.

o **Tip**: Use resource leveling features available in Microsoft Project or Smartsheet to avoid overburdening team members by optimizing resource allocation across tasks.

9. **Assess Risks and Adjust**

   o Throughout the project, evaluate potential risks that may arise, such as changes in scope, delays in delivery, or resource shortages. Many tools allow you to track risks, including creating contingency plans for addressing issues that may arise.

   o **Example**: In Basecamp, you can create a project checklist and highlight potential risks to review with the team. Having a proactive approach to risk management can help prevent issues from escalating.

10. **Project Review and Final Evaluation**

   o After the project is completed, conduct a review to assess what went well and where improvements can be made. Many project management tools offer post-project reports and analytics, allowing you to evaluate project success and learn from any mistakes.

   o **Tip**: Collect feedback from team members and stakeholders using survey tools or built-in feedback features in project management software. Use this input to improve your processes for future projects.

Conclusion

Project planning software offers a range of tools that can help you manage projects efficiently and effectively. By breaking down your project into manageable tasks, assigning roles and responsibilities, setting deadlines, and tracking progress, you'll have a clear roadmap to project success. Whether you are working on a personal project or leading a complex team initiative, choosing the right software and implementing a structured plan will ensure that your project is completed on time, within budget, and to the satisfaction of all stakeholders.

Part 35: Automating Email Campaigns

Email marketing is one of the most effective tools for businesses and organizations to communicate with customers, generate leads, and promote products or services. However, managing email campaigns manually can be time-consuming and prone to errors, especially when dealing with large subscriber lists. Fortunately, automating email campaigns can streamline the process, allowing you to reach your audience efficiently and effectively while saving time and effort.

In this section, we will dive into the process of automating email campaigns, covering the essential steps, tools, and best practices for achieving success.

Why Automate Email Campaigns?

Automating email campaigns brings several key benefits, including:

1. **Time Efficiency**: Instead of sending individual emails to thousands of subscribers manually, automation tools allow you to schedule and send emails in bulk, saving you valuable time.

2. **Consistency**: Email automation ensures that your campaigns are sent out consistently, even when you are busy or unavailable. Regular communication helps build trust and maintain relationships with your audience.

3. **Personalization**: Modern email automation platforms allow for sophisticated segmentation and personalization. You can send tailored content to

specific groups based on their preferences, behavior, or past interactions with your brand, enhancing engagement.

4. **Targeted Campaigns**: With automation, you can create targeted campaigns for different segments of your audience. For example, you could send different content to new subscribers, repeat customers, or people who haven't interacted with your emails in a while.

5. **Performance Tracking**: Most email automation tools provide analytics that track open rates, click-through rates, bounce rates, and other metrics. This allows you to assess the effectiveness of your campaigns and make necessary adjustments.

6. **Scalability**: As your subscriber list grows, manually managing email campaigns becomes increasingly difficult. Email automation tools can easily scale with your business, allowing you to manage large numbers of subscribers without a significant increase in workload.

Steps to Automating Email Campaigns

1. **Select an Email Marketing Platform**

   o The first step in automating your email campaigns is selecting the right email marketing platform. There are many tools available, each offering unique features. Some of the most popular platforms include:

      ▪ **Mailchimp**: Known for its ease of use, Mailchimp offers automation workflows, email templates, and segmentation features.

- **Sendinblue**: Provides email marketing, SMS marketing, and automation tools, ideal for businesses that want a multi-channel approach.

- **ConvertKit**: Focuses on creators and small businesses, offering easy-to-use email automation and segmentation features.

- **ActiveCampaign**: A robust platform offering advanced email marketing, automation, and CRM tools for businesses of all sizes.

- **GetResponse**: Includes automation, landing page creation, and webinar integration, making it a great option for marketers.

o When choosing a platform, consider factors such as ease of use, pricing, available features, integration options, and scalability for future growth.

2. **Build Your Email List**

o Building an email list is one of the first steps in email marketing. Without a solid subscriber base, your campaigns won't have the reach they need. Here are some ways to grow your email list:

- **Lead Magnets**: Offer incentives such as free ebooks, white papers, or

297

exclusive discounts in exchange for email sign-ups.

- **Sign-up Forms**: Use sign-up forms on your website, social media pages, and landing pages to encourage visitors to join your email list.

- **Referral Programs**: Encourage existing subscribers to refer friends and colleagues in exchange for rewards or discounts.

3. **Segment Your Audience**

   o Email segmentation is the process of dividing your email list into smaller groups based on shared characteristics such as demographics, location, interests, behavior, or purchase history. By segmenting your list, you can send more relevant and personalized emails, which increases the chances of engagement.

   o Common segments include:

     - **New Subscribers**: Send a welcome series or introductory emails to build a relationship with new sign-ups.

     - **Inactive Subscribers**: Send re-engagement emails to subscribers who haven't opened your emails in a while.

     - **Frequent Buyers**: Reward loyal customers with exclusive offers or promotions.

- Most email marketing platforms allow you to set up automated workflows that trigger emails based on these segments.

4. **Create Email Campaigns and Workflows**

- **Email Campaigns**: Campaigns are specific email messages you send to your subscribers, such as newsletters, promotions, or event announcements. You can design campaigns using pre-built templates or create custom designs.

- **Workflows**: Workflows are automated email sequences triggered by specific actions or timeframes. For example, when a new subscriber joins your list, you could set up an automated welcome email series that introduces your brand and offers a special discount. Or, when a customer abandons their shopping cart, an automated reminder email could encourage them to complete their purchase.

Here are some common types of automated workflows:

- **Welcome Emails**: A series of emails sent to new subscribers introducing them to your brand and offering an incentive (like a discount or free download).

- **Drip Campaigns**: A series of automated emails sent over a set period to nurture leads and guide them through the buyer's journey.

- **Abandoned Cart Emails**: A triggered email sent to users who added items to their cart but

299

didn't complete the purchase, encouraging them to finalize their order.

- o **Post-Purchase Follow-ups**: Email sequences that follow up with customers after a purchase, asking for feedback, offering related products, or promoting loyalty programs.

5. **Design Engaging Emails**

- o To maximize the effectiveness of your email campaigns, focus on creating visually appealing, well-structured emails. Good design enhances the user experience and increases the chances of readers engaging with the content.

- o **Email Components**:

  - **Subject Line**: Craft a catchy subject line that grabs the reader's attention. Keep it concise and relevant to the email's content.

  - **Pre-header Text**: This text appears next to the subject line in the inbox. Use it to provide additional context or encourage the reader to open the email.

  - **Body Content**: Keep the content concise and valuable. Include images, headings, and calls to action (CTAs) that guide readers toward the next step.

  - **CTA Buttons**: Always include a clear call to action, whether it's to make a purchase, read a blog post, or sign up for an event.

6. Test and Optimize Your Campaigns

- Before sending your emails to your entire list, always conduct A/B tests to determine what works best. Test subject lines, email copy, CTA buttons, and design elements to see what resonates most with your audience.

- **Metrics to Track:**

  - **Open Rate**: The percentage of subscribers who open your email. A low open rate may indicate that your subject line or pre-header text needs improvement.

  - **Click-Through Rate (CTR)**: The percentage of recipients who click on a link or CTA in your email. A high CTR means your email content is engaging and compelling.

  - **Conversion Rate**: The percentage of recipients who take the desired action, such as making a purchase or signing up for a webinar.

  - **Unsubscribe Rate**: The percentage of recipients who opt out of your emails. A high unsubscribe rate can signal that your emails aren't relevant to your audience.

7. Monitor Campaign Performance

- Once your campaigns are live, track their performance using the analytics tools provided by your email marketing platform. This data can help you identify which aspects of your campaigns are working and where improvements are needed.

o Continuously refine your email automation based on data, customer feedback, and industry best practices.

Best Practices for Email Automation

- **Personalization**: Use your subscribers' names, personalize content based on past behavior, and send relevant offers to increase engagement.

- **Timing**: Automate email sends based on optimal times for your audience. Experiment with different times of day and days of the week to find the best windows for engagement.

- **Compliance**: Ensure your emails comply with laws like GDPR and CAN-SPAM, which require you to obtain consent from subscribers and allow them to opt out easily.

Conclusion

Automating email campaigns is an essential skill for any business looking to build strong relationships with its audience, generate leads, and increase sales. By selecting the right tools, segmenting your audience, designing engaging emails, and optimizing performance through continuous testing, you can create highly effective email campaigns that reach the right people at the right time. Automation saves time, ensures consistency, and enhances the customer experience, all while driving business success.

Part 36: Crafting PowerPoint Presentation

PowerPoint presentations are a fundamental tool in business, education, and personal communication. Whether you're pitching a new idea, teaching a class, or presenting findings, the ability to craft effective and engaging PowerPoint slides is essential. A well-designed presentation can captivate your audience, convey your message clearly, and leave a lasting impression.

In this section, we will explore the key aspects of crafting PowerPoint presentations, covering design principles, content organization, visual elements, and tips for engaging your audience.

Why Crafting Effective PowerPoint Presentations Matters

Creating an impactful PowerPoint presentation goes beyond just putting together slides with text and images. It's about designing a visual experience that complements your spoken words, enhances understanding, and keeps your audience engaged throughout the presentation. Here are a few reasons why creating a powerful PowerPoint presentation is crucial:

1. **Clarity of Message**: A well-crafted presentation ensures that your ideas are communicated clearly and concisely, reducing confusion and making your message more memorable.

2. **Engagement**: Visual elements, storytelling, and design strategies can help maintain your audience's interest and engagement, preventing them from losing focus during long presentations.

3. **Professionalism**: A polished, thoughtfully designed presentation conveys professionalism, showing that you have put effort into delivering your message effectively.

4. **Impactful Storytelling**: PowerPoint allows you to tell a story visually through images, videos, and animations, which can make your content more compelling and impactful.

Steps for Crafting a Successful PowerPoint Presentation

Creating a great PowerPoint presentation involves several key steps, from planning your content to refining the design elements. Below, we'll break down the process.

1. Start with Clear Objectives

Before you begin designing your slides, define the objective of your presentation. Ask yourself:

- **What do I want my audience to learn or do after viewing my presentation?**

- **What is the central message I want to convey?**

Setting clear objectives will help you focus on the most important content and avoid overloading your slides with unnecessary information.

2. Organize Content Effectively

A successful presentation is organized logically, guiding your audience through your message without confusion. Structure your content into clear sections, each with a distinct purpose. Typically, a presentation will follow this structure:

- **Introduction**: Introduce yourself, the topic, and the purpose of the presentation. This is where you grab the audience's attention.

- **Main Body**: Break down your content into key points, supporting data, or stories. Organize this section into manageable sections to maintain flow and clarity.

- **Conclusion**: Summarize the key takeaways and provide a call to action or next steps, if applicable.

For each section, ensure that the content flows naturally, with each point building upon the previous one.

3. Choose a Professional Template

The design of your presentation is crucial for creating a professional and cohesive look. While PowerPoint offers a variety of templates, choosing one that complements your message and audience is important. Consider these points:

- **Simple and Clean**: Choose a template with a clean layout that isn't cluttered with unnecessary design elements. This allows your content to stand out.

- **Consistent Colors**: Use a color scheme that aligns with your brand or theme. Stick to a few colors to maintain consistency throughout the presentation.

- **Legibility**: Ensure your text is legible by using high-contrast colors (e.g., dark text on a light background) and large, readable fonts.

- **Branding**: If you're creating a business or corporate presentation, consider using your company's branded template to reinforce professionalism and brand identity.

4. Keep Slides Concise

One of the most common mistakes in PowerPoint presentations is overwhelming the audience with text. Keep your slides concise and use bullet points or short phrases to summarize key points. Avoid long paragraphs of text and focus on making your slides visual aids to support your spoken words.

- **Use Bullet Points**: Break down information into easy-to-read bullet points, highlighting only the most important details.

- **Limit Text**: Aim for no more than 6-7 lines of text per slide. The less text you use, the more attention your audience will give to your speech.

5. Visual Elements and Graphics

Visuals enhance comprehension and engagement. Use images, icons, charts, and graphs to complement your content. Here are some tips for incorporating visuals:

- **Images**: Use high-quality images that are relevant to your message. Images should enhance understanding and illustrate concepts, not just serve as decoration.

- **Charts and Graphs**: Data-heavy presentations benefit from well-designed charts and graphs that simplify complex information and make it easier for the audience to grasp.

- **Icons and Illustrations**: Icons and illustrations can make your presentation more engaging and visually appealing. Use them sparingly to support your message.

6. Incorporating Animations and Transitions

Animations and slide transitions can help keep your audience engaged, but they should be used sparingly and purposefully. Too many flashy animations can be distracting.

- **Simple Animations**: Use animations to emphasize key points or to gradually introduce content to the slide. Avoid excessive movement.

- **Smooth Transitions**: Use simple slide transitions to guide your audience from one section to the next without jarring changes. Choose subtle transitions like "Fade" or "Push" instead of more elaborate effects.

7. Add Multimedia Elements

If appropriate, you can enhance your PowerPoint presentation by adding multimedia elements such as audio and video. These elements can help clarify complex concepts, demonstrate products, or inject energy into your presentation.

- **Videos**: Short video clips that illustrate your points can increase audience retention and keep attention levels high. Be sure to test videos ahead of time to ensure they play smoothly.

- **Audio**: Background music or voice narration can complement the overall presentation. However, ensure that audio does not overpower your voice or distract from your message.

8. Practice Timing and Delivery

Once your PowerPoint slides are ready, practice your delivery. Ensure that the presentation flows smoothly and that you are able to speak confidently without relying heavily on reading from the slides.

- **Timing**: Make sure that you are staying within the allotted time for your presentation. Use the "Rehearse Timings" feature in PowerPoint to time your slides and adjust where necessary.

- **Engage Your Audience**: Use body language, eye contact, and a clear voice to keep your audience engaged. Encourage interaction by asking questions or inviting feedback.

9. Finalizing Your Presentation

Before presenting, take the time to review and finalize your presentation:

- **Proofreading**: Ensure that your content is free from spelling and grammatical errors. Poorly written slides can harm your credibility.

- **Test Your Presentation**: Run through the entire presentation on the device you'll be using to present to make sure everything functions correctly. Check the animations, transitions, and multimedia.

- **Backup**: Always have a backup copy of your presentation stored on a USB drive or cloud storage, in case of technical issues.

Best Practices for Effective PowerPoint Presentations

- **Be Consistent**: Maintain a consistent layout and design across all slides to create a cohesive experience.

- **Focus on Key Points**: Don't overwhelm your audience with too much information. Stick to key takeaways and emphasize the most important points.

- **Engage Your Audience**: Make your presentation interactive by asking questions, incorporating polls, or inviting discussions.

- **Use Simple Fonts**: Choose fonts that are easy to read, such as Arial, Helvetica, or Calibri. Avoid overly decorative fonts that may be hard to read on a screen.

- **Limit the Number of Slides**: Keep your presentation concise by limiting the number of slides to the essentials. Aim for clarity, not quantity.

Conclusion

Crafting a compelling PowerPoint presentation is more than just creating slides—it's about effectively communicating your ideas and engaging your audience. By organizing your content clearly, using visually appealing design elements, and practicing your delivery, you can ensure that your message resonates with your audience. Whether you're presenting to a small group or a large audience, mastering the art of PowerPoint presentations is a valuable skill that will set you apart as a professional communicator.

Part 37: Managing Tasks with Computer Tools

In the fast-paced, ever-evolving world of today, managing tasks efficiently is essential for productivity and success. Whether you're working on personal projects, coordinating with a team, or overseeing a large-scale operation, using the right computer tools can greatly enhance your ability to stay organized, prioritize tasks, and track progress.

This section will explore the various computer tools available for task management, the benefits of digital task management, and how to leverage these tools to stay on top of your responsibilities. From simple to-do lists to advanced project management software, mastering these tools will allow you to streamline your workflows, meet deadlines, and achieve your goals with ease.

Why Managing Tasks with Computer Tools is Essential

1. **Time Management**: The right task management tools can help you stay on top of your priorities and deadlines. By organizing tasks effectively, you reduce the risk of missing deadlines and forgetfulness.

2. **Collaboration**: Many task management tools allow for seamless collaboration, enabling teams to work together efficiently. These tools help in delegating tasks, setting deadlines, tracking progress, and communicating in real-time, regardless of geographical locations.

3. **Task Prioritization**: Task management software enables you to prioritize tasks based on urgency, importance, or deadlines. By organizing tasks into

categories or using methods like the Eisenhower matrix or to-do lists, you can focus on what matters most and avoid feeling overwhelmed.

4. **Increased Productivity**: With task management tools, it's easy to track your progress, see where you need to focus, and avoid distractions. These tools often come with reminders, alerts, and time-tracking features to help you stay on course.

5. **Flexibility**: Digital task management is flexible, allowing for easy modifications, updates, and rescheduling of tasks as circumstances change. Whether you're working on short-term tasks or long-term projects, you can adapt quickly.

Common Task Management Tools and Their Features

There are a variety of tools available to help manage tasks, ranging from simple list-making apps to full-fledged project management platforms. Below are some of the most popular tools for managing tasks:

1. To-Do List Apps

To-do list apps are the simplest form of task management. These tools help you create lists of tasks, set deadlines, and mark off items as you complete them. Some of the most popular to-do list apps include:

- **Todoist**: Todoist is a versatile to-do list tool that helps you organize tasks, set priorities, and track progress. It allows you to categorize tasks with labels, assign due dates, and integrate with other tools such as Google Calendar.

- **Microsoft To Do**: This free task management app integrates with Microsoft 365, providing simple task

311

lists with features like due dates, reminders, and notes. It syncs across devices, making it ideal for personal use.

- **Google Keep**: Google Keep is a note-taking app that also functions as a to-do list. You can create tasks, set reminders, and organize them by color-coded labels for easy tracking.

Key Features:

- Simple and user-friendly interface

- Priority settings and due dates

- Task categorization and labels

- Reminders and alerts

2. Project Management Tools

For more complex projects that involve multiple team members and require detailed tracking, project management software provides a more robust solution. These tools offer features such as task assignments, team collaboration, file sharing, and progress monitoring.

- **Trello**: Trello uses a visual board system to organize tasks into columns or boards. It allows teams to create cards for each task and track progress with due dates, checklists, attachments, and more.

- **Asana**: Asana is a comprehensive project management tool that helps teams plan, track, and manage work. It offers task assignments, project timelines, subtasks, and integrations with other apps like Slack and Google Drive.

- **Monday.com**: This platform is designed for team collaboration and provides a variety of customizable templates for task management. Teams can assign tasks, set due dates, and monitor workflows with visual boards and automated reminders.

Key Features:

- Task assignment and delegation
- Team collaboration and communication
- Visual boards and progress tracking
- File sharing and document management

3. Time Management Tools

Time management tools help you allocate specific time slots for tasks, monitor the time spent on each task, and track your overall productivity. These tools are useful for individuals and teams looking to improve their efficiency.

- **Toggl**: Toggl is a simple time tracking tool that allows you to log time spent on tasks or projects. It helps you measure productivity, identify time sinks, and make adjustments to improve time allocation.

- **RescueTime**: RescueTime runs in the background and tracks how much time you spend on different apps and websites. It provides detailed reports to help you understand where your time is going and suggests improvements to stay focused.

Key Features:

- Time tracking and reporting
- Task categorization and project tracking
- Productivity analytics and insights

4. Collaboration and Communication Tools

Effective task management often requires clear communication between team members. Collaboration tools allow teams to discuss tasks, share updates, and communicate in real-time.

- **Slack**: Slack is a popular communication platform that enables teams to create channels for specific tasks or projects. It integrates with other task management and project management tools, allowing teams to stay up to date with project developments.

- **Microsoft Teams**: Microsoft Teams is a collaboration tool that integrates with the Microsoft 365 suite. It provides chat, video conferencing, and file-sharing features, making it ideal for teams working on tasks together.

- **Basecamp**: Basecamp is a project management and team collaboration tool that helps users manage tasks, communicate, and store files. It combines messaging, task tracking, and scheduling into one platform.

Key Features:

- Instant messaging and communication
- Channel and group discussions
- File sharing and document storage
- Task and project updates

How to Leverage Task Management Tools Effectively

Here are some practical tips for making the most of task management tools:

314

1. **Create Clear Task Categories**: Break tasks into categories based on their priority or type of work (e.g., urgent, medium priority, or low priority). This helps in staying organized and focused on what needs immediate attention.

2. **Set Specific Deadlines and Reminders**: Always set deadlines for each task and use reminders to ensure you don't forget them. Many tools offer automatic notifications or email reminders when tasks are due.

3. **Assign Responsibilities**: If you're working on a team project, assign tasks to the right people. Task management tools allow for easy delegation, ensuring that everyone knows their responsibilities and the status of each task.

4. **Monitor Progress**: Regularly review task completion and overall project progress. This helps to identify any roadblocks or tasks that require attention, allowing you to make adjustments as needed.

5. **Automate Routine Tasks**: Many task management tools allow you to automate routine tasks like recurring deadlines, email alerts, or reminders. Automating repetitive tasks saves time and reduces the chance of overlooking important tasks.

6. **Collaborate and Communicate**: Use collaboration features like comments, file sharing, and messaging to keep everyone on the same page. Constant communication ensures that all team members are informed about task updates and progress.

7. **Review and Reflect**: At the end of each week or month, take the time to review your completed tasks, evaluate your efficiency, and identify areas for

improvement. This reflection helps you optimize your task management approach.

Conclusion

Managing tasks efficiently is essential for staying organized, meeting deadlines, and ensuring that you or your team are moving forward with clarity and purpose. Whether you're managing personal to-do lists or complex team projects, computer tools offer a wide range of solutions to improve task management. By choosing the right tools, setting clear goals, and consistently tracking your progress, you can ensure that your tasks are handled effectively and that your productivity remains high.

Part 38: Creating an Online Store

In today's digital age, e-commerce is booming, and creating an online store is an excellent way to start a business, reach global customers, and build a sustainable brand. Whether you're selling physical products, digital goods, or services, setting up an online store can provide you with the tools and infrastructure you need to manage transactions, track inventory, and communicate with customers.

This section will guide you through the process of creating your own online store, from choosing the right platform to designing your website, managing products, and ensuring a smooth customer experience. You will learn about the various options for building an online store, how to set up payment gateways, and how to optimize your store for search engines to drive traffic.

Why You Should Create an Online Store

1. **Access to a Global Market**: With an online store, you are no longer limited to local customers. You can reach a worldwide audience, which significantly expands your potential customer base.

2. **Low Overhead Costs**: Operating an online store often comes with lower overhead costs than a physical store. There's no need to rent a space or maintain large inventory in a storefront, which means you can operate with fewer expenses.

3. **24/7 Availability**: An online store is open 24/7, allowing customers to browse and shop at their convenience, regardless of time zones. This is a huge advantage over physical stores that have limited hours.

4. **Better Customer Insights**: With e-commerce, you can track and analyze customer behavior, including what products they are interested in, how much time they spend on your site, and their purchasing habits. This data allows you to refine your marketing and sales strategies.

5. **Scalability**: As your business grows, your online store can easily be scaled to handle more products, more traffic, and more orders. E-commerce platforms often offer features that allow for growth without the need for a complete overhaul.

Steps to Create an Online Store

1. Choose the Right E-commerce Platform

Selecting the best platform for building your online store is crucial to its success. There are several popular e-commerce platforms available, each offering different features, ease of use, and pricing structures.

- **Shopify**: Shopify is a user-friendly and highly customizable platform designed specifically for e-commerce. It offers everything from product management and payment gateways to customizable themes and analytics. Shopify is ideal for those who want to start quickly with minimal technical knowledge.

- **WooCommerce**: WooCommerce is a free WordPress plugin that transforms a WordPress website into an online store. It's highly customizable and great for those who are already familiar with WordPress. WooCommerce allows you to sell physical and digital products and supports multiple payment gateways.

- **Wix**: Wix is an easy-to-use website builder that also offers e-commerce capabilities. It's perfect for beginners and offers drag-and-drop functionality, making it simple to design your store without any coding experience.

- **BigCommerce**: BigCommerce is another robust e-commerce platform that is ideal for medium to large businesses. It offers scalability, a wide range of templates, and integrates well with various third-party apps.

Choosing the Right Platform:

- Consider your technical knowledge. If you want ease of use, Shopify or Wix may be better choices.

- If you want more customization options and have experience with WordPress, WooCommerce is a great option.

- Think about your store's growth potential. If you plan on scaling quickly, consider BigCommerce or Shopify, which are designed for growth.

2. Design Your Store

The design of your online store plays a critical role in attracting and retaining customers. A clean, user-friendly, and professional-looking design will encourage customers to browse and complete their purchases.

- **Choose a Template**: Most e-commerce platforms offer a variety of templates, which you can customize to suit your brand's identity. Choose a template that aligns with the type of products you sell and provides a seamless shopping experience.

- **Brand Identity**: Your store design should reflect your brand's personality. Use your brand's colors, logo, and fonts consistently across your website to create a cohesive look.

- **User Experience (UX)**: The layout of your store should be intuitive. Make sure that product categories are clearly defined, search functions are easy to use, and the checkout process is straightforward. A complicated website can lead to abandoned shopping carts.

- **Mobile Optimization**: Ensure that your online store is mobile-friendly, as many customers now shop via smartphones and tablets. Most e-commerce platforms offer responsive templates that adjust to mobile devices.

3. Add Products

Once your store is set up, you can start adding products. The more detailed the product information, the better your customers will be able to make informed purchasing decisions.

- **Product Images**: High-quality images are essential for online stores. Customers can't physically touch or try on products, so high-resolution images that show multiple angles of the product will help build trust and encourage purchases.

- **Product Descriptions**: Write clear, concise, and persuasive product descriptions. Highlight the features, benefits, and specifications of each product. Be sure to include keywords that will help your products rank well in search engines.

- **Pricing**: Be competitive with your pricing, taking into account production costs, competitor pricing, and market demand. Make sure that your prices are clearly displayed and include any shipping or taxes where applicable.

- **Inventory Management**: Keep track of your inventory to avoid overselling products. Most e-commerce platforms offer inventory management features that automatically update stock levels.

4. Set Up Payment Gateways

To accept payments from customers, you'll need to integrate payment gateways into your online store. These gateways process transactions and securely handle payments.

- **PayPal**: PayPal is one of the most widely used payment gateways. It allows customers to pay using their PayPal balance, credit cards, or debit cards.

- **Stripe**: Stripe is another popular payment gateway that allows you to accept credit card payments directly on your site. It is known for its ease of integration and security.

- **Credit/Debit Card Payments**: Some platforms allow you to integrate credit card payment options directly. Make sure your payment process is secure by using SSL certificates to encrypt customer data.

- **Alternative Payment Options**: Consider offering additional payment methods such as Google Pay, Apple Pay, or Buy Now, Pay Later services to cater to different customer preferences.

5. Set Up Shipping and Taxes

Once you have your payment gateway set up, you will need to determine how to handle shipping and taxes.

- **Shipping**: You can set up flat-rate shipping, charge based on the weight of the order, or use real-time shipping rates from carriers like FedEx, UPS, or USPS. You'll also need to decide whether to offer free shipping, discounted shipping, or international shipping.

- **Taxes**: Sales tax regulations vary by region and country. Use your platform's built-in tax features to automatically calculate sales tax based on the customer's location.

6. Launch and Market Your Store

Now that your store is ready, it's time to launch! However, the work doesn't stop there. You'll need to market your store and drive traffic to it.

- **Search Engine Optimization (SEO)**: Optimize your website's content, product descriptions, and images to rank well in search engine results. Use relevant keywords that your target customers are likely to search for.

- **Social Media Marketing**: Leverage social media platforms like Instagram, Facebook, and Pinterest to promote your products. Social media ads can target specific demographics and interests, which can help you reach the right audience.

- **Email Marketing**: Build an email list and send out newsletters, special promotions, or product updates to your subscribers. Personalized email campaigns can help boost sales and customer loyalty.

- **Influencer Marketing**: Partner with influencers or bloggers who align with your brand and can promote your products to their followers.

7. Monitor and Optimize

After launching your online store, continue to monitor its performance. Use analytics tools to track metrics such as website traffic, conversion rates, bounce rates, and sales. Based on these insights, you can make adjustments to your website design, marketing strategies, or product offerings to improve your store's performance.

Conclusion

Creating an online store opens up a world of opportunities for entrepreneurs and businesses. By following the steps outlined above, you can launch a professional-looking, user-friendly e-commerce website and start selling products online. Remember, the success of your online store depends not only on your store's design and product offerings but also on your ability to drive traffic, market effectively, and continuously optimize your store to meet customer expectations.

Part 39: Analyzing Data for Business Decisions

Data analysis has become a fundamental aspect of business decision-making in the modern world. In today's digital age, businesses are overwhelmed with vast amounts of data. The ability to analyze this data effectively can give businesses a competitive edge by improving decision-making, boosting efficiency, and fostering innovation. This section will focus on the importance of analyzing data for business decisions, methods of analyzing data, and the tools that can help you extract meaningful insights to guide your strategies.

Why Data Analysis is Critical for Business Decisions

1. **Informed Decision-Making**: Data-driven decisions are far more reliable than those made based on intuition alone. By analyzing past performance, market trends, and customer behaviors, businesses can make predictions about future outcomes and adjust their strategies accordingly.

2. **Identifying Business Opportunities**: Data analysis helps businesses spot emerging trends and new opportunities. By examining customer preferences, purchasing habits, and industry developments, companies can capitalize on new market opportunities and expand their offerings.

3. **Improving Operational Efficiency**: Analyzing operational data helps identify inefficiencies within processes. By understanding which areas are underperforming, businesses can streamline their

operations, reduce costs, and allocate resources more effectively.

4. **Enhancing Customer Experience**: Data analysis allows businesses to understand their customers better, which can lead to improved customer experiences. By tracking customer satisfaction, behavior, and feedback, businesses can tailor their products, services, and marketing strategies to meet customer expectations more effectively.

5. **Competitive Advantage**: Businesses that can harness the power of data are better positioned to outperform competitors. By monitoring competitors, analyzing market trends, and adjusting business strategies in real-time, companies can stay ahead of the curve.

6. **Risk Management**: Data analysis helps in assessing risks, such as market fluctuations, supply chain disruptions, and customer churn. By predicting potential risks, businesses can take preventive measures and mitigate negative impacts.

Steps for Analyzing Data for Business Decisions

1. Define Your Goals and Questions

Before diving into data analysis, it's essential to define the goals of your analysis and the questions you want to answer. Data analysis is most effective when it's focused on specific business objectives. These could include:

- Improving sales performance
- Optimizing marketing campaigns
- Identifying cost-saving opportunities
- Enhancing customer retention

Clearly defining your goals will help you focus on the most relevant data, avoid unnecessary distractions, and increase the chances of drawing meaningful insights.

2. Collect the Right Data

Data analysis begins with the collection of relevant data. Businesses can gather data from various sources, including:

- **Sales Data**: Information on transactions, customer behavior, and product performance.

- **Customer Data**: Demographic details, feedback, reviews, and interaction history.

- **Website Analytics**: Traffic patterns, conversion rates, and user behaviors on your website.

- **Financial Data**: Profit and loss statements, balance sheets, and cash flow reports.

- **Market Data**: Trends, competitor performance, and industry benchmarks.

Data should be collected in a structured way, ensuring that it is clean, accurate, and relevant to the business objectives. The use of customer relationship management (CRM) tools, data warehousing systems, and other automated data collection methods can help businesses collect large volumes of data efficiently.

3. Clean and Prepare the Data

Raw data is often messy, incomplete, or inconsistent. Cleaning and preparing the data is a critical step before analysis can begin. This process involves:

- **Handling Missing Data**: Missing data can skew results. Depending on the nature of the missing data, you can either remove it, fill it in with estimates, or use other techniques to account for it.

- **Standardizing Formats**: Ensuring consistency in units, formats, and measurements across all data sources.

- **Removing Outliers**: Outliers are extreme values that can distort the analysis. Identifying and handling them can help improve the accuracy of results.

- **Consolidating Data**: If data is stored in multiple places, it may need to be consolidated into a single format or database for easier analysis.

4. Analyze the Data

Once the data is cleaned and prepared, it's time to analyze it. There are several methods and techniques for analyzing business data, depending on the type of data and the insights you want to obtain.

- **Descriptive Analysis**: This involves summarizing and describing the main features of a dataset. Common techniques include calculating averages, percentages, and trends. Descriptive statistics help businesses understand what has happened in the past.

- **Diagnostic Analysis**: Diagnostic analysis seeks to explain why something has happened. For example, if sales have declined, diagnostic analysis could explore factors like changes in consumer preferences, marketing effectiveness, or competitor activities.

- **Predictive Analysis**: Predictive analysis uses historical data to forecast future trends. Using machine learning algorithms and statistical models, businesses can predict customer behavior, demand fluctuations, and potential risks.

- **Prescriptive Analysis**: Prescriptive analysis goes beyond predictions by offering recommendations for future actions. Using optimization techniques, it helps businesses decide the best course of action to achieve their goals, such as improving sales or reducing costs.

- **Sentiment Analysis**: This technique analyzes customer feedback, reviews, and social media mentions to determine the general sentiment toward a product, service, or brand. It provides insight into customer satisfaction and loyalty.

5. Visualize the Data

Data visualization is the process of representing data in graphical form. Visualizing data helps to identify patterns, trends, and outliers quickly. Common tools for data visualization include:

- **Charts and Graphs**: Bar charts, pie charts, line graphs, and histograms are simple ways to represent trends, comparisons, and distributions.

- **Dashboards**: Dashboards aggregate key metrics and display them in real-time, allowing businesses to monitor performance at a glance. Many businesses use platforms like Tableau, Power BI, or Google Data Studio to create customized dashboards.

- **Heat Maps**: Heat maps visualize the intensity of data across a geographic area or within specific segments, making it easier to spot patterns.

6. Interpret the Results

After conducting the analysis and visualizing the data, the next step is to interpret the results. Interpretation involves understanding what the data is telling you and how it can inform business decisions. It's essential to ask questions like:

- What does this data tell me about the market, my customers, and my operations?

- Are there any clear trends or patterns that can guide future strategies?

- What are the implications of this data for the short-term and long-term goals?

This step also involves communicating the findings clearly to stakeholders, ensuring that decision-makers can understand the insights and act upon them.

7. Make Data-Driven Decisions

The ultimate goal of data analysis is to make informed business decisions that improve outcomes. Using the insights gained from data analysis, businesses can make decisions in areas such as:

- **Product Development**: Analyze customer feedback and sales data to identify opportunities for product improvements or new product offerings.

- **Marketing Strategies**: Optimize marketing campaigns by analyzing customer behavior, targeting the right audience, and improving messaging based on data insights.

- **Operational Efficiency**: Streamline operations by identifying bottlenecks, inefficiencies, or cost-saving opportunities through data analysis.

- **Financial Management**: Make more accurate financial projections, allocate resources effectively, and manage cash flow by analyzing financial data.

Tools for Data Analysis

There are many tools available to help businesses analyze data effectively:

- **Microsoft Excel**: One of the most widely used tools for basic data analysis. It offers various functions for data manipulation, pivot tables, and basic statistical analysis.

- **Google Analytics**: Used for analyzing website data, Google Analytics provides insights into traffic sources, user behavior, and conversion rates.

- **Tableau**: A powerful data visualization tool that helps create interactive dashboards and reports.

- **Power BI**: A Microsoft tool that integrates well with Excel and other business applications to create advanced visualizations and reports.

- **SPSS and SAS**: Used for more advanced statistical analysis and modeling.

Conclusion

Data analysis is an invaluable skill in today's business world. By effectively analyzing data, businesses can make informed decisions that drive growth, increase efficiency, and improve customer satisfaction. By following the steps outlined in this section, you can gain the insights you need to make data-driven decisions that will positively impact your business's bottom line. Whether you are just starting or looking to enhance your analytical skills, mastering data analysis tools and techniques will empower you to make smarter, more strategic business choices.

Part 40: Managing Customer Relations Digitally

In the modern business landscape, effective customer relationship management (CRM) is a cornerstone of success. As businesses continue to expand their digital footprint, managing customer relations digitally has become not only a necessity but also a competitive advantage. By leveraging technology, companies can build stronger, more personalized connections with customers, improve customer satisfaction, and enhance retention rates. This section will explore how businesses can utilize digital tools and strategies to manage customer relations effectively, including CRM software, data analytics, automation, and customer service best practices.

The Importance of Managing Customer Relations Digitally

1. **Enhanced Customer Experience**: Digital customer relationship management tools allow businesses to personalize communication, offer tailored solutions, and respond to customers in real-time. By analyzing customer data, businesses can offer targeted services that meet specific needs and preferences, improving customer satisfaction.

2. **Streamlined Communication**: Digital platforms make it easier for businesses to communicate with customers across multiple channels, such as email, live chat, social media, and mobile apps. This ensures that customers can reach the business in a way that is most convenient for them, enhancing the overall experience.

3. **Improved Customer Retention**: By continuously tracking and nurturing relationships with customers through digital platforms, businesses can build long-lasting connections and loyalty. Digital CRM tools can help businesses proactively address issues, anticipate customer needs, and offer solutions that keep customers engaged and satisfied.

4. **Efficiency and Cost-Effectiveness**: Digital tools automate repetitive tasks, such as follow-up emails, appointment reminders, and customer support, which saves time and reduces operational costs. Automation also ensures that businesses can handle large volumes of customer interactions without compromising on quality.

5. **Data-Driven Insights**: Digital CRM tools gather and store valuable data on customer behaviors, preferences, and interactions. This data allows businesses to make informed decisions, tailor marketing efforts, and identify opportunities to improve products and services.

6. **Scalability**: As businesses grow, managing customer relationships manually becomes increasingly difficult. Digital CRM systems scale seamlessly to accommodate more customers, ensuring that businesses can maintain high-quality relationships as their customer base expands.

Key Digital Tools for Managing Customer Relations

1. Customer Relationship Management (CRM) Software

CRM software is the most powerful tool for managing customer relationships digitally. These platforms centralize all customer data and interactions in one place, providing businesses with a comprehensive view of each customer. Some of the most popular CRM tools include:

- **Salesforce**: Known for its robust features, Salesforce offers a cloud-based CRM solution that integrates with other business tools, allowing businesses to manage sales, customer service, marketing, and more.

- **HubSpot CRM**: HubSpot is a user-friendly CRM system designed for businesses of all sizes. It offers tools for sales automation, marketing, and customer service, along with reporting and analytics capabilities.

- **Zoho CRM**: Zoho CRM is a versatile platform that helps businesses manage customer relationships through features such as lead and contact management, sales forecasting, and multichannel communication.

- **Microsoft Dynamics 365**: A comprehensive CRM tool that integrates well with other Microsoft Office products, allowing businesses to manage customer interactions, sales, and marketing efforts.

CRM software allows businesses to track and manage customer inquiries, sales, follow-ups, and customer service requests, ensuring that each interaction is recorded and no opportunities are missed.

2. Email Marketing Automation

Email marketing is a critical component of digital customer relationship management. Automating email campaigns allows businesses to engage customers with personalized content, promotions, and updates without needing to manually send each message. Email marketing automation platforms include:

- **Mailchimp**: Mailchimp offers email marketing automation, segmentation, and analytics tools. It allows businesses to create personalized email campaigns based on customer behavior and preferences.

- **ActiveCampaign**: ActiveCampaign combines email marketing with automation and CRM tools. It enables businesses to automate customer journeys and send targeted emails at the right time.

- **Sendinblue**: A comprehensive email marketing platform, Sendinblue offers tools for automation, SMS marketing, and transactional emails, helping businesses build stronger relationships with customers.

3. Live Chat and Chatbots

In today's fast-paced world, customers expect immediate responses to their inquiries. Live chat and chatbots provide instant communication between businesses and customers, helping address issues quickly and efficiently. Popular tools include:

- **Zendesk Chat**: A live chat software solution that allows businesses to offer real-time support to customers on their websites, helping resolve issues immediately.

- **Intercom**: A customer messaging platform that offers live chat, chatbots, and messaging automation, allowing businesses to engage customers across multiple channels and provide personalized support.

- **Tidio**: Tidio offers live chat and chatbot solutions to help businesses automate responses and provide round-the-clock support, ensuring customers can get assistance whenever they need it.

Live chat and chatbots streamline customer service by providing instant responses to customer inquiries, helping resolve issues quickly and improving overall satisfaction.

4. Social Media Management Tools

Social media is a powerful platform for engaging with customers and building relationships. Managing customer interactions across multiple social media channels can be challenging, but social media management tools make it easier. Tools like:

- **Hootsuite**: A social media management platform that allows businesses to schedule posts, monitor conversations, and track performance across social media platforms.

- **Buffer**: Buffer helps businesses manage social media content, track engagement, and analyze performance across Facebook, Instagram, Twitter, and LinkedIn.

- **Sprout Social**: A social media management tool that offers features for publishing, monitoring, and reporting on social media activities, helping businesses engage with customers and analyze their social media presence.

Social media management tools enable businesses to maintain consistent communication with customers, address inquiries, and respond to feedback, all while improving engagement.

5. Customer Feedback Tools

Understanding customer satisfaction and identifying areas for improvement is crucial for maintaining strong relationships. Digital feedback tools help businesses collect insights directly from customers. Popular tools include:

- **SurveyMonkey**: A platform that enables businesses to create surveys and collect customer feedback on a variety of topics, from product quality to customer service experiences.

- **Typeform**: Typeform helps businesses create user-friendly surveys, quizzes, and forms that engage customers and gather valuable feedback.

- **Qualtrics**: A powerful tool for collecting and analyzing customer feedback, Qualtrics provides businesses with actionable insights to improve products, services, and customer relationships.

Collecting customer feedback is essential for improving relationships. Feedback tools allow businesses to monitor customer satisfaction and adjust their strategies based on insights.

6. Customer Support Platforms

A strong customer support system is essential for digital customer relationship management. Platforms such as:

- **Freshdesk**: Freshdesk provides tools for managing customer support tickets, organizing inquiries, and automating responses, ensuring that customers receive timely assistance.

- **Zoho Desk**: Zoho Desk is a helpdesk software that helps businesses track and manage customer queries, ensuring that each ticket is addressed promptly.

- **Help Scout**: Help Scout offers email-based customer support, live chat, and collaboration features, helping businesses provide excellent support and maintain strong customer relations.

Customer support platforms help businesses manage and resolve customer issues quickly, ensuring that customers feel heard and valued.

Best Practices for Managing Customer Relations Digitally

1. **Personalize Interactions**: Use customer data to personalize interactions, whether it's through targeted emails, personalized recommendations, or customized responses. Personalization builds stronger connections with customers.

2. **Respond Promptly**: In the digital world, customers expect fast responses. Use live chat, chatbots, and automated email systems to provide quick replies to customer inquiries.

3. **Be Proactive**: Monitor customer behavior and anticipate their needs. Proactively reach out to offer assistance, updates, or solutions before issues arise.

4. **Collect and Act on Feedback**: Regularly collect customer feedback and use it to improve products, services, and processes. Customers appreciate when their input is valued and acted upon.

5. **Maintain Consistency Across Channels**: Ensure that your brand messaging, tone, and customer service are consistent across all digital channels, including email, social media, live chat, and your website.

6. **Provide Self-Service Options**: Empower customers to solve issues on their own with knowledge bases, FAQs, and instructional videos. Offering self-service options enhances customer satisfaction and reduces the need for direct support.

Conclusion

Managing customer relations digitally has transformed how businesses interact with and serve their customers. By utilizing CRM tools, email marketing, live chat, social media management, and customer feedback platforms, businesses can build stronger, more personalized relationships that lead to improved customer satisfaction and loyalty. Embracing these digital tools not only enhances operational efficiency but also provides businesses with the insights needed to make data-driven decisions and maintain a competitive edge in the marketplace. Digital customer relationship management is no longer optional—it's essential for thriving in the digital economy.

Introduction to Section 5: Educational Tools

In the ever-evolving digital age, technology has revolutionized the way we learn and teach. Whether you're an educator, student, or lifelong learner, educational tools have become indispensable in facilitating knowledge acquisition and skill development. This section, "Educational Tools," is designed to guide you through the vast array of digital tools available for enhancing education, both inside and outside the classroom.

Educational tools empower users to engage with content in interactive, creative, and efficient ways. From learning management systems (LMS) that streamline course delivery, to tools for creating interactive content, and resources that aid in collaboration and knowledge sharing, these tools are transforming traditional educational practices. They allow educators to personalize learning experiences for students, track progress, and adapt to varying learning styles. For learners, these tools provide opportunities to access resources, collaborate with peers, and engage in a self-paced, interactive environment.

In this section, we will explore a wide variety of educational tools tailored for different learning environments and objectives. Topics covered will include tools for creating engaging digital lessons, platforms for interactive learning, collaborative tools for group projects, and software that helps both teachers and students assess and track educational progress. Whether you're looking to create compelling educational content, manage learning experiences, or improve teaching efficiency, this section will provide you with the knowledge and resources to leverage digital tools in meaningful and effective ways.

By the end of this section, you'll have a comprehensive understanding of the tools that can enhance educational processes, foster better engagement, and contribute to more effective learning outcomes. Whether you're a teacher seeking to improve classroom interaction, a student aiming to excel in your studies, or someone passionate about lifelong learning, the tools explored here will equip you with the essential digital skills to navigate today's educational landscape. Let's embark on a journey to explore the world of educational technology and unlock the potential of digital learning!

Part 41: Designing Flashcards for Study

Flashcards have long been an effective tool for reinforcing memory and enhancing learning. Their simplicity, versatility, and effectiveness make them an invaluable resource for students of all ages, from elementary school to graduate-level studies. With the advancements in technology, creating flashcards is no longer limited to paper and pen. Digital flashcards allow for greater flexibility, customization, and accessibility, making studying more efficient and interactive.

In this section, we will guide you through the process of designing flashcards for study, focusing on how to leverage both traditional and digital tools for creating flashcards that are not only effective but also engaging. Whether you are studying for a language exam, preparing for a professional certification, or memorizing historical facts, flashcards can be tailored to meet your specific needs.

Why Use Flashcards for Studying?

Flashcards are a simple yet powerful tool for reinforcing knowledge and improving recall. Here are some reasons why flashcards are effective for studying:

1. **Active Recall**: Flashcards are a prime example of the active recall method, where learners retrieve information from memory rather than passively reading notes. This strengthens neural connections and aids long-term retention.

2. **Spaced Repetition**: When used with a spaced repetition system (SRS), flashcards can optimize

learning by repeating information at increasing intervals, which helps prevent forgetting.

3. **Focused Learning**: Flashcards allow learners to focus on individual concepts, helping break down complex material into digestible, bite-sized pieces.

4. **Portable and Convenient**: Digital flashcards are easily accessible on your phone, tablet, or computer, allowing you to study on the go, at any time.

5. **Customization**: Flashcards can be tailored to fit any subject, learning level, or personal preference. You can incorporate images, sounds, and even videos to make them more engaging.

Designing Flashcards for Effective Study

When designing flashcards, it's important to focus on the content, structure, and presentation to maximize their effectiveness. Below are key tips for creating the most effective study flashcards:

1. Keep it Simple and Focused

Each flashcard should focus on a single concept, term, or question. Avoid overcrowding the card with too much information. The key is to break down larger topics into smaller chunks to facilitate easier learning.

Example:

- **Front**: "What is the capital of France?"

- **Back**: "Paris"

2. Use Clear and Concise Language

Ensure that the language you use on the flashcards is clear and easy to understand. Avoid jargon, complex sentence structures, and excessive details. The goal is to prompt a simple recall of the key information.

Example:

- **Front**: "What is the formula for the area of a triangle?"
- **Back**: "Area = ½ × base × height"

3. Incorporate Visuals

For visual learners, adding images, diagrams, or charts to the flashcards can enhance comprehension and memory. A picture can often convey complex concepts more effectively than words alone.

Example:

- **Front**: Image of a triangle with labeled base and height.
- **Back**: "Area = ½ × base × height"

4. Use Mnemonics and Memory Aids

Mnemonics or memory aids can be incorporated into the flashcards to help recall complex information. Rhymes, acronyms, or funny associations can make studying more enjoyable and memorable.

Example:

- **Front**: "What is the acronym for the Great Lakes?"
- **Back**: "HOMES (Huron, Ontario, Michigan, Erie, Superior)"

5. Include Question-and-Answer Format

Flashcards are most effective when structured as a question on the front and the answer on the back. This reinforces active recall and helps test your knowledge.

Example:

- **Front**: "What is the Pythagorean theorem?"
- **Back**: "$a^2 + b^2 = c^2$"

Digital Flashcards Tools

While traditional paper flashcards are great, digital tools offer many advantages, such as portability, accessibility, and the ability to use multimedia elements (images, audio, etc.). There are several digital tools and apps that make designing and studying with flashcards even easier:

1. Anki

Anki is a powerful flashcard app that uses spaced repetition to help you memorize information more effectively. It allows users to create custom decks, add multimedia (images, audio, and videos), and sync across multiple devices. Anki is ideal for long-term memorization and is widely used by students in fields such as medicine, languages, and law.

2. Quizlet

Quizlet is another popular flashcard tool that allows users to create flashcards, access shared decks, and play interactive study games. It also supports various study modes such as "Learn," "Write," and "Test," making it a versatile tool for students. The "Match" game is particularly fun for reinforcing your learning while challenging your recall speed.

3. Cram

Cram is a simple-to-use flashcard tool that offers both digital and printable flashcards. It allows users to organize flashcards into folders and track progress. It also provides a "Cram mode" that helps with repetition and memorization.

4. Brainscape

Brainscape uses a unique method of spaced repetition to help you memorize faster. You can create flashcards or search for pre-made decks on various subjects. The app tracks your learning progress, so you can focus on the areas where you need the most improvement.

5. StudyBlue

StudyBlue is another app that allows users to create digital flashcards, share them with others, and track their study progress. It also supports multimedia, so you can include images and audio to make your flashcards more interactive.

Interactive Flashcard Tips

While designing digital flashcards, you can also incorporate interactive elements to make the study process more engaging. Here are some ideas to consider:

1. **Audio**: For subjects like language learning, adding pronunciation or sound clips can enhance recall. For example, add a sound clip on the back of a flashcard with a word in the target language.

2. **Animations or GIFs**: Use simple animations or GIFs to illustrate complex concepts, such as chemical reactions or biological processes.

3. **Multiple Choice or Fill-in-the-Blank**: Instead of just using a question-answer format, include multiple-choice questions or fill-in-the-blank questions to provide additional variety and test comprehension.

4. **Progress Tracking**: Many digital flashcard apps track your learning progress, so you can focus on weaker

areas. Make sure to regularly review the flashcards marked as "difficult."

Using Flashcards with Spaced Repetition

To maximize the effectiveness of flashcards, use a spaced repetition system (SRS). SRS algorithms optimize the timing of when you should review each flashcard based on how well you know the content. If you find a card easy, you'll review it less frequently. If you struggle with a card, you'll review it more often until it is fully memorized.

Most digital flashcard apps, such as Anki and Quizlet, incorporate spaced repetition, allowing you to track your progress and adapt the frequency of reviews.

Conclusion

Designing effective flashcards is an excellent way to reinforce learning and boost retention. Whether you are preparing for exams, learning a new language, or mastering a complex subject, flashcards can help simplify the process and make studying more efficient. By keeping the content simple, using visuals and mnemonic devices, and leveraging digital tools, you can create flashcards that cater to your specific learning style. By using flashcards consistently with spaced repetition, you can enhance your memory and achieve your study goals faster and more effectively.

Figure 26: Online Quiz

Part 42: Creating Online Quizzes

Creating online quizzes is a powerful and engaging way to assess knowledge, reinforce learning, and gather feedback. Whether you're an educator, a business owner, or just someone interested in sharing knowledge, online quizzes offer a flexible platform for creating interactive, fun, and informative tests.

In this section, we will explore the process of designing effective online quizzes, provide practical tips for structuring your quizzes, and introduce popular online quiz-making tools. Whether you want to test knowledge in a classroom, engage your audience for marketing purposes, or design a fun quiz for a website, we've got you covered.

Why Create Online Quizzes?

Online quizzes have a wide range of benefits, making them an excellent tool for various purposes:

1. **Engagement and Interaction**: Quizzes can make learning and engagement more interactive and enjoyable. They can break the monotony of traditional learning methods and offer a fun challenge for users.

2. **Instant Feedback**: With online quizzes, users can receive instant feedback, making the learning process more dynamic and informative. Immediate results help learners understand where they need improvement and guide their next steps.

3. **Customization**: Online quizzes can be easily tailored to different topics, difficulty levels, and target audiences, offering flexibility for both the creator and the participant.

4. **Data Collection and Analysis**: Quizzes can be used to gather valuable data. This is especially useful in business settings where feedback and responses can guide product development, marketing strategies, and customer satisfaction analysis.

5. **Easy Distribution**: Online quizzes are accessible from anywhere, anytime, as long as there is an internet connection. They can be shared via social media,

websites, email, or through embedded links, making them highly accessible.

6. **Scalability**: Unlike traditional paper-based quizzes, online quizzes can be taken by a virtually unlimited number of participants without the need for additional effort from the quiz creator.

Types of Online Quizzes

When creating online quizzes, it's essential to consider the type of quiz you want to create. Here are some common types of online quizzes:

- **Multiple Choice**: Participants select the correct answer from a list of options. This type of quiz is ideal for testing factual knowledge.

- **True or False**: Participants answer with either "True" or "False." These quizzes are quick and effective for testing simple knowledge.

- **Fill in the Blanks**: Participants are asked to fill in missing words or phrases, testing their recall and understanding of the material.

- **Matching**: Participants match items from two lists. This is a great way to test associations or relationships between concepts.

- **Open-Ended**: Participants provide a free-text response, making it useful for testing comprehension or critical thinking.

- **Image-Based**: This type of quiz uses images instead of text, such as identifying landmarks, animals, or products. It's great for more visually focused topics.

- **Ranking/Rating**: Participants rank or rate items according to certain criteria, useful for gathering opinions or preferences.

Steps for Creating an Online Quiz

Creating a successful online quiz involves careful planning and attention to detail. Follow these steps to ensure that your quiz is both effective and engaging.

1. Define the Purpose of the Quiz

Before you start creating a quiz, define its purpose. Ask yourself:

- Is this quiz meant to assess knowledge or serve as a learning tool?

- Are you gathering feedback or measuring engagement?

- Is it for fun or a serious assessment?

Knowing the purpose will help you design a quiz that meets your objectives.

2. Choose the Topic and Scope

Select a topic that aligns with your purpose. Whether you're creating a quiz to test knowledge on a subject, to promote a product, or for entertainment purposes, make sure the topic is relevant to your audience.

Determine the scope of the quiz—whether it's covering a broad subject or a narrow niche—and set a clear boundary for the amount of information you want to test. A quiz should be neither too long nor too short; aim for a manageable number of questions (e.g., 10-20).

3. Create the Quiz Questions

Write clear, concise questions that match the difficulty level of your audience. Here are some tips for crafting great quiz questions:

- Use clear and simple language.

- Keep the questions relevant to the topic.

- Avoid tricky or misleading questions.

- Mix question types (multiple choice, true/false, open-ended) to maintain variety and engagement.

Make sure each question is valuable to the quiz's overall goal. For example, if you're assessing knowledge, ensure the questions are challenging but not too difficult. If you want to gauge opinion, use rating or ranking questions.

4. Craft Engaging Answer Options

For multiple-choice or true/false questions, offer a range of answer choices. In multiple-choice questions, provide plausible but incorrect options, also known as "distractors," to make the quiz more challenging. For true/false questions, ensure that the statements are clearly factual.

If the quiz is open-ended, prepare an answer key in advance for easy grading and feedback.

5. Add Immediate Feedback

One of the major advantages of online quizzes is the ability to provide immediate feedback. If the quiz serves an educational purpose, offer explanations for the correct answers, helping participants understand why they got an answer right or wrong. This is essential for reinforcing learning.

6. Design and Format the Quiz

351

The layout and design of your quiz can significantly affect the user experience. A clean, simple interface ensures that participants can focus on the content, not the design. Incorporate visual elements like images, icons, and colors to make the quiz visually appealing, but avoid cluttering the page.

7. Test the Quiz

Before launching your quiz to a larger audience, test it yourself or with a small group. Check for technical issues, ensure the questions and answers are clear, and verify that the scoring system works properly.

8. Share and Promote the Quiz

Once your quiz is ready, share it with your target audience. Use platforms like social media, email newsletters, and websites to distribute your quiz. Encourage participants to share the quiz with others to increase engagement.

Popular Tools for Creating Online Quizzes

Several online tools make quiz creation simple and intuitive. These platforms typically offer user-friendly interfaces, customizable templates, and analytics tools to track performance. Here are a few of the most popular options:

1. Google Forms

Google Forms is a free and easy tool for creating online quizzes. It supports multiple question types, allows for instant feedback, and integrates with Google Sheets for data collection and analysis. Google Forms is ideal for basic quizzes.

2. Quizlet

Quizlet is a popular tool that allows you to create custom quizzes and share them with others. It has a large library of pre-made quizzes and flashcards, making it a great choice for both study purposes and entertainment quizzes.

3. Typeform

Typeform is known for its user-friendly interface and sleek, modern design. It offers a variety of question types and customization options. Typeform allows you to create quizzes that are visually appealing and interactive.

4. Kahoot!

Kahoot! is a fun, game-like quiz platform that's perfect for classroom or team environments. It supports live, real-time quiz-taking, and users can compete against one another, making it ideal for educational settings.

5. SurveyMonkey

SurveyMonkey is a robust survey tool that can also be used to create quizzes. It offers advanced question types, detailed analytics, and customization options for a professional quiz experience.

6. ProProfs Quiz Maker

ProProfs offers an easy-to-use quiz builder with features like quizzes with instant scoring, feedback, and customizable templates. It's great for business, education, and customer feedback quizzes.

7. Quizizz

Quizizz is similar to Kahoot! and is designed to make quizzes more engaging. It offers multiplayer quiz modes, gamification features, and real-time feedback, making it a fun choice for classrooms and group settings.

Conclusion

Creating online quizzes is an excellent way to assess knowledge, engage your audience, and create interactive learning experiences. By carefully crafting your questions, utilizing the right tools, and providing immediate feedback, you can create quizzes that are both effective and fun. Whether you're designing quizzes for education, business, or entertainment, online quizzes offer a versatile platform for achieving your goals.

Figure 27: An eBook book cover

Part 43: Building Interactive eBooks

In the digital age, traditional books are being transformed into interactive eBooks that offer a dynamic, engaging, and immersive experience. Interactive eBooks are more than just digital versions of paper books—they incorporate multimedia elements such as audio, video, hyperlinks, animations, quizzes, and interactive graphics to enhance the reader's experience. Whether you're an educator, business professional, or aspiring author, creating an interactive eBook can provide your audience with a more engaging and informative way to consume content.

In this section, we will explore the importance of interactive eBooks, the process of creating them, and the tools available to build an interactive eBook from scratch.

Why Build an Interactive eBook?

Interactive eBooks have revolutionized the way content is consumed and shared. Here are some key reasons why you should consider building one:

1. **Engagement**: Interactive eBooks capture the reader's attention by offering more than just text. Adding multimedia elements such as videos, animations, and quizzes makes the content more engaging and helps to hold the reader's attention longer.

2. **Multimedia Integration**: You can integrate a wide range of multimedia elements that traditional books cannot offer, such as audio narrations, embedded videos, images, and clickable links. This is especially useful for educational eBooks, where visuals and multimedia can enhance understanding.

356

3. **Interactivity**: Features like clickable links, embedded forms, and navigation buttons allow readers to interact with the eBook in ways that increase user engagement and make the content more accessible.

4. **Improved Learning**: Interactive eBooks can include features such as quizzes, flashcards, and embedded resources that aid in learning and retention. This makes them an excellent choice for educators and trainers.

5. **Adaptability**: Interactive eBooks can adapt to different platforms and devices, such as tablets, smartphones, and computers. They provide a cross-platform experience that allows users to engage with the content on any device.

6. **Customizability**: You can customize the design and functionality of your interactive eBook to fit your brand, style, or personal preferences, creating a unique reading experience for your audience.

7. **Enhancing Content**: Interactive features such as clickable table of contents, footnotes, and chapter links improve navigation, making it easier for readers to explore different parts of the book quickly.

Steps for Building an Interactive eBook

Creating an interactive eBook requires planning and careful consideration of the elements that will make it both informative and engaging. Follow these steps to build your own interactive eBook.

1. Define Your Purpose and Audience

Before diving into the technical aspects, it's essential to determine the purpose of your interactive eBook and your target audience. Ask yourself:

- What is the goal of the eBook? Is it educational, entertainment-focused, or a business tool?

- Who is your target audience? Are they students, professionals, hobbyists, or general readers?

- What kind of multimedia elements will best serve the purpose of your eBook? Will you use videos, audio clips, images, quizzes, or interactive diagrams?

By clearly defining the purpose and audience, you can design an eBook that aligns with their needs and expectations.

2. Plan the Structure and Content

Once you've defined the purpose, plan the structure and content of your eBook. Think about the following:

- **Table of Contents**: Create a clear and organized table of contents to help readers navigate through the eBook.

- **Chapters and Sections**: Divide the content into chapters or sections to maintain clarity and organization.

- **Multimedia Elements**: Decide where multimedia elements such as videos, audio, images, and interactive graphics will fit into the eBook to enhance the content.

- **Interactive Features**: Plan how you want the reader to interact with the eBook. Will you include quizzes, hyperlinks, clickable buttons, or other interactive features?

3. Choose the Right eBook Creation Tool

There are many software tools and platforms available that can help you build an interactive eBook. Some popular ones include:

- **Adobe InDesign**: This professional tool offers advanced features for creating eBooks with interactive elements, including hyperlinks, videos, and buttons. It's perfect for authors who are comfortable with design and layout software.

- **Apple iBooks Author**: Apple's iBooks Author is a free tool designed for creating interactive eBooks that are specifically for iOS devices. It allows users to add multimedia, quizzes, widgets, and interactive features.

- **Kotobee Author**: Kotobee is a user-friendly tool that allows you to create interactive eBooks with embedded multimedia, widgets, quizzes, and even 3D content. It supports various formats and platforms, making it an excellent choice for creating cross-platform eBooks.

- **Canva**: Canva is a simple tool with drag-and-drop functionality that allows you to design interactive PDFs. While it's less feature-rich than InDesign or Kotobee, it's great for beginners who want to create visually appealing, interactive PDFs with limited technical knowledge.

- **Book Creator**: Book Creator is a popular platform that allows authors to create multimedia-rich eBooks for iOS, Android, and the web. It supports adding text, images, audio, video, and interactive elements.

- **Sigil**: Sigil is an open-source eBook editor for EPUB files, and it supports the creation of interactive eBooks with hyperlinks, multimedia, and other interactive features.

4. Add Multimedia Elements

The key to building an interactive eBook lies in its multimedia components. Here's how to incorporate multimedia effectively:

- **Videos**: Embed videos that illustrate key concepts or provide additional context. Educational eBooks often use explainer videos, while entertainment eBooks may include trailers or behind-the-scenes footage.

- **Audio**: Add audio narrations, sound effects, or background music to enhance the experience. This can be particularly useful for language learning eBooks or guided tours.

- **Images and Graphics**: Use high-quality images and graphics to complement the text and make the content more visually appealing. Include interactive diagrams, charts, or infographics that readers can click for additional details.

- **Animations**: Integrate animations to explain complex ideas or to simply make the reading experience more engaging. These can be incorporated as GIFs or interactive HTML5 elements.

- **Interactive Forms**: Add forms, such as quizzes or surveys, that allow readers to interact with the content. For example, you can include multiple-choice questions at the end of each chapter for self-assessment.

5. Implement Interactive Features

Interactive features help make your eBook dynamic and engaging. These can include:

- **Hyperlinks**: Add internal and external links to provide more information or navigate readers to other sections within the eBook.

- **Navigation Buttons**: Implement buttons that allow readers to jump to specific sections or chapters, providing an easy way to navigate through the content.

- **Interactive Buttons**: Use clickable buttons for various functions, such as playing audio or video, submitting feedback, or redirecting to external websites.

- **Pop-Ups and Tooltips**: Include tooltips and pop-up windows that offer additional information, images, or definitions without overwhelming the main content.

6. Test Your eBook

Before publishing your eBook, thoroughly test it to ensure that all multimedia elements and interactive features are functioning as expected. Test your eBook on different devices and platforms to ensure compatibility and responsiveness. Pay attention to loading times, especially for larger multimedia files, and make sure everything works smoothly across various screen sizes.

7. Publish and Share

Once your interactive eBook is ready, you can publish and distribute it on various platforms:

- **Amazon Kindle**: If you're creating an eBook for a large audience, consider publishing it on platforms like Amazon Kindle, which offers a broad reach.

- **Apple Books**: If you're using iBooks Author, you can publish your interactive eBook on Apple Books, reaching iOS users.

- **Web and Social Media**: Share your eBook on your website or social media platforms, providing downloadable versions or links to online readers.

Conclusion

Building an interactive eBook is a creative and rewarding way to deliver content that captivates your audience and provides a richer, more engaging experience. By incorporating multimedia, interactivity, and customization, you can create a truly dynamic reading experience. With the right tools, planning, and execution, your interactive eBook can stand out in the digital marketplace and provide readers with a memorable, impactful experience.

Part 44: Developing eLearning Modules

In the modern world, eLearning has become one of the most effective ways to impart knowledge and skills. Whether for academic institutions, corporate training, or self-paced learning, eLearning modules provide learners with the flexibility and interactivity that traditional teaching methods cannot offer. Developing eLearning modules involves the creation of comprehensive online learning experiences, which can include multimedia elements, interactive assessments, and user-friendly navigation.

In this part of the guide, we will explore the essential steps in developing eLearning modules, from the initial planning stages to the final implementation and evaluation. We will also discuss the best practices and tools available to ensure the modules are engaging, effective, and accessible for all learners.

Why Develop eLearning Modules?

eLearning modules offer many benefits to both educators and learners. Here are some key reasons why eLearning has become a go-to option in modern education:

1. **Accessibility**: eLearning allows students to access the content from anywhere in the world, at any time, using any device. This flexibility is crucial for learners with busy schedules or those who live in remote areas.

2. **Cost-Effectiveness**: By reducing the need for physical classrooms and printed materials, eLearning modules can lower educational costs, especially in a corporate or organizational context.

3. **Customization**: With eLearning, you can design content that caters to different learning styles. The modules can be customized to include various multimedia elements, interactive exercises, and assessments.

4. **Engagement**: Interactive content like quizzes, simulations, and gamified learning experiences can significantly boost learner engagement and retention rates.

5. **Tracking and Analytics**: Most eLearning platforms provide robust tracking tools that allow instructors to monitor learner progress and assess the effectiveness of the training. This data is invaluable for improving the learning process over time.

6. **Scalability**: eLearning modules can be easily scaled to accommodate a large number of learners without the need for additional resources, making them ideal for large organizations or global reach.

Steps to Develop an Effective eLearning Module

Developing an eLearning module involves several critical steps, from planning the content to delivering and evaluating the finished product. Here's a step-by-step guide:

1. Define Learning Objectives

Before creating any content, it's essential to define the learning objectives. What should learners be able to do after completing the module? These objectives will guide the content creation process and help ensure that the module aligns with the intended goals.

To define clear learning objectives, ask yourself the following questions:

- What knowledge or skills do I want the learner to gain from this module?

- What real-world applications will these skills or knowledge have?

- How will I measure the learner's success in achieving these objectives?

Use the SMART criteria (Specific, Measurable, Achievable, Relevant, Time-bound) to help make your learning objectives clear and actionable.

2. Conduct a Needs Analysis

Once you've defined your learning objectives, the next step is to conduct a needs analysis. This will help you understand the learner's current knowledge, skills, and learning preferences.

Key considerations include:

- **Learner Demographics**: What is the educational background of the learners? What are their ages, learning styles, and technology literacy levels?

- **Content Gap**: What knowledge gaps exist, and how can the module fill these gaps?

- **Technological Requirements**: What devices and software will the learners be using to access the module? Will they need access to a specific eLearning platform?

By understanding these aspects, you can design a module that is tailored to the learner's needs.

3. Create a Course Outline

Once the learning objectives are clear, create a detailed course outline. The outline should break down the module into digestible sections or units, each focused on achieving a specific objective. You should consider the following:

- **Content Breakdown**: Divide the content into logical chunks (e.g., introduction, theory, practical exercises, assessments).

- **Learning Pathway**: Define the sequence in which the learner should progress through the content. Make sure the learning flow is logical, starting with foundational concepts and advancing to more complex ones.

- **Interactive Elements**: Plan where to incorporate interactive elements like quizzes, simulations, and case studies that will reinforce learning.

- **Multimedia Integration**: Determine where videos, audio, images, and other multimedia elements should be added to enhance learning.

A clear course outline will help keep the content organized and ensure that all objectives are covered.

4. Develop Content

Content development is the most time-consuming part of building an eLearning module. You will need to create various forms of content, including:

- **Text-Based Content**: Write clear, concise, and engaging text that explains the concepts. Break up large paragraphs into shorter, digestible sections. Use bullet points and headings to make the text more readable.

- **Visuals**: Incorporate relevant images, infographics, diagrams, and charts that visually represent the concepts being taught. Visuals can significantly enhance understanding and retention.

- **Audio and Video**: Use audio and video elements where appropriate to explain complex concepts, provide demonstrations, or introduce expert opinions. This is especially helpful for auditory learners.

- **Interactive Features**: Incorporate interactive features such as clickable buttons, drag-and-drop activities, simulations, and interactive diagrams that allow learners to engage with the content actively.

5. Choose an eLearning Authoring Tool

To build your eLearning module, you'll need an authoring tool that allows you to create, edit, and organize your content. Several popular eLearning authoring tools include:

- **Articulate Storyline**: A versatile tool that allows you to create highly interactive eLearning courses with ease. It offers drag-and-drop functionality and supports multimedia integration.

- **Adobe Captivate**: Ideal for creating responsive eLearning modules, Adobe Captivate supports a wide range of interactive features, including quizzes, simulations, and drag-and-drop exercises.

- **Lectora**: Known for its user-friendly interface, Lectora is a great tool for designing eLearning courses. It supports multimedia integration and offers robust quiz and assessment features.

- **iSpring Suite**: This tool is a PowerPoint-based authoring platform that allows you to create interactive eLearning courses directly from PowerPoint. It's ideal for beginners.

- **Camtasia**: While primarily used for video editing, Camtasia also offers features that allow you to add interactivity to videos, making it a great choice for creating engaging eLearning videos.

Choose the tool that best fits your content type and technical skills.

6. Implement Assessments

Assessments are a vital component of eLearning modules, as they measure learner progress and reinforce learning. Consider including the following types of assessments:

- **Quizzes**: Multiple-choice, true/false, and fill-in-the-blank questions can be used to test learners' understanding of the content.

- **Surveys and Polls**: Use surveys to gather feedback from learners on the module content and learning experience.

- **Practical Exercises**: Implement real-world scenarios, case studies, or simulations that allow learners to apply what they've learned.

- **Final Exam**: A final exam can be used to evaluate learners' overall grasp of the material covered in the module.

7. Test the Module

Testing the module is crucial to ensure that it works as expected. It's important to check for:

- **Functionality**: Ensure that all interactive features, multimedia elements, and navigation work smoothly.

- **Usability**: The interface should be intuitive and user-friendly. Learners should be able to easily navigate through the module without confusion.

- **Compatibility**: Test the module on various devices (PCs, tablets, smartphones) and browsers to ensure it's compatible across all platforms.

- **Content Accuracy**: Review the content for accuracy, clarity, and consistency. Ensure that there are no errors or missing information.

8. Deploy and Track Learner Progress

Once the module is complete and tested, deploy it on your chosen eLearning platform. Popular platforms for delivering eLearning content include:

- **Moodle**: An open-source learning management system (LMS) widely used for hosting eLearning courses.

- **Canvas**: A cloud-based LMS that offers various features for course management and learner assessment.

- **TalentLMS**: An easy-to-use, cloud-based LMS designed for corporate training.

Track learners' progress and performance using the tracking and analytics features of the eLearning platform. Use this data to improve the module in future versions and to adjust the learning experience for different types of learners.

Conclusion

Developing an eLearning module can be a rewarding project that enhances your learners' experiences and provides them with valuable, engaging content. By defining clear objectives, using the right authoring tools, incorporating multimedia and interactive elements, and testing the module for usability and functionality, you can create an eLearning course that meets the needs of your audience. Whether you're creating training for employees, students, or self-learners, an eLearning module offers an effective and scalable way to deliver education and training.

Part 45: Making Educational Infographics

Infographics have become one of the most effective and engaging ways to present information visually. They help simplify complex concepts, data, and ideas by transforming them into easily digestible, eye-catching visuals. In the realm of education, infographics can be powerful tools to enhance learning by illustrating key ideas, processes, and relationships in a clear and memorable format.

This part will provide you with a comprehensive guide to creating educational infographics, covering the basics of design, tips for making them impactful, tools you can use, and best practices to ensure that your infographics effectively convey the message to your intended audience.

Why Use Educational Infographics?

Infographics are widely used in education due to their ability to:

1. **Simplify Complex Information**: Infographics break down complicated data or concepts into clear, easy-to-understand visuals. This is especially useful in subjects that involve heavy statistics, data analysis, or processes.

2. **Enhance Engagement**: People are naturally drawn to visuals. Infographics combine text and images to capture attention and engage learners more effectively than traditional text-heavy materials.

3. **Increase Retention**: Studies show that visuals aid in better memory retention. By presenting information

through visual means, learners are more likely to remember and recall the content later.

4. **Appeal to Multiple Learning Styles**: Infographics support visual learners, but can also incorporate auditory elements, helping to cater to different learning styles.

5. **Facilitate Easy Comparison**: Infographics are great for comparing facts, trends, or data sets side by side in an easily digestible format, making them ideal for lessons in history, science, business, and more.

6. **Encourage Interaction**: Infographics are often used in interactive learning environments, where learners can manipulate or interact with the content, such as clicking on specific parts to reveal more information.

Steps to Create an Effective Educational Infographic

Creating an educational infographic involves a combination of thoughtful planning, design principles, and the use of the right tools. Follow these steps to create an impactful educational infographic:

1. Define the Goal and Audience

Before starting the design process, it's crucial to define the objective of your infographic and understand the needs of your audience. This will help shape the overall content, tone, and style of your infographic.

- **Goal**: What is the key message or concept you want to convey? Are you aiming to summarize a process, explain a concept, display statistical data, or compare information?

- **Audience**: Who will be viewing the infographic? Are they students, teachers, professionals, or general learners? Understanding your audience helps you tailor the complexity, tone, and visuals to match their needs.

2. Gather Data and Information

The next step is to collect the necessary data or information that will form the basis of your infographic. This can include:

- **Statistics**: Collect data points, facts, or research findings that are relevant to the subject.

- **Processes and Steps**: If you're explaining a process, outline the steps in a logical sequence.

- **Comparisons**: If comparing different concepts, gather all the points of comparison to highlight key differences or similarities.

- **Visual Elements**: Think about how you might visualize the data. Would charts, graphs, icons, or diagrams work best for your content?

Ensure that the information you use is accurate and sourced from reputable materials. Infographics are more credible when they contain verified and high-quality data.

3. Choose a Template or Layout

Choosing the right layout is essential to ensuring your infographic is visually appealing and easy to follow. The layout will depend on the type of information you're presenting and how you want to structure the content. Common layouts include:

- **Timeline**: Useful for displaying events, historical data, or progress in a chronological order.

- **Process Flow**: Ideal for explaining a step-by-step process or sequence of actions.

- **Comparison**: Works well for side-by-side comparisons of two or more ideas, concepts, or items.

- **Statistical**: A layout that presents data in charts, graphs, and numeric formats.

- **List or Hierarchical**: Best for ranking items or concepts in a list form or showing a hierarchy (e.g., from most important to least important).

Tools like Canva, Piktochart, and Adobe Spark offer a wide range of pre-designed templates, making it easier to choose a layout that aligns with your content.

4. Select the Right Visual Elements

Incorporating appropriate visuals can elevate the quality of your infographic and make the information more accessible. Visuals should:

- **Enhance Understanding**: Use charts, diagrams, and icons to illustrate your data or concepts. Visual aids are particularly helpful when explaining abstract or difficult concepts.

- **Be Consistent**: Stick to a consistent color palette, typography, and icon set to maintain a cohesive look throughout the infographic.

- **Be Simple and Clear**: Avoid clutter. Every visual element should have a purpose and contribute to the overall message of the infographic. A clean, organized design ensures the infographic is easy to follow and understand.

Here are some common visual elements to consider:

374

- **Icons**: Use icons to represent concepts or actions. They provide a quick, recognizable way of conveying information.

- **Charts and Graphs**: Bar graphs, pie charts, and line graphs are excellent tools for presenting numerical data or comparisons.

- **Images and Illustrations**: Select high-quality images or illustrations that align with the theme of the infographic.

- **Shapes and Lines**: Use boxes, arrows, and other shapes to separate sections and guide the viewer's eyes through the content.

5. Organize the Information Effectively

Structure your infographic in a way that allows your audience to easily navigate the content. The layout should follow a logical flow that makes sense based on the subject matter. Key considerations for organizing your information include:

- **Hierarchy**: Make sure the most important information stands out. Use font sizes, bold text, and color contrasts to highlight key points.

- **Readability**: Use large, readable fonts for text. Avoid overwhelming the viewer with too much text. Use bullet points, short sentences, and clear headings.

- **Spacing**: Don't overcrowd the design. Use sufficient white space to allow each section to "breathe" and ensure the infographic is easy to read.

6. Add Text to Support Visuals

Text plays an important role in guiding your audience through the infographic. Use concise, clear language to explain key points or data. Here are some tips for adding text:

- **Headings**: Add headings for each section of the infographic to provide structure and help the reader navigate the information.

- **Short Descriptions**: Provide short descriptions or captions to explain the visuals. Keep the text concise, focusing on the most important information.

- **Quotes or Statistics**: If relevant, include notable statistics or quotes that reinforce the content.

Make sure that the text complements the visuals, without overpowering them.

7. Choose Color Schemes and Fonts

The right color palette and fonts can dramatically affect the impact of your infographic. Consider these points:

- **Color Palette**: Choose a color scheme that aligns with the subject matter. For example, for an environmental infographic, green tones may work well. Make sure the colors are complementary and contrast well against each other for readability.

- **Typography**: Use simple, easy-to-read fonts. Stick to one or two complementary fonts for consistency. Use bold for headings and regular font styles for the body text. Avoid using too many font styles in one design.

8. Review, Edit, and Test

Once your infographic is designed, review it carefully. Ensure that:

- The visuals align with the educational goal.

- The text is clear and free of errors.

- The infographic is visually balanced, with appropriate use of space and elements.

Testing your infographic by sharing it with a few individuals from your target audience can provide valuable feedback before you finalize it.

Tools for Creating Educational Infographics

There are several tools available that make designing educational infographics easy, even for beginners. Some popular ones include:

- **Canva**: A user-friendly tool that offers a wide variety of templates, icons, and customization options.

- **Piktochart**: A platform that specializes in creating infographics, presentations, and reports with easy-to-use templates and tools.

- **Venngage**: This tool offers customizable templates and a library of icons and charts to help you create data-driven infographics.

- **Adobe Spark**: A versatile tool for creating infographics, social media posts, and videos. Adobe Spark also offers templates and design assets.

- **Visme**: A powerful tool for creating infographics with a large library of templates, charts, and design elements.

Conclusion

Educational infographics are powerful tools for simplifying complex concepts, engaging learners, and enhancing memory retention. By following the steps outlined in this guide—defining your goals, collecting data, selecting visuals, and choosing the right design—you can create impactful infographics that communicate information in an easy-to-understand, visually appealing way. The use of the right tools will further simplify the process, ensuring that your educational infographics are not only effective but also professional in appearance.

Part 46: Recording and Editing Tutorials

Creating high-quality tutorials involves more than just demonstrating a process or teaching a concept; it also requires a blend of technical skills, clear communication, and effective use of tools for recording and editing. Whether you're creating instructional videos for YouTube, educational platforms, or internal training, the process of recording and editing tutorials can significantly impact how your audience engages with your content. This guide will walk you through the steps of recording and editing tutorials, from planning to finalizing your video.

Why Recording and Editing Tutorials Are Important

Tutorials are one of the most effective ways to teach and share knowledge. The combination of visual and auditory elements in tutorial videos can make learning more engaging and easier to understand. Effective recording and editing enhance the educational value of your content, ensuring that the message is clear, the pace is appropriate, and the video quality is professional.

Key benefits include:

1. **Improved Engagement**: Well-recorded and edited tutorials keep the learner's attention, making the material more interesting and easier to follow.

2. **Clear Communication**: Editing allows you to remove unnecessary elements and improve the flow of information, making the tutorial more understandable.

3. **Professional Quality**: Editing can elevate the production quality of your tutorial, making it look polished and high-quality.

Steps to Recording and Editing Tutorials

1. Plan Your Tutorial Content

Before you start recording, it's essential to plan your tutorial carefully. Planning helps you stay focused, organized, and ensures that your content is concise and effective. Follow these steps:

- **Define the Objective**: What is the purpose of your tutorial? Identify the specific concept or task you want to teach.

- **Audience**: Understand the needs of your target audience. Tailor the language and complexity of your tutorial based on their knowledge level.

- **Break It Down**: Outline the key steps or points you will cover. Break down the tutorial into clear sections, so viewers can follow along easily.

- **Script or Outline**: Although some tutorials are improvised, creating a script or outline can help ensure you cover everything and maintain a logical flow. A script is especially helpful for more complex tutorials or when precision is needed.

2. Set Up Your Recording Environment

Your recording environment plays a crucial role in the quality of your tutorial. A well-prepared setup ensures that you capture clear audio and crisp video. Here are the key elements to focus on:

- **Lighting**: Ensure the area is well-lit, preferably with natural light or soft artificial lighting. Avoid harsh shadows or overly bright lights that could obscure your subject.

- **Background**: Choose a clean, uncluttered background, or use a green screen if you're planning to overlay a custom background during editing.

- **Audio**: Use a high-quality microphone to ensure clear and professional-sounding audio. External microphones, such as lapel mics or condenser mics, are usually much better than built-in computer mics.

- **Camera Setup**: If you're recording yourself, set the camera at eye level and ensure you're in focus. For screen tutorials, use screen recording software (discussed in the next section) to capture on-screen actions.

3. Recording the Tutorial

Recording is the first step in creating your tutorial. Depending on your tutorial type, the recording process may vary. Below are a few tips based on different tutorial formats:

- **Screen Recording Tutorials**: If you're recording a software tutorial, consider using screen recording tools like OBS Studio, Camtasia, or ScreenFlow. These tools capture your screen while also allowing you to add voiceovers. Here's how to make it effective:

  o Record in a resolution that suits your audience, typically 1080p for clear detail.

  o Highlight your mouse cursor or clicks if demonstrating software navigation.

381

- o Use annotations or on-screen text to reinforce key points.

- o Record short segments to minimize mistakes and improve clarity.

- **On-Camera Tutorials**: If you're teaching something in person or through a physical demonstration:

  - o Use a tripod or stable surface to keep the camera steady.

  - o Speak clearly, and remember to maintain eye contact with the camera to engage your viewers.

  - o Use gestures and body language to help illustrate your points.

- **Voiceover Tutorials**: If you want to explain a process without being on-camera, you can combine screen recording with a voiceover. Speak naturally and avoid monotony to keep your audience engaged.

- **B-Roll Footage**: If necessary, capture extra footage (B-roll) that can be used to illustrate a concept more effectively. For example, if demonstrating how to use a tool, you may want to show close-ups of the tool in action.

4. Editing Your Tutorial

Editing is where you refine your recorded footage and create a polished, engaging tutorial. The goal is to eliminate distractions, correct mistakes, and enhance the instructional value of the video. Here are some essential editing steps:

- **Choose Editing Software**: Select an editing tool that suits your needs and expertise. Some popular options include:

  o **Beginner Tools**: iMovie, Shotcut, or Windows Video Editor.

  o **Intermediate Tools**: Adobe Premiere Pro, Final Cut Pro, or Camtasia.

  o **Advanced Tools**: DaVinci Resolve, which is free but offers professional-level features.

- **Trim and Cut**: Start by trimming any unnecessary sections, such as pauses, mistakes, or irrelevant footage. Ensure the tutorial is concise but still covers all important details.

- **Add Transitions**: Use smooth transitions between different sections of your tutorial. Avoid overusing transitions, as they can be distracting. Simple fades or cuts between scenes work best for most educational content.

- **Audio Enhancement**: Clean up the audio by removing background noise, enhancing volume levels, and normalizing the sound. Use audio editing software like Audacity or Adobe Audition to reduce hums, clicks, and static noises.

- **Add Text Overlays**: Text can help clarify your points. Add titles, subtitles, and annotations to reinforce what you're teaching. For example, you might add text to highlight key steps or important tips.

- **Highlight Key Points**: Use visual elements like arrows, circles, or zooms to emphasize important areas on the screen, especially in screen-recording tutorials.

- **Include Music (Optional)**: Adding background music can help create a more pleasant viewing experience. Be sure to choose royalty-free music, and keep the volume low to avoid overpowering the spoken content.

- **Include Callouts and Captions**: If needed, insert callouts or captions to further explain specific sections of the tutorial. Captions are particularly useful for accessibility, helping those with hearing impairments follow along.

- **Exporting Your Video**: Once you're happy with your tutorial, export the video in a high-quality format suitable for your platform. Common formats include MP4, MOV, and AVI. Choose the appropriate resolution based on where you'll be sharing the tutorial (e.g., 1080p for YouTube).

5. Publishing and Sharing Your Tutorial

Once your tutorial is edited and ready, it's time to share it with your audience. Choose the best platform for your content:

- **YouTube**: Ideal for public tutorials. Optimize your video title, description, and tags for searchability.

- **Vimeo**: Great for high-quality tutorials, especially if you plan to share them with a specific group.

- **Social Media**: Platforms like Facebook, Instagram, and LinkedIn can be used for shorter tutorials or highlights.

- **Educational Platforms**: If you're creating a more formal tutorial, consider platforms like Udemy, Teachable, or Coursera for course creation.

- **Personal Websites**: You can also upload tutorials directly to your own website or blog for a more controlled distribution.

6. Collect Feedback and Improve

After publishing your tutorial, engage with your audience and ask for feedback. Look at metrics like views, likes, and comments to gauge how well the tutorial was received. You can use this feedback to make adjustments in future tutorials, such as improving pacing, content clarity, or video quality.

Tips for Creating Engaging and Effective Tutorials

1. **Keep it Simple**: Don't overwhelm your audience with too much information at once. Break the tutorial into manageable steps.

2. **Be Clear and Concise**: Focus on clarity—avoid using jargon unless necessary, and explain technical terms as you go.

3. **Be Interactive**: Encourage viewers to follow along with the tutorial, ask questions, or attempt tasks themselves.

4. **Engage with Your Audience**: Respond to comments or questions after publishing your tutorial to foster a community and show your commitment to helping others learn.

5. **Use Visuals**: Wherever possible, use diagrams, animations, or images to make your points clearer.

6. **Stay Consistent**: If you're planning to create a series of tutorials, maintain a consistent style, tone, and pacing to build familiarity with your viewers.

Conclusion

Recording and editing tutorials can be an incredibly rewarding endeavor that not only helps others learn but also enhances your own teaching and presentation skills. By carefully planning your content, using the right tools, and refining your video through editing, you can create tutorials that are clear, engaging, and impactful. Whether you're teaching a complex concept, showing a practical skill, or sharing your expertise, well-crafted tutorials have the power to educate, inspire, and engage audiences around the world.

Figure 28: Simulation Class

Part 47: Building Simple Simulations for Teaching

Simulations are powerful tools for teaching and learning because they provide an interactive environment where learners can engage with real-world scenarios in a controlled, virtual setting. By building simple simulations, educators can help students understand complex concepts, practice skills, and explore potential outcomes without the risks or limitations of real-world experimentation. This part of the guide will walk you through the process of creating simple simulations that can enhance your teaching strategy and improve your students' learning experience.

What are Simulations and Why are They Important?

Simulations are interactive models that replicate real-world processes, systems, or phenomena, allowing students to manipulate variables, observe outcomes, and make decisions. They can be used across a variety of subjects, from science and mathematics to history, economics, and business.

Key benefits of simulations in teaching include:

1. **Active Learning**: Simulations promote active engagement by allowing students to explore, experiment, and learn by doing.

2. **Risk-Free Exploration**: Learners can experiment with different variables or scenarios without real-world consequences. For example, simulating financial investments or biological processes can help students understand the impact of their decisions.

3. **Complex Problem-Solving**: Simulations provide opportunities to practice complex decision-making and problem-solving skills in a realistic context.

4. **Immediate Feedback**: Interactive simulations often provide immediate feedback, allowing learners to assess their actions and adjust their approach accordingly.

5. **Visualization of Concepts**: For abstract or difficult concepts, simulations can provide a visual and dynamic representation, making it easier for students to grasp complex ideas.

Steps to Build Simple Simulations for Teaching

1. Define the Learning Objectives

Before starting to build a simulation, clearly define what you want your students to learn. Ask yourself:

- What concept or process am I teaching?

- What outcomes or results should students observe as they interact with the simulation?

- What skills do I want students to develop (problem-solving, critical thinking, data analysis)?

For example, if you're teaching physics, you may want a simulation where students can experiment with different forces on an object and see how those forces affect its motion. If you're teaching economics, you might create a market simulation where students control supply and demand and observe how pricing changes.

2. Choose the Right Tool or Platform

Selecting the right platform to build your simulation depends on the complexity of the simulation, your technical skills, and the needs of your audience. Here are some tools and platforms that you can use to build simple simulations:

- **Scratch**: A visual programming language designed for beginners, Scratch allows you to create interactive stories, games, and simulations. It's especially useful for teaching younger audiences or people new to programming.

- **SimCityEDU**: This version of the popular SimCity game is designed for educational purposes and allows users to create simulations of urban planning and development.

- **PhET Interactive Simulations**: Developed by the University of Colorado Boulder, PhET provides free interactive simulations in various subjects such as physics, chemistry, biology, and mathematics.

- **Unity**: If you're comfortable with programming, Unity is a powerful game development platform that can be used to create immersive and interactive simulations.

- **Excel/Google Sheets**: For more data-driven simulations, spreadsheets can be used to build financial models, decision-making scenarios, or mathematical simulations.

- **Coggle or MindMeister**: If you want to create interactive, visual simulations that demonstrate processes or concepts, mind-mapping tools can be helpful.

3. Design the Simulation

The design phase involves creating the structure of your simulation, ensuring it aligns with your learning objectives. Here are a few key steps to keep in mind when designing your simulation:

- **User Interaction**: Determine how users will interact with the simulation. Will they input data, make decisions, or change variables? Consider what controls or input methods are necessary (buttons, sliders, drop-down menus, etc.).

- **Scenarios and Variables**: Create realistic scenarios that reflect the learning objectives. Include key variables that students can manipulate. For example, if you're building a climate simulation, variables might include temperature, humidity, and carbon emissions.

- **Feedback Mechanisms**: The simulation should offer feedback based on the user's actions. For example, if a student adjusts the speed of a car in a physics simulation, the simulation might show how the car's motion changes, or how distance and time are affected. Feedback can be in the form of text, visual changes, or data displays.

- **Realism and Relevance**: Make sure that the simulation accurately represents the concept you're teaching. It should provide enough realism to make the activity engaging, but it doesn't need to be overly complex. Focus on the most important aspects that help students understand the learning goal.

4. Build the Simulation

Once you have your design in place, you can start building the simulation. The steps will depend on the platform or tool you've chosen, but in general, the process involves:

- **Setting up the user interface (UI)**: Create the necessary buttons, sliders, text fields, and other controls that allow users to interact with the simulation.

- **Programming the logic**: This step involves defining how the simulation works. If you're using a tool like Scratch, this might involve dragging and dropping coding blocks. In more advanced platforms like Unity, you would write code to manage the simulation's logic, such as handling user input, calculating outcomes, and displaying feedback.

- **Testing the Simulation**: Once the simulation is built, test it thoroughly to ensure that it works as expected. Check for bugs, errors, or logic issues. Consider testing it with a small group of students to gather feedback before rolling it out to a larger audience.

5. Integrate Educational Content

Once the simulation is functional, you can integrate educational content such as:

- **Instructions and Guidelines**: Provide clear instructions on how to use the simulation. You might want to explain the rules of the simulation or give hints on how to achieve certain goals.

- **Learning Prompts**: Include prompts or questions that encourage students to reflect on their decisions during the simulation. For example, "What happened when you increased the pressure? Why do you think that is?"

- **Assessment**: You can design the simulation to include assessment elements like quizzes or challenges. For example, if you're teaching chemistry, the simulation might ask students to identify compounds formed based on certain conditions.

6. Provide Access and Use

Once the simulation is ready, it's time to make it available to your students. If you're using an online platform or tool, share the link or provide access through a learning management system (LMS). If you're building something on your computer, you may need to upload it to a platform like Google Drive, Dropbox, or your personal website.

Encourage students to interact with the simulation and apply what they've learned in class. You might also offer additional resources or support for students who need help.

7. Evaluate and Improve

After your students have interacted with the simulation, gather feedback and evaluate its effectiveness. Ask students about their experience:

- Did they find the simulation engaging and helpful?

- Were there any technical issues or areas of confusion?

- Did the simulation help them achieve the learning objectives?

Use this feedback to refine and improve the simulation for future use.

Types of Simple Simulations for Teaching

- **Science Simulations**: These can include simulations of chemical reactions, biological processes, or physics experiments. For example, you could create a simulation where students can experiment with different force variables and observe how they affect an object's motion.

- **Economic Simulations**: Teach students about supply and demand, market prices, or financial budgeting by creating simulations of a market or business environment.

- **Mathematics Simulations**: Use simulations to help students understand complex math concepts, such as graphing equations, probability simulations, or geometry explorations.

- **Social Studies Simulations**: Recreate historical events or social processes where students can explore different scenarios and outcomes. For example, you could simulate historical events like the civil rights movement, or teach about government decision-making through a political simulation.

- **Language Learning Simulations**: Simulate real-world conversations or situations where students can practice their language skills in a controlled setting. For instance, students could use a simulation to order food in a restaurant or navigate through an airport using their target language.

Conclusion

Building simple simulations for teaching is a creative and effective way to engage students, enhance their learning experience, and help them grasp difficult concepts. By following a structured approach—defining learning goals, selecting the right tools, designing engaging interactions, and testing—teachers can create simulations that provide a meaningful learning experience. Whether you're teaching science, economics, history, or any other subject, simulations can make learning more interactive, engaging, and impactful.

Part 48: Developing Classroom Games

Classroom games are a dynamic and engaging way to enhance learning, boost student participation, and foster a collaborative environment. When designed effectively, educational games can transform the learning experience, making it both enjoyable and effective. Games allow students to apply concepts in a hands-on, interactive manner, while encouraging healthy competition and critical thinking. This part of the guide will help you develop classroom games that are educational, fun, and impactful.

Why Classroom Games Are Effective for Learning

Classroom games promote several benefits that support the educational development of students:

1. **Active Learning**: Games require active participation, helping students engage with the material in a more meaningful way.

2. **Motivation and Engagement**: Game-based learning provides an element of fun and excitement, keeping students motivated and engaged throughout the lesson.

3. **Collaboration and Teamwork**: Many classroom games require students to work together, fostering collaboration and teamwork.

4. **Reinforcement of Concepts**: Games allow students to reinforce what they've learned by applying it in different contexts, enhancing their retention.

395

5. **Feedback and Reflection**: Games provide immediate feedback, allowing students to adjust their understanding and strategies as they progress.

6. **Development of Problem-Solving Skills**: Many games encourage critical thinking, decision-making, and strategy, which are essential skills both in and out of the classroom.

Types of Classroom Games

Before designing a game, it's important to decide which type of game best suits your educational goals. Here are some common types of classroom games you can develop:

1. **Quiz Games**: These are fast-paced games where students answer questions to score points. They can be played individually or in teams, encouraging competition and quick thinking.

2. **Role-Playing Games (RPGs)**: Students take on different roles and make decisions based on the context of a scenario. This type of game is excellent for exploring historical events, literary characters, or real-world situations.

3. **Board Games**: Create a customized board game with spaces, cards, and challenges related to the lesson. These can help reinforce concepts in a playful and interactive way.

4. **Word Games**: Games like word search, crossword puzzles, or spelling bees can help reinforce vocabulary, language skills, and spelling.

5. **Simulation Games**: These mimic real-world situations where students can make decisions and see

the outcomes. They can be used to teach business, economics, or environmental issues.

6. **Memory and Matching Games**: These games help improve recall and recognition skills. Students must match terms, images, or definitions based on the lesson.

7. **Physical or Outdoor Games**: Incorporating physical activity into learning can keep students engaged, especially for kinesthetic learners. These games may involve challenges, tasks, or scavenger hunts.

Steps to Develop Classroom Games

1. Identify the Educational Objective

Start by identifying the core learning objectives you want your game to achieve. These objectives should align with your curriculum and the material you want students to learn. For example, if you're teaching a math lesson, your game could help reinforce concepts like multiplication, addition, or fractions. If you're focusing on history, the game might involve questions about historical events, dates, or people.

Ask yourself the following questions:

- What do I want my students to learn or practice through the game?

- What skills do I want the students to develop (e.g., problem-solving, collaboration, quick thinking)?

- How will the game reinforce these learning objectives?

2. Choose the Game Format

Depending on your class size, subject, and the nature of your learning objectives, choose the format for the game. Here are some popular formats:

- **Individual Play**: Best for games that test knowledge or personal skills (e.g., quizzes, spelling bees, word searches).

- **Team-Based Play**: Encourages collaboration and teamwork, and is great for larger classes (e.g., team trivia, relay races).

- **Classroom Competitions**: Create an overall competition that involves multiple rounds or stages (e.g., a tournament-style competition with elimination rounds).

- **Digital Games**: Use online game creation tools or apps to design interactive learning experiences for students. Tools like Kahoot!, Quizizz, or JeopardyLabs can be used to build digital quiz games or interactive trivia.

3. Create the Rules and Structure

Clearly define the rules of the game so that students understand how to play and what is expected of them. The rules should be simple, fair, and easy to follow. Some key aspects to consider:

- **Game Objective**: What is the main goal of the game? Do students aim to answer the most questions correctly, complete challenges, or earn the most points?

- **Scoring System**: How will points be awarded? Will there be bonuses for correct answers or challenges? Are there penalties for wrong answers?

- **Time Limits**: Set time limits for each turn or round to keep the game moving and maintain energy in the classroom.

- **Team or Individual Play**: If the game is team-based, how will you organize the teams? Consider using random groupings, allowing students to choose their own teams, or even rotating teams for each round.

- **Challenges or Levels**: To add excitement, create different levels or challenges that increase in difficulty as students progress.

For example, in a math game, the first round could involve simple addition, while the second round might be multiplication. Or in a history game, questions might become progressively more difficult as players advance.

4. Design the Game Components

Create or gather the materials you need to play the game. This might include:

- **Question Cards or Lists**: Prepare questions, scenarios, or challenges that are aligned with your learning objectives. For a quiz game, this could be a list of questions with correct answers. For a role-playing game, write out different scenarios that the students must navigate.

- **Game Boards or Digital Tools**: For board games, design a layout with spaces, cards, or other game mechanics. For digital games, use an online tool to create the game structure and user interface.

- **Prizes or Rewards**: Offering small rewards or incentives, such as stickers, certificates, or extra credit, can increase the excitement and motivate students to participate.

If you're using a digital platform, familiarize yourself with the interface and ensure that the game elements are easy for students to navigate.

5. Test the Game

Before you launch the game in your classroom, test it out yourself or with a colleague to ensure it runs smoothly. Make sure the instructions are clear and that the game mechanics are functioning properly. It's helpful to test the game with a small group of students to get their feedback on the gameplay experience. Look for any potential issues, such as:

- Are the questions too easy or difficult?

- Does the game move at a good pace?

- Is the scoring system clear and fair?

Based on feedback, you may need to adjust the game's complexity, the number of rounds, or the format.

6. Facilitate the Game in the Classroom

Once the game is ready, it's time to play! As the facilitator, it's important to keep things organized and fun. Here are some tips for managing the game:

- **Keep the Energy High**: Keep the game moving by maintaining a lively atmosphere and encouraging students to stay engaged. Offer praise and positive reinforcement throughout the game.

- **Monitor Student Participation**: Make sure every student has an opportunity to participate, especially in team-based games. Rotate students if necessary, so everyone has a chance to answer questions or take turns with tasks.

- **Encourage Collaboration**: If you're playing a team game, encourage students to work together and share ideas. Team games are a great way to build communication and teamwork skills.

- **Provide Feedback**: Give immediate feedback as students answer questions or complete challenges. Positive reinforcement can help build students' confidence and understanding of the material.

7. Reflect and Evaluate

After the game, take time to reflect on the experience and evaluate its effectiveness. Ask students for feedback about the game:

- Did they enjoy it?

- What aspects of the game helped them learn?

- Was the game challenging, and did it help them apply the material?

Based on their responses, you can adjust the game for future lessons, making it even more effective and engaging.

Examples of Simple Classroom Games

- **Jeopardy**: Create a Jeopardy-style game with categories related to your lesson. Students select a category and answer questions of increasing difficulty for points.

- **Pictionary**: In this drawing and guessing game, students draw pictures related to lesson topics, while others try to guess the correct answer.

- **Bingo**: Create Bingo cards with terms or concepts from the lesson. As you call out the answers or definitions, students mark off the corresponding squares.

- **Trivia**: Use a trivia-style quiz with multiple-choice questions or open-ended questions. Divide the class into teams, and award points for correct answers.

- **Escape Room**: Create a classroom "escape room" challenge where students need to solve puzzles or answer questions to unlock the next clue, eventually leading them to "escape."

- **Scavenger Hunt**: Hide items or clues related to the lesson around the classroom or school. Students must find them by answering questions or completing tasks.

Conclusion

Developing classroom games is an excellent way to bring energy, excitement, and engagement into the learning environment. Games help students actively participate, build teamwork skills, and apply their knowledge in a hands-on way. By following a structured process for game development, from identifying learning objectives to creating rules and evaluating the game's impact, you can create fun and effective educational experiences that reinforce classroom material and enhance student learning.

Part 49: Creating an Academic Portfolio

An academic portfolio is a powerful tool that showcases your educational journey, achievements, and growth as a student. It is a collection of your work that demonstrates your skills, knowledge, and progress over time. Whether you're a high school student applying for college, a university student compiling your achievements for future opportunities, or a professional looking to showcase your qualifications, an academic portfolio is an essential asset in presenting your academic profile.

This section will guide you through the process of creating an academic portfolio, including its purpose, what to include, and how to organize and present your materials effectively.

Why Create an Academic Portfolio?

An academic portfolio serves as a dynamic representation of your academic abilities, progress, and potential. It is more than just a record of grades and test scores; it's an opportunity to reflect on your learning, document key achievements, and showcase your strengths and growth. Here are some reasons why an academic portfolio is beneficial:

1. **Showcase Your Achievements**: A portfolio allows you to display your best work and document your academic success over time.

2. **Reflect on Your Growth**: By collecting and reviewing your work, you can assess your development, identify strengths, and recognize areas for improvement.

3. **Provide Evidence for Opportunities**: Whether applying for scholarships, internships, college admissions, or job opportunities, an academic portfolio is a powerful way to present yourself to potential decision-makers.

4. **Organize Your Work**: A portfolio helps keep your academic work in one place, making it easier to access and share when necessary.

5. **Demonstrate Skills and Knowledge**: An academic portfolio can demonstrate your competency in specific areas, including critical thinking, problem-solving, creativity, and research skills.

Components of an Academic Portfolio

An academic portfolio can take many forms, from a physical binder filled with documents to a digital portfolio hosted online. Regardless of format, your portfolio should contain the following key components:

1. Introduction or Personal Statement

The introduction or personal statement is your opportunity to introduce yourself and explain the purpose of your portfolio. This section should provide:

- **Who you are**: A brief summary of your academic background, interests, and goals.

- **Purpose of the Portfolio**: What you want to achieve with this portfolio (e.g., applying for college, presenting your work, reflecting on your progress).

- **Reflection**: A short paragraph reflecting on your learning journey and how this portfolio represents your growth.

2. Table of Contents

A table of contents helps the viewer navigate through your portfolio easily. It should list the major sections and documents included in your portfolio, along with page numbers or hyperlinks if it's a digital portfolio. Organize your portfolio logically for easy access to information.

3. Resume or Curriculum Vitae (CV)

Include an updated resume or CV that highlights your academic qualifications, extracurricular activities, achievements, internships, volunteer work, and any relevant experiences. This document should provide an overview of your background, education, and accomplishments outside of the classroom.

4. Academic Achievements

This section should highlight your most significant academic accomplishments, including:

- **Grades or Transcripts**: A summary of your GPA or academic performance in key courses.

- **Awards and Honors**: Any academic awards, scholarships, or recognitions you've received.

- **Test Scores**: Relevant standardized test scores, such as SAT, ACT, GRE, or subject-specific tests.

- **Coursework**: Include any particularly important or relevant courses that demonstrate your depth of knowledge in your field of study.

5. Samples of Work

One of the most important sections of your portfolio is the collection of work samples that showcase your skills and accomplishments. Depending on your field of study, you can include:

- **Research Papers and Essays**: Include your best academic writing, research papers, and essays that demonstrate your writing, analysis, and research skills.

- **Projects**: Present any major projects you've completed, whether individual or collaborative. Include summaries, images, or even links to final project presentations.

- **Creative Works**: If applicable, include any artistic or creative works such as presentations, artwork, music, or videos that demonstrate your creativity.

- **Lab Reports or Case Studies**: For STEM or technical fields, include lab reports or case studies that highlight your ability to conduct experiments, analyze data, and draw conclusions.

6. Reflection and Self-Assessment

This section is an opportunity to reflect on your academic journey and your learning. It should include:

- **Personal Reflection**: Write about your experiences, what you've learned, and how you've grown over time. Discuss challenges you've faced and how you've overcome them.

- **Skills Development**: Identify and describe the academic and personal skills you've developed, such as problem-solving, communication, leadership, and research.

- **Future Goals**: Explain your academic and career goals, and how you plan to achieve them. This could include future projects, further studies, or career aspirations.

7. Letters of Recommendation

Including letters of recommendation from professors, teachers, or mentors can add credibility to your academic portfolio. These letters can speak to your character, work ethic, academic abilities, and achievements.

8. Extracurricular Activities

This section should include any non-academic achievements that support your academic growth and demonstrate your leadership, time management, and collaboration skills. Include:

- **Clubs and Organizations**: Any clubs, societies, or professional organizations you are a part of.

- **Volunteering or Community Service**: Include any volunteer work that highlights your commitment to service or social causes.

- **Sports and Other Hobbies**: Participation in sports or other extracurricular activities can demonstrate discipline, teamwork, and dedication.

Formatting Your Academic Portfolio

Your portfolio should be well-organized, clean, and easy to navigate. Whether it's a physical binder or a digital portfolio, here are some tips on formatting it effectively:

- **Consistency**: Use consistent fonts, colors, and styles throughout your portfolio. This creates a polished, professional look.

- **Clear Sections**: Divide your portfolio into clear sections with headers and subheaders for easy navigation.

- **Professional Appearance**: Make sure the presentation is neat and visually appealing. Avoid clutter and ensure each section is well-organized.

- **Visuals**: For a digital portfolio, include relevant images, infographics, or video clips that help illustrate your work.

- **Accessibility**: If creating a digital portfolio, ensure that it's easily accessible and can be shared with potential employers, academic institutions, or collaborators. Use platforms like WordPress, Wix, or LinkedIn to create an online portfolio.

How to Organize a Digital Academic Portfolio

Creating a digital academic portfolio offers the advantage of easy sharing and customization. Here's how you can organize your portfolio online:

1. **Choose the Right Platform**: Decide whether you want to use a website builder (e.g., Wix, WordPress) or a portfolio-specific platform (e.g., Behance, LinkedIn).

2. **Domain Name**: If possible, get a personalized domain name that reflects your name or area of expertise.

3. **Upload Documents and Samples**: Upload your academic documents, work samples, and other materials as PDFs, images, or videos.

4. **Use Interactive Elements**: Include links to your online projects, blogs, or social media profiles. Add interactive features such as clickable tables of contents and easy navigation tools.

5. **Optimize for Mobile**: Make sure your portfolio is mobile-friendly and accessible on various devices.

6. **Share and Update Regularly**: Share your digital portfolio with academic institutions, potential employers, or colleagues. Update it regularly with new accomplishments and work samples.

Conclusion

An academic portfolio is not just a collection of documents; it's a powerful tool that reflects your academic identity, achievements, and growth. By carefully curating and presenting your work, you can demonstrate your strengths, commitment, and potential to schools, employers, or any other stakeholders. Whether digital or physical, a well-organized and reflective academic portfolio is an essential asset for showcasing your educational journey and setting yourself apart for future opportunities.

Figure 29: Newsletters:

Part 50: Producing School Newsletters Digitally

In today's digital age, creating and distributing school newsletters digitally has become an essential tool for keeping students, parents, teachers, and the wider community informed about important school events, updates, and achievements. Digital newsletters offer convenience, flexibility, and the ability to reach a larger audience in a timely and cost-effective manner.

This section will guide you through the process of producing school newsletters digitally, covering the tools, best practices, content organization, and tips for creating engaging and informative newsletters that will capture the attention of your readers.

Why Create a Digital School Newsletter?

School newsletters serve several key purposes, including:

- **Communication**: They are an effective way to communicate with parents, students, and the community, keeping them informed about school events, upcoming activities, important announcements, and achievements.

- **Engagement**: Digital newsletters can help create a sense of community by involving readers in the school's activities and showcasing student work, projects, and events.

- **Cost-Effectiveness**: Compared to printed newsletters, digital newsletters save on printing and distribution costs, making them a more affordable option for schools.

411

- **Environmentally Friendly**: By going digital, schools reduce paper waste, contributing to sustainability efforts.

- **Timely Updates**: Digital newsletters can be easily updated and distributed quickly, ensuring that important information reaches recipients promptly.

Steps to Producing Digital School Newsletters

1. Plan Your Newsletter Content

Before you begin creating the newsletter, you should have a clear plan for the content and structure. Consider the following:

- **Audience**: Determine who the primary audience for your newsletter is (parents, students, teachers, or the broader community). Tailor the content to their needs and interests.

- **Purpose**: Identify the primary purpose of your newsletter (e.g., sharing school events, celebrating student achievements, announcing upcoming activities, etc.).

- **Frequency**: Decide how often the newsletter will be published (weekly, bi-weekly, monthly, etc.) and stick to a consistent schedule.

- **Sections**: Break your content into clear sections to make it easy for readers to navigate. Common sections for a school newsletter might include:

  o **Principal's Message**: A brief message from the school principal or other school leaders.

- o **Upcoming Events**: Information on upcoming school events, activities, and important dates.

- o **Student Achievements**: Highlighting student accomplishments, awards, and projects.

- o **Classroom News**: Updates from different grade levels, teachers, or specific classes.

- o **Community News**: Local community events, programs, or initiatives relevant to the school.

- o **Health and Wellness Tips**: Offering advice on physical, emotional, and mental well-being for students and families.

2. Choose the Right Tools and Platforms

There are various digital tools and platforms available for creating and distributing newsletters. Here are some options to consider:

a. Newsletter Design Tools

- **Canva**: Canva is a user-friendly graphic design tool that offers a range of templates for school newsletters. It allows you to customize designs easily and add text, images, and other media. You can export the newsletter as a PDF, image, or even a link to share digitally.

- **Adobe Spark**: Adobe Spark is another design tool that allows you to create visually appealing newsletters with pre-made templates. It offers customization features and is ideal for visually-rich content.

- **Microsoft Publisher**: For users comfortable with Microsoft Office, Publisher offers templates for newsletters that can be customized with school branding, images, and content.

- **Mailchimp**: This tool is a popular option for creating and sending professional-looking email newsletters. Mailchimp allows for easy integration with email lists, templates for newsletters, and analytics to track performance.

b. Email Platforms

- **Google Docs**: Google Docs is a simple way to create a text-based newsletter, and it's especially useful for collaborative projects. You can share the document via email or download it as a PDF.

- **Mailchimp**: In addition to creating newsletters, Mailchimp provides powerful email campaign tools to send newsletters to a specific mailing list. It tracks open rates and click-throughs, offering insights into how effective the newsletter is.

- **Constant Contact**: Another widely-used email marketing tool, Constant Contact is designed to help create, manage, and send newsletters to large email lists. It includes templates, design tools, and tracking features.

3. Organize the Layout and Design

The layout and design of your newsletter are critical in capturing and retaining the reader's attention. Consider these tips to ensure your newsletter is visually appealing and easy to read:

- **Use Clear Headings and Subheadings**: Make your sections easy to navigate by using bold headings and subheadings. This helps readers quickly find the information they are most interested in.

- **Keep Text Short and Concise**: While you may have a lot of information to share, keep the text concise and to the point. Use bullet points, short paragraphs, and clear language.

- **Incorporate Images**: Visual elements like photos, charts, or illustrations can make your newsletter more engaging. Include images of school events, student projects, and classroom activities to give it a personal touch.

- **Branding**: Use your school's logo, colors, and fonts to maintain a consistent and professional look throughout the newsletter.

- **Call to Action (CTA)**: If you want readers to take action (e.g., RSVP for an event, participate in a fundraiser, or visit the school website), make sure to include a clear call to action with links or buttons.

4. Proofread and Review the Newsletter

Before sending out the newsletter, carefully proofread the content to ensure accuracy and professionalism. Look for spelling and grammatical errors, ensure that all links are working, and verify event dates and times. It's also a good idea to ask a colleague or another member of the school community to review the newsletter for clarity and to check for any overlooked errors.

5. Distribute the Newsletter

Once your newsletter is ready, it's time to distribute it. There are a few different methods you can use:

415

a. Email Distribution

- **Mailing Lists**: If you already have a list of email addresses for parents, teachers, and other stakeholders, you can send the newsletter via email. Tools like Mailchimp, Google Groups, or Constant Contact allow you to send newsletters to large email lists.

- **Email Attachments or Links**: You can send the newsletter as an attachment (e.g., a PDF file) or include a link to the digital version of the newsletter hosted on your school's website or cloud storage.

b. School Website or Blog

- **Post it Online**: If your school has a website or blog, you can upload the newsletter there, allowing parents and the community to access it at any time.

- **Dedicated Newsletter Page**: Consider creating a dedicated page for school newsletters, where past issues are also archived for easy access.

c. Social Media

- **Share on Social Media**: Use the school's social media platforms to share highlights or links to the newsletter. You can share images or snippets of content from the newsletter with a link to the full issue on the school website.

- **Facebook, Instagram, and Twitter**: These platforms can be used to engage with a wider community, sharing the newsletter's content with followers, parents, and students.

Best Practices for Effective Digital School Newsletters

To ensure your school newsletters are effective, follow these best practices:

- **Consistency**: Publish newsletters on a consistent schedule so that your readers know when to expect them. This could be monthly, bi-weekly, or aligned with the school term.

- **Engage Readers**: Include interactive elements such as polls, surveys, or contests to engage readers and encourage participation.

- **Use Data**: If you're using email tools like Mailchimp, track open rates, click rates, and other analytics to gauge how well the newsletter is performing. This data can help you refine future newsletters.

- **Personalize Content**: If possible, customize the content for different audiences (e.g., one version for parents, one for teachers, etc.). This ensures that the information is relevant to the readers.

- **Keep it Visual**: Use images, infographics, and colorful layouts to make the newsletter visually appealing. A well-designed newsletter can increase reader engagement and retention.

Conclusion

Creating a digital school newsletter is an effective and modern way to communicate with students, parents, and the wider community. By carefully planning your content, choosing the right tools, and adhering to design principles, you can create a newsletter that keeps everyone informed and engaged.

Whether it's sharing upcoming events, celebrating student achievements, or providing important announcements, digital newsletters help build a strong connection between the school and its community.

Summary of Possibilities with Computer Craft

Computers have revolutionized how we approach creativity, productivity, and innovation, opening a universe of possibilities through computer craft. This field encompasses a vast range of activities, from creating digital art to programming complex systems, solving everyday problems, and building advanced projects. Here is a detailed summary of what can be achieved with computer craft:

1. Creative Expression

Computer craft allows individuals to channel their creativity into various forms of digital art and design:

- **Digital Art**: Use tools like Adobe Photoshop or Procreate to create stunning illustrations, digital paintings, and graphic designs.

- **3D Modeling**: Design intricate 3D objects and animations using software like Blender or Autodesk Maya.

- **Music Production**: Compose, mix, and produce music tracks with digital audio workstations (DAWs) such as FL Studio, Logic Pro, or Ableton Live.

- **Filmmaking and Video Editing**: Craft professional-grade videos with editing tools like Adobe Premiere Pro or Final Cut Pro.

2. Educational Endeavors

Computers provide numerous opportunities for enhancing education and knowledge sharing:

- **Creating Online Courses**: Share expertise through video lectures, interactive quizzes, and resource materials on platforms like Udemy or Coursera.

- **Designing Infographics**: Use tools like Canva or Piktochart to visually represent information, making learning more engaging.

- **Developing eLearning Modules**: Create interactive lessons and simulations to teach complex topics effectively.

3. Everyday Problem Solving

Computer craft makes managing daily tasks easier and more efficient:

- **Organizing Files**: Develop systems to store and categorize files, ensuring easy retrieval.

- **Creating Calendars and Schedules**: Use software like Microsoft Outlook or Google Calendar to plan and manage tasks.

- **Automating Tasks**: Employ tools like IFTTT or Zapier to automate repetitive actions, saving time and effort.

4. Advanced Technological Projects

For tech enthusiasts, computer craft provides avenues to experiment with cutting-edge technologies:

- **IoT Development**: Build Internet of Things (IoT) systems to control smart devices and automate home setups.

- **Blockchain Applications**: Experiment with decentralized apps, cryptocurrencies, and smart contracts.

- **Augmented Reality (AR) and Virtual Reality (VR)**: Create immersive environments and experiences for gaming, education, or training.

- **Cybersecurity**: Explore tools and techniques to secure systems and networks against cyber threats.

5. Gaming and Entertainment

Gaming enthusiasts can unleash their creativity and technical skills in this exciting domain:

- **Game Development**: Create 2D or 3D games using engines like Unity or Unreal Engine.

- **Modding**: Customize existing games to add new features, environments, or characters.

- **Streaming and Content Creation**: Share gameplay videos or tutorials on platforms like Twitch or YouTube.

6. Community Building and Sharing

Computers enable individuals to connect with others and create meaningful online communities:

- **Hosting Virtual Meetups**: Organize webinars, workshops, or group discussions using platforms like Zoom or Microsoft Teams.

- **Digital Advocacy**: Run campaigns to raise awareness and drive social change.

- **Crowdsourcing and Crowdfunding**: Use platforms like Kickstarter or GoFundMe to support innovative projects or causes.

7. Personal and Professional Development

Through computer craft, individuals can enhance their skills and advance their careers:

- **Programming and Coding**: Develop applications, websites, or software to solve specific problems or create new experiences.

- **Data Analysis**: Use tools like Python, R, or Excel to interpret and visualize data for informed decision-making.

- **Portfolio Building**: Showcase skills through digital portfolios, highlighting accomplishments and expertise.

8. Environmental and Social Impact

Computer craft can also be a force for good, addressing global challenges and improving lives:

- **Sustainable Design**: Use simulation software to create eco-friendly products or systems.

- **Volunteer Networks**: Organize community efforts and outreach programs using digital tools.

- **Educational Access**: Develop open-source learning platforms to provide education to underserved communities.

Conclusion

The possibilities with computer craft are limited only by imagination and willingness to learn. From personal hobbies like crafting memes and editing family photos to ambitious projects like developing IoT systems or creating virtual reality experiences, computer craft offers endless opportunities for creativity, problem-solving, and growth. Whether you're an artist, educator, gamer, entrepreneur, or tech enthusiast, computer craft equips you with the tools to bring your visions to life and make a tangible impact in both your personal and professional spheres.

Encouragement to Explore and Innovate Further

The world of computer craft is vast and ever-evolving, offering limitless opportunities to learn, create, and innovate. Whether you're a beginner exploring basic tools or a seasoned expert diving into advanced projects, the journey of computer craft is one of endless discovery. Each skill you acquire opens doors to new possibilities, empowering you to express your creativity, solve problems, and make a meaningful impact.

Don't be afraid to experiment and push boundaries. Every great innovation started with someone daring to try something new. Use the resources at your disposal—online tutorials, forums, software, and communities—to deepen your knowledge and expand your horizons. Remember, the most groundbreaking ideas often come from combining existing tools and concepts in fresh and unexpected ways.

Take small steps, celebrate your progress, and embrace challenges as opportunities to grow. The digital world is a playground for your imagination, and the only limits are the ones you set for yourself. Whether you're building a game, designing a smart home, or creating an educational tool, your contributions have the potential to inspire and transform.

So, dive in with curiosity and confidence. Explore, innovate, and share your creations with the world. You have the power to shape the future, one digital craft at a time. Your journey in computer craft could lead to innovations that not only enrich your life but also positively impact others around you. The possibilities are endless—embrace them!

Resources for Continuing Education and Skill Development

To grow your skills and explore the vast world of computer craft, it's important to leverage the right resources. Here is a curated list of tools, platforms, and communities to support your learning journey:

1. Online Learning Platforms

- **Coursera**: Offers courses on programming, digital design, video editing, and more from top universities and institutions.
  Website: www.coursera.org

- **edX**: Provides free and paid courses in technology, multimedia, and advanced digital skills.
  Website: www.edx.org

- **Udemy**: A wide range of affordable, beginner-friendly to expert-level courses on various topics, including game design, coding, and graphic design.
  Website: www.udemy.com

- **Skillshare**: Features creative and technical classes, such as animation, graphic design, and photography editing.
  Website: www.skillshare.com

2. Free Educational Resources

- **Khan Academy**: Great for understanding foundational programming and digital creativity.
  Website: www.khanacademy.org

- **GitHub**: Open-source projects and guides to help you understand coding and collaborative development.
  Website: www.github.com

- **FreeCodeCamp**: A nonprofit platform for learning coding, web design, and data analysis.
  Website: www.freecodecamp.org

- **MIT OpenCourseWare**: Access to free courses in computer science and technology from one of the world's leading institutions.
  Website: ocw.mit.edu

3. YouTube Channels

- **CrashCourse**: Engaging educational videos on technology and computer science topics.
  Channel: CrashCourse

- **Tech With Tim**: Tutorials on Python, game development, and other coding tools.
  Channel: Tech With Tim

- **The Futur**: Learn design, creativity, and branding through professional insights.
  Channel: The Futur

4. Blogs and Online Communities

- **Medium**: Follow technology and creativity writers for tutorials and industry insights.
  Website: www.medium.com

- **Stack Overflow**: A forum where you can ask coding-related questions and learn from experts.
  Website: stackoverflow.com

- **Reddit Communities**: Subreddits like r/learnprogramming, r/VideoEditing, and r/DIY offer valuable advice and discussions.
  Website: www.reddit.com

5. Software and Tools for Practice

- **Codecademy**: Interactive coding exercises for beginners and intermediate learners.
  Website: www.codecademy.com

- **Canva**: A user-friendly tool for designing marketing materials, e-cards, and infographics.
  Website: www.canva.com

- **Blender**: Open-source software for 3D animation and design.
  Website: www.blender.org

- **Trello/Asana**: Tools for project management to practice planning and task organization.
  Trello: www.trello.com
  Asana: www.asana.com

6. Certifications and Accreditation

- **Google Certifications**: Offers credentials in digital marketing, IT support, and cloud computing.
  Website: grow.google/certificates

- **Microsoft Learn**: Free resources and certifications for Microsoft products and technologies. Website: learn.microsoft.com

- **Adobe Certified Professional**: Certification for Adobe tools like Photoshop, Premiere Pro, and Illustrator. Website: www.adobe.com

7. Books and Manuals

- **"The Art of Computer Programming" by Donald Knuth**: A classic for understanding algorithms and programming.

- **"You Don't Know JS" by Kyle Simpson**: A deep dive into JavaScript for web developers.

- **"Designing Data-Intensive Applications" by Martin Kleppmann**: For those exploring advanced systems and applications.

8. Local Meetups and Hackathons

Join local tech meetups or participate in hackathons to network with like-minded individuals and sharpen your practical skills. Platforms like **Meetup.com** and **Devpost.com** are great for finding these events.

9. Experiment and Share

The best way to learn is by doing. Work on personal projects, share your creations on platforms like GitHub or Behance, and seek feedback. This hands-on approach will not only improve your skills but also build your confidence.

With these resources at your fingertips, you can continue your journey in computer craft, deepening your expertise and unlocking new opportunities. Stay curious, stay persistent, and remember—every expert was once a beginner. The tools to transform your passion into mastery are now in your hands!

www.ingramcontent.com/pod-product-compliance
Lightning Source LLC
Chambersburg PA
CBHW052143070326
40689CB00051B/3157